WHY UKRAINE MUST WIN

WHY UKRAINE MUST WIN

Thomas Cromwell

East West Publishing
Washington, DC

East West Publishing, Washington, DC

EastWestPublishing.org

Library of Congress Control Number: 2023903709

ISBN Paperback: 979-8-9877993-0-7
ISBN Hardcover: 979-8-9877993-2-1
ISBN eBook: 979-8-9877993-1-4

Published on March 1, 2023
Version 2 Published on May 1, 2023
Version 3 Published on April 4, 2024

Printed in the United States of America

Contents

APPENDICES

Preface

Ukraine is the Front Line in the Global Battle of Good Against Evil

The Russian invasion of Ukraine is the culmination of a series of aggressive moves by Vladimir Putin as he seeks to reconstitute the empire that unraveled upon the collapse of the Soviet Union. Although Russia is already the largest country by size in the world, evidently it is not big enough for Putin, who has for years been working to reclaim territories lost by Moscow at the beginning of the 1990s.

After finding that the world did not respond forcefully to his military adventures when he crushed a Chechen uprising in 1999 and occupied parts of Georgia in 2008 as well as Crimea and the Donbas in 2014, Putin apparently believed that he could get away with an all-out attack on the parts of Ukraine that he did not already control.

No doubt encouraged by the weak leadership demonstrated by Washington in its rushed and poorly-executed withdrawal from Afghanistan in 2021, on February 24, 2022 Putin launched a massive invasion of Ukraine by land, sea and air. He called it a "special military operation," but it was, of course, the beginning of an all-out war against Ukraine.

Wars are a Common Feature of Our World

As Winston Churchill pointed out, human history is one of constant wars:

> The story of the human race is war. Except for brief and precarious interludes, there has never been peace in the world; and before history began, murderous strife was universal and unending.[1]

Wars occur because there is evil in the world, evil that seeks to dominate good. However, not all conflicts have equal significance for the world. Those which are related to the defense or preservation of fundamental human rights and liberties have the most durable ramifications for humanity.

The specific causes for a particular war will naturally vary from one conflict to another, but the ultimate purpose for fighting injustice and aggression is always to diminish evil and advance the cause of good.

Why the War in Ukraine is of Particular Importance

In the 20th century we witnessed wars on an unprecedented scale that involved many countries across the globe. The First World War was supposed to be the war to end all wars because of its horrors, but before the guns fell silent on the Western Front the Russian Revolution had brought Tsarist rule to a bloody end and started what became decades of Communist-initiated conflicts across the world. And just 21 years after WWI ended, an even more expansive and deadly global war was started by the vengeful megalomaniac Adolf Hitler and his Nazi Party.

The world that emerged from WWII was in many ways better than the world before it was fought. Since that war ended we have witnessed great advances in science and technology that have transformed our standard of living for the better. Poverty has been radically reduced and health greatly improved.

But during the same period, the Cold War was fought to keep Communism at bay as the armies of brutal regimes plunged one nation after another into the misery of atheistic tyranny. The toll of the Cold War in lives lost was as great as that of the two previous world wars combined.

The fall of the Soviet Union and the collapse of its empire at the end of

---

1. Winston S. Churchill. November 14, 1937. *Mankind is Confronted by One Supreme Task*. News of the World.

the 1980s and beginning of the 1990s marked an important milestone in the global contest between good and evil. However, the Marxist ideologies that underpinned the Communist world (and still do today) were not eradicated. They spread through western institutions and remained the ruling ideology of Communist China, North Korea, Cuba and other states.

Russia emerged from the Soviet Union minus the socialist republics that it had once controlled, and without a string of subservient European satellites and an international network of Communist parties and regimes. But the leadership in Moscow never had to confront its own evil past, resulting in it remaining a belligerent state that continued to threaten its neighbors.

Putin inherited much of the aggressive imperial spirit of Soviet Russia, and he never really accepted the loss of empire. His ambition became to reclaim what Russia had lost, and in particular to regain control of Belarus and Ukraine. For both countries he tried to manipulate the political establishment to accept his leadership. This has worked in Belarus, but not in Ukraine, leading to Putin's incremental aggression against Kyiv with the ultimate purpose of Russia absorbing Ukraine into its federation.

The Global Significance of Victory for Ukraine

Thus the war now raging in Ukraine is the result of the Cold War never having been brought to a successful conclusion. It has fallen to Ukraine to stand up to Russian aggression, placing it on the front line in the global battle between good and evil—at least in the relative sense of those words. Thus Ukraine is where these two irreconcilable forces are now face-to-face and engaged in a contest for control over the future of humanity.

The war is reminiscent of the fighting in both the world wars of the last century. The brutality of the Russian invaders, the massive casualties they have inflicted, and the widespread destruction of Ukrainian cities and infrastructure are hauntingly similar to the carnage wrought by German and Soviet armies in those earlier wars.

These parallels point to the unique situation Ukraine has been thrust into and the reason why the valiant response of its leaders and people is so important for the world.

In this book we make the case for all righteous people and powers in the world to come to the support of Ukraine, because Ukraine really is fighting this bloody war to preserve the rules- and values-based civilization that we now still enjoy. There should be no confusion as to which side is in the right, and Ukraine must be given all the assistance necessary for it to win this war as soon and as thoroughly as possible.

A decisive victory over Russia could become a global turning point for good, benefiting people everywhere, and especially those still languishing under the tyranny of dictatorial regimes.

Introduction

A Barbaric Invasion

Vladimir Putin's invasion of Ukraine on February 24, 2022 was an act of evil. It stunned Ukraine and sent shock waves around the world. How could this 20th century-type aggression take place in peaceful 21st century Europe?

Putin and his Foreign Minister Sergey Lavrov had vehemently denied any intension to invade, even though Russian troops had been massing along the Ukraine border for months.[1] The Russians—having inherited considerable skills in disseminating propaganda from Soviet time—simply lied. That is, until they did invade, at which point they got busy making up reasons to justify their barbaric attack on a peaceful neighbor.

Russia's armies crossed Ukraine's border from the north, east and south. Initially, they met little resistance from a Ukrainian army that was unprepared for this onslaught. A dumbstruck world watched with dismay as what seemed like Ukraine's inevitable collapse unfolded.

The military experts all predicted Ukraine would only be able to last for a few days. For example, Mark Milley, the US chairman of the joint chiefs

---

1. Vladimir Isachenkov and Yuras Karmanau. January 17, 2022. *Russia denies looking for pretext to invade Ukraine*. AP.

of staff, told Congress that he thought Kyiv would not be able to hold out for more than 72 hours.[2]

The eyes of the world were on Ukraine and NATO: What would Ukraine do? What would NATO do?

A Hero is Born

The answer to the first question came on February 25, the second day of the invasion, as Russian armor advanced on the capital Kyiv and other cities across Ukraine. That evening, President Volodymyr Zelensky stepped onto the street outside his office to speak to his nation and the world. He was calm and measured, and immediately addressed the most pressing issue on everyone's mind: would he try to save his own life and escape the capital? Or would he stay and fight?

Holding a smartphone in his hand, he made what would become a selfie of historic importance for his country. In a simple, 32-second statement, he said what all Ukrainians needed to hear: Zelensky and the other top leaders of Ukraine were going nowhere:

> Good evening everyone.
>
> The head of the presidential party is here. Prime Minister Shmyhal is here. Podolyak [a presidential advisor] is here. The president is here. We are all here. Our soldiers are here. The citizens of the country are here.
>
> We are all protecting our independence, our country, and we are going to continue to do so. Glory to the defenders of Ukraine. Glory to Ukraine.[3]

The rest of the civilized world also needed to hear this. If Ukraine's leadership was standing strong, then the rest of the world had good cause to

---

2. Jacqui Heinrich and Adam Sabes. February 5, 2022. *Gen. Milley says Kyiv could fall within 72 hours if Russia decides to invade Ukraine: sources.* Fox News.

3. Volodymyr Zelensky. February 25, 2022. *We are all here.* https://www.youtube.com/watch?v=617zPYju5VQ

come to Ukraine's aid. Which they soon started to do, answering the second question: what would NATO do in response to the invasion?

A couple of days later, Zelensky provided further confirmation of his resolve. When the American government offered to help him escape from his embattled capital, Zelensky responded with a quip that perfectly captured his defiance in the face of the Russian horde:

"The fight is here; I need ammunition, not a ride."[4]

Many thought Zelensky, a former comedian and actor, would quickly crumble under Russian pressure. But his brief message on February 25 would prove to be just the first of daily briefings he shared with his countrymen and the world that were consistently encouraging, on bad days and good.

He would prove unflagging in his support for his people, and especially the Ukrainians who were on the front lines, sacrificing their lives, whom he visited frequently. And he would prove unflagging in his outreach to a world that has what Ukraine needs to survive the Russian onslaught and expel Putin's army from Ukraine.

Zelensky became a hero overnight. Not since Winston Churchill walked the streets of bombed-out London and rallied a wavering nation to fight the Nazis at all costs and for as long as necessary, had a leader appeared who was so unquestionably willing to put his own life at risk to save his country from an unthinkably dreadful future.

Some may scoff at this comparison, but the parallels are not insignificant. In Britain's darkest hour there was little reason to hope that Hitler's armies could be kept at bay. They had already overrun the Netherlands, Belgium and France, and were massed right across the English Channel, poised to invade.

Churchill rallied the British not with proof that they could prevent or

---

4. Sharon Braithwaite. February 26, 2022. *Zelensky refuses US offer to evacuate, saying 'I need ammunition, not a ride.'* CNN.

turn back an invasion, but based on the principle that as a people they had to fight the evil of Nazism, whatever the cost and for however long it took to achieve victory.

Churchill recognized in Hitler an evil and dangerous man, someone who could not be persuaded with diplomacy to give up his irrational imperialist ambitions. He had to be thoroughly defeated on the battlefield so that his only option would be to surrender unconditionally.

Hitler revealed his true character when he violated the norms of civilized behavior and broke a string of commitments made at Versailles by rearming Germany and then using that army to invade other countries. Churchill read him correctly.

Putin has likewise violated civilizational norms and broken a string of international commitments, including Russia's signature on the 1994 Budapest Memorandum that offered assurances to Ukraine that Russia, America and Britain would honor Kyiv's independence and territorial integrity in exchange for Ukraine giving up its nuclear weapons for 'safe-keeping and decommissioning' in Russia.

The Memorandum includes these two paragraphs that commit the three signatories to respect Ukraine's sovereignty. Russia first violated this commitment with its occupation and annexation of Crimea in 2014, and then its full invasion of February 24, 2022:

1. The United States of America, the Russian Federation, and the United Kingdom of Great Britain and Northern Ireland, reaffirm their commitment to Ukraine, in accordance with the principles of the CSCE [Commission on Security and Cooperation in Europe] Final Act, to respect the Independence and Sovereignty and the existing borders of Ukraine.

2. The United States of America, the Russian Federation, and the United Kingdom of Great Britain and Northern Ireland, reaffirm their obligation to refrain from the threat or use of force against the territorial integrity or political independence of Ukraine, and that none of their

weapons will ever be used against Ukraine except in self-defense or otherwise in accordance with the Charter of the United Nations.[5]

Furthermore, once the Russian army entered Ukraine it immediately began to commit a range of war crimes by targeting civilians and civilian infrastructure with rockets, drones and artillery fire, using illegal munitions—such as phosphorus bombs—and by raping men, women and children, torturing prisoners and forcibly relocating Ukrainian civilians to Russia. In short, Russia has resorted to the barbaric practices that have been associated with its military since the Soviet era.

A Moral Challenge to the West

It is not common in our brave new secular world to think of the behavior of people and nations in terms of good and evil. Most Western leaders prefer transactional arguments over moral imperatives. But what can you call Russia's behavior in Ukraine if not evil? It echoes the actions of the Soviet Union, which President Ronald Reagan rightly called an "Evil Empire."[6]

The benefit of recognizing the behavior of a nation as evil is that this perspective provides a moral basis for making strategic and cost-benefit calculations. After all, in the final analysis it is the impact on our civilization, good or bad, that determines whether or not a conflict justifies the shedding of our blood and expenditure of our treasure in defense of a righteous side.

Any effort to accommodate evil will inevitably lead to its empowerment and resurgence. This is what Reagan understood, and it explains why he broke with decades of the Western policies of containment and détente. He laid out his Cold War policy towards Communist states in the simplest of all terms, based on his own moral compass and his understanding of the fundamental values of Western civilization: "We win. They lose."[7]

---

5. See the full text of the 1994 Budapest Memorandum in Appendix 2.

6. Ronald Reagan. March 8, 1983. *Speech to the National Association of Evangelicals.*

7. Ronald Reagan. 1977. Reagan told Richard Allen (later his national security advisor): *My theory of the Cold War is that we win and they lose.*

Earlier, in a 1964 speech, he had elaborated on his view that the West's contest with the Soviet Union was essentially moral in nature, and that the core issue facing the West was whether or not it was willing to pay the price to defeat evil:

> You and I have the courage to say to our enemies, "There is a price we will not pay. There is a point beyond which they must not advance." …Winston Churchill said, "The destiny of man is not measured by material computations. When great forces are on the move in the world, we learn we're spirits — not animals." And he said, "There's something going on in time and space, and beyond time and space, which, whether we like it or not, spells duty."[8]

Duty indeed, a moral duty to protect the innocent from the evils of tyrants, aggressors and oppressors. If we want to preserve our rules-based international order we cannot afford to let Russia achieve its unjust goals in Ukraine.

In the current crisis brought about by Russia's aggression, thankfully many NATO members have concluded that Russia must be driven out of Ukraine. This is for the sake of Ukraine itself, since it has every right to enjoy full sovereignty over all its territory. But it is also for the sake of the world. A victorious Russia would be encouraged to continue on the path of aggression against other countries, and other despotic regimes would be encouraged to imitate the Russians—for example, Beijing would be incentivized to try and conquer Taiwan.

A Lack of Clarity has Delayed NATO's Response

It took some time for NATO to react to the seriousness of the situation with the resolve, speed and scale required, although the response of some ex-Soviet states and satellites was an exception to this pattern. The countries that have experienced Russian aggression and oppression in the past know all too well what to expect if Russia succeeds in expanding onto their territories.

---

8. Ronald Reagan. October 27, 1964. *A Time for Choosing*. Ronald Reagan Presidential Library and Museum.

(Estonia, for example, has committed one percent of its GDP to providing support to Ukraine.[9] This amounts to almost 50 percent of its own defense budget.[10])

Thus commitments to send arms to the capable but grossly outgunned Ukrainian army have been halting, and generally made only after a new round of Russian atrocities. A too-prevalent mindset behind this dithering and the delays it produces is the reluctance to provoke Putin by helping Ukraine defeat Russia as quickly and fully as possible. Many Western leaders wring their hands over the purported dangers of escalation instead of committing promptly and fully to the earliest possible victory by Ukraine.

The United States has been the most generous with its support for Ukraine, but far too slow getting the armaments Ukraine needs to the battlefield. These delays reflect the Biden administration's lack of clarity and decisiveness in its foreign policy. Dithering is justified as sensible caution in the name of avoiding escalation of the conflict.

Furthermore, while there is a broad bipartisan consensus of support for Ukraine in Washington, there are also some influential voices among conservatives who are opposed to supporting Ukraine—at least at the current level, if at all. The loudest of these voices is that of Tucker Carlson, a prominent *Fox News* anchor. In Congress his views are echoed by Matt Gaetz, Marjorie Taylor Greene, and a few others. These pundits and politicians are apparently blind to the injustice of the invasion, immune to the terrible suffering inflicted on the Ukrainian people by Russia, and unable to see the historical and civilizational importance of this conflict. They are clearly helping the Russian cause, although they would likely deny this.

The same is true of a number of major European NATO members, who have also contributed significantly to Ukraine's war effort, but only after

---

9. Press Release. January 19, 2023. *Estonia's military support to Ukraine will increase to more than 1% of GDP.* Stenbock House, Government of Estonia.

10. W. J. Hennigan. February 16, 2023. *'Don't Play With Us.' Estonia Sends Message to Russia With Ukraine Aid.* Time Magazine. https://time.com/6256280/estonia-aid-russia-ukraine/

the US has led the way. Germany is Exhibit 1 in this group. The government of SPD Chancellor Olaf Scholz has been doing a lot of hand-wringing and foot-dragging over providing heavy weapons to Ukraine, weapons that would give a critical advantage to Ukraine on the battlefield.

The reason given by Scholz has been fear of escalating the war—as if Putin has not already escalated this conflict to the maximum he can by throwing every weapon he's got—short of nuclear weapons—into the invasion.

For most European countries that suffered grievous losses of life and massive destruction from Hitler's aggression some eight decades ago, followed by decades of Soviet occupation and intimidation, the Russian threat to European peace and stability is immediate—and very good reason to do everything they can to help Ukraine defeat Russia.

You would think that Germany above all other European states would be the most eager to show the world that this time around it is on the right side of history and eager to lead European opposition to Russia's barbarism. Sadly, it has not been so. The Scholz administration appears to always look for political cover before taking action to help Ukraine.

Furthermore, America and its European allies have imposed a number of restrictions on the use of the weapons they have provided. For example, the highly effective HIMARS have only been provided with shells with a range of 80 kilometers, while Ukraine really needs the 300 kilometer-range ATACMS shells that can reach Russian military depots and infrastructure in Crimea and staging areas in Russia itself. They have also been reluctant to supply Western fighter jets, or even to permit third countries to do so.

The argument that providing these weapons would escalate the conflict is specious. It is Russia that is in violation of international laws and agreements, and has used the full range of its conventional weapons in its invasion of Ukraine. Why shouldn't Ukraine have the right to use a similar range of weapons to defend itself, including against legitimate military targets in Russia itself?

Foot-dragging by nations which have the wherewithal to help Ukraine win is immoral. It condemns the Ukrainian people and other innocents caught up in this war to more suffering—and possibly death—by guaranteeing the prolongation of the conflict. These delays are clearly beneficial to Russia's cause.

The Criminal Case Against Putin and Russia

On March 17, 2023, the International Criminal Court (ICC) indicted Vladimir Putin and a member of his government for forcibly removing Ukrainian children to Russia. This makes Putin an international pariah, a criminal wanted in the 123 member countries of the ICC. He will no doubt steer clear of those countries, but the point has been made: the mark of Cain has been stamped on his forehead.

Meanwhile, the evidence of war crimes committed by Russia in Ukraine is massive, and increasing every day. It points to Putin wanting to erase the very identity and nationhood of Ukraine. As we will explain in Chapter 5, Putin is indeed responsible for Russia committing all the war crimes that justify the label of genocide. He deserves to be tried for these crimes.

Ukraine Must Win

This book is critical of the containment mentality and practices that have influenced the Western responses to Russia's invasion. We advocate for a policy that is unequivocal in identifying Russia as the aggressor in this conflict, and Ukraine as the victim of aggression. Based on this clear distinction between evil and good, respectively, Ukraine's allies should do everything in their power to help Ukraine win this war as quickly and completely as possible.

General Ben Hodges, the former commander of the US Army in Europe, is one of the clearest thinkers on Ukraine. He has consistently called for NATO and other supporters of Ukraine to be unequivocal and outspoken about the need for Kyiv to defeat Russia decisively, so that it can regain control over all the territory Russia has occupied since 2014.

Such a decisive victory will not only deter future Russian aggression, it will also deter other bad actors from contemplating similar aggression. Communist China in particular will be made to weigh very carefully the costs of using military force to incorporate Taiwan into the People's Republic.

In one media interview after another, Hodges repeats his call for Ukraine's allies to be united and clear in their resolve to help Ukraine win. For example, he told the *Kyiv Post*: "We need to decide that we want Ukraine to win."[11] This mindset translated into official NATO policy is indeed the key to enabling Ukraine to be victorious in the shortest amount of time possible, thereby minimizing its already staggering losses of people and property.

Once this determination is made, all the decisions regarding what weapons systems to send to Ukraine, and when, will be answered: send Kyiv what it needs to win this war as soon as possible. And, as Hodges says, don't let Russian propaganda and threats of retaliation deter you from this good cause.

It is time for moral clarity and principled decision-making. It is time for Western leaders to shake off the immobilizing spell cast by Russia's propaganda and to end decades of wrongheaded policies that have favored appeasement over principle.

Ukraine can win. Ukraine must win. Ukraine will win.

---

11. Ben Hodges in an interview with the Kyiv Post. January 20, 2023. *We Need to Decide That We Want Ukraine to Win.* Kyiv Post.

Chapter 1

Why Ukraine Must Win Over Russia's Evil Decisively

Good Cannot Compromise with Evil

So long as you view the world as a place where people and nations are arrayed in shades of gray, devoid of characteristics that make one objectively better than the other, you will not understand the importance of the more virtuous side winning a conflict decisively.

Good and evil are real, and evil must be thoroughly defeated if a good world is to emerge. This principle may sound simplistic, but it is true, and has been born out in history.

What do we mean by evil? It is an active force that draws its destructive energy from the perversion and misuse of good—which it seeks to destroy. By good we mean all that aligns with our original purpose as human beings made by a good Creator.

Evil is constantly looking for ways to win over good, which by its nature threatens evil's existence. Thus so long as evil has the means, it will use them to attack good. It has no other purpose.

We recognize evil as it operates within our own nature, constantly seeking to destroy the intrinsic goodness of God's image imprinted on our original being. And we recognize it in the world around us in the aggression of the stronger against the weaker, and in the oppression, torture and murder of innocents by ruthless, ungodly people and regimes.

Evil by its very nature cannot tolerate good and therefore cannot coexist with good. Thus when evil defeats good, it seeks to secure its victory by crushing completely the good it has conquered, never resting until this destruction is complete. Conversely, good cannot coexist with evil, since the whole purpose of evil is to destroy good.

This is why it is so important for good to win its conflicts with evil decisively. If the evil side is losing but allowed to live to fight another day, it will sue for peace only so that it can regroup and rearm. Think of how this principle operates in our own lives. If we do not resolutely tackle and defeat bad habits and behavior, they will linger with us while looking for ways to regain their positions of influence in our lives.

The 20th century saw Socialist, Communist and fascist incarnations of evil unleash merciless aggressions against the world, killing tens of millions of innocents and ruining the lives of unknown millions more. The death toll from these conflicts was greatly increased because in WWI and the Cold War the Allies stopped short of defeating the forces of evil as swiftly and decisively as possible.

WWI Taught Us How Not to End Wars

The Treaty of Versailles ended World War I but it did not end the German nationalism that had been so destructive in the war and which later inspired the militarism of Adolf Hitler and like-minded Germans who brought it back to life in the Nazi Party that they founded.

The conventional wisdom on Versailles is that it ultimately failed to secure peace in Europe because it imposed draconian, impossible-to-fulfill demands for reparations on the losing Germans. However, as noted historian Victor Davis Hanson pointed out in 2019, the Germans were allowed to keep their conquests in Russia that were 50 times the territory Berlin had to return to the Allies in France and elsewhere. Hanson also noted that the reparation terms were not at all unusual for the times, and would have been expected by Germany.

The real reason for the treaty's failure was that Germany's surrender was conditional when it should have been unconditional:

> Versailles certainly failed to keep the peace. Yet the problem was not because the treaty was too harsh, but because it was flawed from the start and never adequately enforced.

> The Versailles Treaty was signed months after the armistice of November 1918, rather than after an utter collapse of the German Imperial Army. The exhausted Allies made the mistake of not demanding the unconditional surrender of the defeated German aggressor.

> That error created the later German myth that its spent army was never really vanquished, but had merely given up the offensive in enemy territory. Exhausted German soldiers abroad were supposedly "stabbed in the back" by Jews, communists and traitors to the rear.

> The Allied victors combined the worst of both worlds. They had humiliated a defeated enemy with mostly empty condemnations while failing to enforce measures that would have prevented the rise of another aggressive Germany.

> England, France and America had not been willing to occupy Germany and Austria to enforce the demands of Versailles. Worse, by the time the victors and the defeated met in Versailles, thousands of Allied troops had already demobilized and returned home.

> The result was that Versailles did not ensure the end of "the war to end all wars."

> As embittered Marshal Ferdinand Foch of France, supreme commander of the Allied forces, presciently concluded of the Versailles settlement: "This is not peace. It is an armistice for 20 years."

> Foch was right.[1]

Once in power, Hitler violated the Versailles treaty again and again while

---

1. Victor Davis Hanson. July 25, 2019. *The Lessons of the Versailles Treaty*. Arkansas Democrat Gazette.

leaders in Allied countries looked the other way and did nothing. Knowledge of the Nazi's massive rearming was initially met with bemusement, and only once the evidence of Hitler's military intentions became overwhelming did the Allies begin to take their own rearmament seriously.

In late September 1938, The United Kingdom, France and Italy signed the Munich Agreement with Germany under which Berlin annexed the western region of Czechoslovakia, known as the Sudetenland, which was home to a population of some three million people, predominantly ethnic Germans.

When Hitler announced that this was his last territorial claim in northern Europe, most of Europe sighed with relief that a war in Czechoslovakia had been avoided. And British Prime Minister Neville Chamberlain returned from Munich boasting that the agreement assured "peace in our time."

As we all now know, Hitler lied and Europe was shown to be a dupe. The Allies had been so intent on avoiding another war that they had made a huge concession to the person who would prove to be the principal creator of European wars, signaling to Hitler that his enemies would choose peace on his terms over another major European conflict.

Germany had lost WWI but now it was dictating the terms of the post-WWI order to the war's victors!

Fortunately We Applied the Lesson of WWI in WWII

Always angered at Germany's defeat in WWI—in which he had fought as a lowly corporal—Hitler was intent on reversing that loss and gaining *lebensraum* for the fatherland. A year after Munich, on September 1, 1939, he unleashed a blitzkrieg on Poland, starting World War II in earnest.

In contrast to the failed Treaty of Versailles, World War II came to an end when Hitler's Third Reich surrendered unconditionally to the Allies on May 7, 1945, followed by the unconditional surrender of Nazi ally Japan, on September 2, 1945.

The Allies occupied Germany and Japan to make sure that the terms of surrender were carried out by the losing nations. As a result, both countries went through profound national soul-searching and reformation, relinquishing their imperial ambitions and militarism, and eventually emerging as peaceful nations who joined the Allies in countering new threats from a new set of belligerent nations and alliances.

Chapter 2

A Post-WWII Era of Compromise With Evil

The Rise of the Soviet Empire

Following the surrender of Germany and Japan, the world was very different from what it had been before the war's onset. The British Empire was no longer a dominant military force capable of projecting its power to far corners of the earth; and the United States had replaced it as leader of the free world.

Meanwhile, having received enormous amounts of materiel and other support from Washington under President Franklin Delano Roosevelt's Lend-Lease program, Moscow was able not only to drive Hitler's armies from Russian territory, but also to occupy much of eastern and central Europe.

The Soviet Union was now an ascendent superpower and lost no time breaking the promises Stalin had made to FDR and Winston Churchill at Yalta by preventing free elections in countries it had 'liberated' from Nazi Germany. Instead Moscow established its hegemony over them as vassal states. These countries were East Germany, Poland, Hungary, Czechoslovakia, Romania and Bulgaria. (The Soviets had invaded and occupied the Baltic States—Lithuania, Latvia and Estonia—in June, 1940, and annexed them in August that year.)

Furthermore, in East Asia, where Moscow entered the war with Japan on August 8, 1945—just 25 days before Tokyo surrendered to US forces—Stalin committed similar violations of agreements made at Yalta and Potsdam by occupying Japanese-controlled territory and then preventing free elections from taking place.

Thus on August 9, the day after Moscow declared war on Tokyo, the Soviets unleashed an army of 1.6 million men to capture Japanese-occupied territories in China, Korea and Japan. The main target was Manchuria where the Japanese had established the puppet state of Manchukuo. After the Japanese surrendered on August 15—after just a week of fighting—the Soviets handed massive stockpiles of Japanese weapons to Mao's army, greatly assisting it in the war it was fighting with Chiang Kai-shek's *Kuomintang* forces.[1]

The same day that Stalin invaded Manchuria, his forces also invaded Japanese-occupied Korea, where they moved south to the 38th parallel, the line that had been agreed with America as the demarcation between Soviet and US-occupied territories. Stalin would renege on his commitment to hold free elections in North Korea. Instead he keep his army there until 1948, by which time a Communist dictatorship had been established under Kim Il Sung.[2]

Moscow wanted to occupy Japan's northern home island of Hokkaido, but faced with strong American opposition it 'only' occupied Japan's Kuril Islands, which it has kept to this day. (In 1875 Japan had ceded the southern part of Sakhalin to Russia in exchange for the Kuril Islands, and since WWII Tokyo has maintained its claim to the islands.)

Conventional wisdom holds that it was necessary for the Western Allies to make concessions to Stalin so that the USSR could help them defeat Germany, initially, and then Japan. This may be true, but it is also true that Stalin needed the massive support he received from America—beginning before

---

1. Andrew Salmon. August 11, 2020. *Red Storm on Rising Sun*. Asia Times.

2. Editors. November 13, 2009. *American troops arrive in Korea to partition the country*. History.com.

Washington had entered the war itself—to drive Hitler's army from Russian territory, and therefore needed the Allies more than they needed him. (Britain also contributed materiel to Stalin, including planes and tanks, but on a much smaller scale.)

The US Embassy in Moscow maintains on its website a list of materiel sent to Russia during WWII. It includes 400,000 jeeps and trucks, 14,000 airplanes, 8,000 tractors, 13,000 tanks, 1.5 million blankets, 15 million pairs of boots, 107,000 tons of cotton, 2.7 million tons of petrol products and 4.5 million tons of food.[3]

But Stalin was a master at extracting ever more concessions from the West. Thus in addition to receiving this mountain of supplies from America, he also demanded territorial concessions (the Baltic States and parts of Poland), as well as agreement for Soviet armies to occupy countries in Europe and territories in Asia.

A big part of the problem was that the Western Allies took Stalin at his word when he committed to holding free elections in the lands he occupied at the end of the war—in Europe and Asia. He clearly had no intention of doing so, but the Allies did not insist on free elections and the withdrawal of Soviet armies from these territories. Instead, they accepted as a fait accompli continued Soviet occupation and the installation of puppet Communist regimes.

In hindsight, it was not necessary for the Allies to make the concessions they did to Stalin, in Europe and Asia. Nor was it necessary for them to agree to the creation of the United Nations with a Soviet veto power (which we discuss in Chapter 15). Making these accommodations for Stalin proved to be dangerously shortsighted since they led to the birth of a mighty Soviet Empire which for 45 years would remain the primary perpetrator of evil in the world, and which gave birth to a successor evil empire in Communist China.

---

3. *World War II Allies: U.S. Lend-Lease to Soviet Union*, 1941-1945. US Embassy & Consulates in Russia.

Weakness in Washington

As ever-mounting evidence shows, FDR was not nearly as cautious of the Soviets as he should have been. One of his first moves as a new president in 1933 was to establish diplomatic relations with Moscow for the first time. This would open the doors for the Soviets to flood Washington with agents whose business it was to weaken America's opposition to the USSR and—once the two countries became allies fighting Hitler—to encourage the American government to make support for the Soviet Union a foreign policy priority.

According to several books on this period—including those reporting the revelations of Washington's Venona project which decoded cables between Moscow and its agents in the United States—there were hundreds of Soviet agents operating in the country during WWII and its aftermath.[4] The Venona program was initiated by the Army Signal Corps—precursor to the National Security Administration. By the time it was shut down in 1980, Venona had identified some 350 Soviet agents that had operated in the United States since the program was launched in 1943.[5] There were many agents before the program started, and likely many others never caught by Venona.

Some agents had senior posts in the administration, including in the White House, State Department, Treasury Department, Defense Department, the WWII era Office of War Information and the Office of Strategic Services—precursor to the CIA. They also penetrated sensitive programs like the Manhattan Project—which developed America's first nuclear weapons—as well as US embassies, labor unions, media companies and defense contractors.

When a repentant former Soviet agent, Whittaker Chambers, in 1939 informed FDR via his advisor Adolf A. Berle of the existence of an extensive Soviet spy apparatus in Washington (Chambers provided a long list of the

---

4. One of the best sources on this issue is the 1999 book *Venona: Decoding Soviet Espionage in America*, by John Early Haynes and Harvey Klehr.

5. History of the FBI. *World War, Cold War*, 1939-1953. FBI. https://www.fbi.gov/history/brief-history/world-war-cold-war

agents he was aware of personally), the president dismissed the warning. Later, Chambers learned what had happened when Berle passed the information to FDR:

> Berle had taken my information to the President at once. The President had laughed. When Berle was insistent, he had been told in words which it is necessary to paraphrase, to "go jump in the lake."[6]

Chambers' network included many key officials in Washington, including senior State Department officer Alger Hiss (who played important roles at Yalta and in the founding of the United Nations), and senior Treasury Department official Harry Dexter White (who played a key role in the founding of the IMF and World Bank at Bretton Woods).

As Diana West points out in her book *American Betrayal*, under the constant pressure of pro-Soviet members of the FDR administration, including the president's closest advisor, Harry Hopkins, Moscow got more Lend-Lease assistance than did any other American ally in WWII, including Britain.[7]

FDR Refused to Recognize Stalin as a Monster

Franklin Roosevelt comes across as an intellectually vain man. He was an early model of Western leaders (think Kissinger, Nixon, Clinton, Merkel, Macron.) who believed they could 'manage' Communist and other dictators with their charm and brilliance. (FDR's decision to run for a fourth term as president when he knew his body could no longer stand the strain of office reflected his far too great opinion of himself and his importance for America and the world.)

It was this arrogance that led to FDR's lack of caution towards the Soviet Union, his dismissal of credible reports of extensive Soviet espionage in Washington, and his belief that he could do business with Stalin to bring

---

6. Whittaker Chambers. 1952. *Witness*. p405.

7. Diana West. 2013. *American Betrayal: The Secret Assault on Our Nation's Character*. p42.

about the convergence of Western democracies and free markets with the totalitarian regime and Socialist economy of the Soviet Union.

Someone who did understand Stalin extremely well was William C. Bullitt, the first US ambassador to Moscow, where he was posted from December 13, 1933 to May 16, 1936. He followed this stint with four years as ambassador to France, but he continued to advise FDR, whom he had supported for president in 1932.

On January 29, 1943 Bullitt wrote a letter to FDR warning that Stalin was not a changed man, and that it was a dangerous mistake to believe the propaganda that he was as the basis for a policy of appeasement towards the Soviet Union. Bullitt said the United States should not "permit our war to prevent Nazi domination of Europe to be turned into a war to establish Soviet domination of Europe."[8]

At the time, Russian propaganda was pushing the line that Stalin was a changed man. As Diana West explains:

> The basic story, repeated over and over again, was that Stalin had changed, Stalin had no interest in territorial gains or world revolution, and Stalin was taking the Soviet Union in the direction of democracy and liberty.[9]

West notes that this view of Stalin was fabricated by Moscow on behalf of Stalin himself, and disseminated internationally by the Comintern—the abbreviated name for the Communist International, which was the Soviet organization responsible for managing Communist parties throughout the world, making sure that they all followed Moscow's line:

> What Bullitt understood early on, however, was that these lies were no "mistake." Instead—and this is critical—they were exactly "the view being propagated by the Comintern." He elaborated, "It is the communist party line in Great Britain, the United States and all other countries where there are communist parties. It is the line of fellow

8. Ibid, p198.

9. Ibid, p199.

travelers and many 'liberals'. Since Stalin personally sets the party line, it is what Stalin wants us to believe about him… The most careful search for factual evidence to support the thesis that Stalin is a changed man reveals none."[10]

In response to this thoughtful and serious letter, FDR offered possibly the most naïve statement on Stalin ever made by a Western leader. He simply referred to the opinion of Harry Hopkins, who had long professed sympathies for the Soviet Union—and might have been an agent for Moscow.[11] Here is FDR's response:

Bill, I don't dispute your facts, they are accurate. I don't dispute the logic of your reasoning. I just have a hunch that Stalin is not that kind of a man. Harry says he's not and that he doesn't want anything in the world but security for his country, and I think that if I give him everything I possibly can and ask nothing from him in return, *noblesse oblige*, he won't try to annex anything and will work with me for a world of democracy and peace.[12]

Remember, this was after FDR must have known a great deal about Stalin's purges in the 1930s, and the Gulag. He should have also known about the extent of Soviet propaganda, which had been so active at the outset of the war—first to persuade America to stay out of the war with Hitler because Stalin had a mutual non-aggression pact with Germany, but then, after Hitler launched Operation Barbarossa in June 1941, took a 180 degree turn to encourage Washington to back Britain and the Soviet Union as allies opposing Hitler.

Even at this time, Moscow's propaganda was incredibly effective. FDR's hunch, which was based on it, proved to be absolutely unfounded, and the

---

10. Ibid, p199.

11. Ibid, p182.

12. William C. Bullitt. August 30, 1948. *How We Won the War and Lost the Peace.* Life, p94.

policies he pursued based on it would prove catastrophic for the post-WWII world.

The damage done by FDR because of his refusal to recognize Stalin for who he really was became evident to several senior US officials who dealt with the Soviet dictator. Russia expert George F. Kennan first went to Moscow as a deputy to Ambassador Bullitt. Much later, after years of observing Stalin and Roosevelt's approach to him, Kennan had these critical things to say about the war-time president:

> I mean by that FDR's well-known conviction that although Stalin was a rather difficult character, he was at bottom a man like everyone else; that the only reason why it had been difficult to get on with him in the past was because there was no one with the right personality, with enough imagination and trust to deal with him properly; that the arrogant conservatives in the Western capitals had always bluntly rejected him, and that his ideological prejudices would melt away and Russian cooperation with the West could easily be obtained, if only Stalin was exposed to the charm of a personality of FDR's caliber. There were no grounds at all for this assumption; it was so childish that it was really unworthy of a statesman of FDR's standing.[13]

Kennan repeated his criticism of FDR in a 1996 interview with CNN:

> President Franklin Roosevelt rarely betrayed all of his reasons for doing anything to other people. I think that his hopes about Russia were largely unrealistic during the wartime period. I don't think FDR was capable of conceiving of a man of such profound iniquity, coupled with enormous strategic cleverness as Stalin. He had never met such a creature and Stalin was an excellent actor and when he did meet with leading people at these various conferences, he was magnificent, quiet, affable, reasonable.[14]

---

13. George F. Kennan. 1960. *Russia and the West Under Lenin and Stalin.* Little Brown. Quoted in Ernst Topitsch. 1987. *Stalin's War.* St Martin's Press, p129.

14. George F. Kennan. June 1996. *Interview of George F. Kennan.* CNN Cold War Series.

The Soviets Used Nukes to Intimidate the West

Once Moscow's spies in America and Britain had secured the secrets of the Atom bomb, in 1949 the USSR was able to make nuclear weapons itself. Stalin used his possession of these weapons to blackmail his erstwhile WWII allies—the United States and other Western states. He intimidated them into accepting his de facto occupation of European countries and generally emasculated the West by threatening to use nuclear weapons if they opposed him.

In the meantime, the Soviet Union aggressively expanded its global empire by employing conventional weapons and terror. A favorite strategy was to instigate and then support Marxist insurgencies called national liberation movements, especially in developing countries with unstable governments.

Soviet belligerence towards the West during the Cold War was on full display when Nikita Khrushchev spoke to the United Nations in 1960. He accused the West, and America in particular, of pursuing neo-colonialism and a provocative nuclear policy that was endangering civilization. In words echoed by the Kremlin today, he argued that Moscow could not be expected to curb its own nuclear weapons programs unless the West stopped its nuclear 'provocation'.[15] (As always, the side actually engaged in evil blames the innocent side for the sins that are its own.)

The Fallacy of Containment

As the US State Department's Office of the Historian records, American policy towards the Soviet threat in the post WWII era was guided by the desire to contain, rather than defeat, the Communist juggernaut:

> George F. Kennan, a career Foreign Service Officer, formulated the policy of "containment," the basic United States strategy for fighting the cold war (1947-1989) with the Soviet Union.

---

15. Nikita Khrushchev. 1960. *Speech to the United Nations General Assembly.* United Nations, General Assembly, Official Records, Fifteenth Session, pp68-84.

Kennan's ideas, which became the basis of the Truman administration's foreign policy, first came to public attention in 1947 in the form of an anonymous contribution to the journal *Foreign Affairs*, the so-called "X-Article." "The main element of any United States policy toward the Soviet Union," Kennan wrote, "must be that of a long-term, patient but firm and vigilant containment of Russian expansive tendencies." To that end, he called for countering "Soviet pressure against the free institutions of the Western world" through the "adroit and vigilant application of counter-force at a series of constantly shifting geographical and political points, corresponding to the shifts and maneuvers of Soviet policy." Such a policy, Kennan predicted, would "promote tendencies which must eventually find their outlet in either the break-up or the gradual mellowing of Soviet power."[16]

Thus the US served as the leading supplier of military assistance to countries on the Soviet periphery. This started with the Truman Doctrine, which provided assistance to post-WWII Turkey and Greece to prevent them from establishing Communist governments under Moscow's control. And once NATO was created, in 1949, America became the anchor for the alliance that protected it and most of Western Europe—as well as Turkey and Greece—from Soviet aggression.

All around the world there were Soviet-lit fires that Washington tried to extinguish. In Africa and Latin America, for example, the parties to many conflicts were Soviet and US proxies. Hence in Angola, for example, Washington provided support to Jonas Savimbi's UNITA rebels fighting the Soviet-backed government of José Eduardo dos Santos, and in Nicaragua America supported the Contras in their fight with the Soviet-supported Sandinista government of Daniel Ortega.

But there were also several major wars that the American military engaged in directly to counter Soviet-backed Communist regimes, notably in Korea, Vietnam and Afghanistan.

---

16. State Department article on George F. Kennan: https://history.state.gov/milestones/1945-1952/kennan

The Korean War Established a Terrible Cold War Precedent

The war in Korea marked the first significant US military encounter with a Communist state that was backed militarily by Moscow. The war started when Stalin, now armed with nuclear weapons, in 1950 approved an invasion of South Korea by the North—a Soviet client since 1945.

In a sign of things to come, Dean Acheson, the US secretary of state, in a January 12, 1950 speech to the National Press Club in Washington indirectly encouraged the invasion when he announced that the US defense perimeter in Asia included Japan and the Philippines but not South Korea and Taiwan. Given Stalin's worries that an invasion of South Korea by the North might prompt a US military response, Acheson's speech provided reassurances that undoubtedly encouraged him to give dictator Kim Il Sung the go-ahead.[17]

(This unwise speech by Acheson was echoed in early 2022 when US President Joe Biden suggested that the US response to a Russian invasion of Ukraine would be determined by the extent of the Russian military operation and occupation of Ukrainian territory.[18] This was no doubt music to Putin's ears, since it appeared to offer Russia a measure of Western acceptance for his invasion.)

The North Korean Army crossed the 38th Parallel that separated North from South Korea on June 25, 1950. On the same day, the UN Security Council voted for an Allied mission to support South Korea—a vote made possible because Russia had walked out of the Council in protest over the seating of the Republic of China (Taiwan) instead of a representative of the People's Republic of China.

The South was unprepared for the Northern onslaught and lost control of most of its territory in a matter of weeks. However, with the mandate provided by the UN resolution, America led a coalition of 21 allies who came

---

17. Miles Maochun Yu. March 9, 2017. *Green, Yellow, Or Red—What Color Was Dean Acheson's Speech?* Hoover Institution.

18. Joe Biden. January 19, 2022. *Remarks by President Biden in Press Conference*. The White House.

to the defense of South Korea, an alliance commanded by American General Douglas MacArthur.

Following MacArthur's surprise naval landing at Inchon on September 15, 1950, the South quickly recovered its territory up to the 38th Parallel. MacArthur then convinced President Harry Truman that the allied army should push all the way north to the Yalu River, which forms the border with Communist China. This second offensive made good progress until November 25, when a massive Chinese army of 200,000 soldiers crossed into North Korea to support Pyongyang.

The Allies were forced back to the 38th Parallel. MacArthur, wanted permission from Washington to blockade China and bomb Chinese military targets north of the Yalu as well as the bridges over the river. But Truman refused permission, citing the possible entry of the Soviet Union into the conflict. On December 19, 1950, Truman administration officials informed MacArthur that Washington no longer planned to fight for the reunification of Korea.

MacArthur saw this as a betrayal of Korea, but Truman was personally angered by MacArthur's independence and fired him, appointing General Matthew Ridgeway as a replacement.

Thus Washington's pattern of seeking the containment of Communism rather than victory over it was established. The thinking behind this decision was elaborated in an April 11, 1951 speech Truman gave to the nation:

> He began by defending his overall policy in Korea, declaring, "It is right for us to be in Korea." He excoriated the "communists in the Kremlin [who] are engaged in a monstrous conspiracy to stamp out freedom all over the world." Nevertheless, he explained, it "would be wrong—tragically wrong—for us to take the initiative in extending the war... Our aim is to avoid the spread of the conflict." The president continued, "I believe that we must try to limit the war to Korea for these vital reasons: To make sure that the precious lives of our fighting men are not wasted; to see that the security of our country and the free world is not needlessly jeopardized; and to prevent a

third world war." General MacArthur had been fired "so that there would be no doubt or confusion as to the real purpose and aim of our policy."[19]

There you have it. Harry Truman appeared 'presidential'. He wanted to avoid a third world war. He wanted to avoid a nuclear confrontation. He reasoned that it was better to end a conflict short of victory than to risk an escalation of the war. Surely this was wise and statesmanlike? Surely his position demonstrated maturity and restraint and would save lives?

History would prove otherwise. Truman's weakness set Korea on the path to the perennial North-South conflict that has continued for 70 years now, and remains a key ingredient in the instability of Asia. It also condemned millions of Koreans in the North to live under a brutal dictatorship that has been unable to feed its own people and yet invests massive resources into military spending, including for the development of nuclear weapons and missiles, which it uses to constantly threaten aggression against other states.

Furthermore, the compromise with Communism in Korea would establish a pattern for conflicts with the Soviet Union and other Communist states. This Western uncertainty and equivocation in the face of aggression fueled further aggression and resulted in more human suffering. Sadly, these subsequent conflicts would end up taking many more American lives—and consuming much more American treasure—than the likely cost that would have been incurred to liberate all of Korea.

The evil of the Kim Il Sung regime in Pyongyang that Truman left in place would soon become evident.

On May 12, 1952, General Mark W. Clark took over the United Nations Command from Ridgeway, and became the lead negotiator with North Korea. Clark would later describe his experience with the North Koreans in an interview he gave for a 1970 film narrated by John Wayne, called *War-*

---

19. Editors. November 13, 2009. *President Truman relieves General MacArthur of duties in Korea.* History.com.

hawk: No Substitute for Victory, which was intended to draw lessons for the Vietnam war from America's experience in Korea:

> After being at Panmunjom, being in charge of the negotiations there, and our people being insulted almost daily, I finally pled with my government to let me break off the negotiations at Panmunjom and place on the conference table a reasonable American position, one on which we could sign an armistice. And finally Washington permitted me to do so. We walked out. And then I called in my commanders, the Navy, the Airforce and the Army, and we discussed for days: How could we hurt the enemy within the limitations imposed upon us? And one by one—with the exception of the Yalu River bridges—I had these limitations taken off.

> Our hands were untied. And we hit the dams and we took out their power. We hit their dams and inundated their fields. We attacked Pyongyang, the capital of North Korea, after notifying the people that we were coming. And we just pounded them until it hurt them. And then, about three months later, Kim Il Sung sent me a message and said "Let's go back to the conference table, and let's trade prisoners of war, our sick and wounded." That's something we had asked to do many months before. And then we got down to business and began to work on an armistice.[20]

Clark had recognized that so long as the North Koreans could drag out the armistice negotiations at no cost to themselves, they would do so. This gave them time to regroup and rearm, at which point they could once more pursue their ultimate ambition of controlling the whole Korean peninsula. The renewed bombing of North Korean targets pushed Pyongyang to negotiate seriously. (Clark had wanted to bomb the bridges over the Yalu River for the obvious reason that this would effectively cut North Korea off from its main supporter, Communist China. This would have brought Kim Il Sung back to negotiations even more quickly.)

------

20. Mark W. Clark. 1970. *Warhawk: No Substitute for Victory.* Amazon Prime, Time Stamp 53:09.

It was at this point, in December 1952, that President-elect Eisenhower visited Korea. Clark presented him with a plan to defeat the North with air and naval power primarily. However, as with Eisenhower's concessions to the Soviet Union at the end of WWII, the new president decided to follow Truman's lead and settle for a divided Korea. Clark was instructed to resume armistice negotiations, which he did with success.

The South Koreans and the rest of the world should thank Clark for his resolve. Without his personal determination to force an armistice on North Korea by making the cost of refusing to negotiate in earnest too high for Pyongyang to pay, Korea would likely have gone the way Vietnam went 20 years later, with the whole peninsula falling under Pyongyang's brutal Communist rule.

US Containment Policies Assured a Communist Victory in Vietnam

Continuing his interview for *Warhawk*, General Clark connected the failure to win the war in Korea outright with the disaster that was unfolding in Vietnam at the time the film was made:

> And as I signed that Korean armistice I was convinced that had we stepped out, and had we had the courage to win our first test of arms with Communism, and win decisively, we would not be in the predicament, the mess we find ourselves in at the present time in Vietnam.

He was correct, as MacArthur had been before him. Many of the commanders in Vietnam also understood this basic truth about Communism: you could not defeat it through diplomacy that was not preceded by a military victory, or accompanied by a clear capability and credible threat to employ the military in a conflict.

American involvement in Vietnam started in earnest under President John F. Kennedy and continued under President Lyndon B. Johnson. But Richard M. Nixon—who in 1968 won the presidency based, in part, on his promise to end the war with honor—would own the debacle that unfolded in Vietnam. His national security advisor, and later secretary of state, was

Henry Kissinger, a Harvard academic who from the outset believed the war in Vietnam was unwinnable.

As Niall Ferguson wrote in his biography of Kissinger:

> It has long been assumed that Henry Kissinger "supported" the Vietnam War throughout the 1960s—and that this was one of the reasons Richard Nixon offered him the job of national security adviser. This view is incorrect. As his private papers and diaries make clear, Kissinger realized by 1966 at the latest that the U.S. intervention in defense of South Vietnam was a doomed enterprise and that only a diplomatic solution would end the conflict.[21]

Granted extraordinary negotiating powers by Nixon, Kissinger in 1971 undertook what became two years of negotiations with the North Vietnamese in Paris, a period during which America suspended the bombing of military targets in the North. The Paris Peace Accords, signed on January 27, 1973, won Kissinger and his North Korean counterpart, Le Duc Tho, a Nobel Peace Prize. But the Peace Accords were nothing to celebrate. The North Vietnamese had successfully worn down the Americans without making any significant concessions to get what they wanted.

As Foreign Service officer John Negroponte later joked:

> We bombed the North Vietnamese into accepting our concessions.[22]

Jessica Rotondi expanded on this in an article for History.com:

> The Paris Peace accords leading to a ceasefire in Vietnam were signed on January 27, 1973. To critics, "peace with honor" didn't look that different from options available when Nixon first took power: "Kissinger and Nixon wasted four years of negotiations with the

---

21. Niall Ferguson. October 10, 2015. *The Kissinger Diaries: What He Really Thought About Vietnam.* Politico Magazine.

22. Thomas Meaney. May 11, 2020. *The Myth of Henry Kissinger: Nixon's Secretary of State was a far less remarkable figure than his supporters, his critics—and he himself—believed.* The New Yorker.

Vietnamese communists, agreeing to virtually the same peace terms in 1973 that were on the table in 1969," argues [Robert K.] Brigham. In total, 2.5 million to 3 million Vietnamese and other Indochinese and 58,000 Americans died in Vietnam. Hundreds more were missing in action.[23]

South Korea was saved from Communism because of the resolve of generals MacArthur and Clark as well as other military commanders, but the whole of Vietnam was lost to Communism because of Washington's lack of determination to defeat the North.

The US military has long had more than sufficient capability to win wars against Communism decisively, but political leaders in Washington have repeatedly been intimidated by Soviet threats into settling for less. In Vietnam, this losing mindset was the basis for Nixon and Kissinger's diplomacy, which failed abysmally. To quote again from Rotondi quoting Brigham:

Kissinger wanted to make sure the war ended in Paris and not in Saigon. He had very little faith in the Vietnamese armed forces. He understood U.S. Congress didn't have a stomach for the conflict and wanted the U.S. to withdraw without looking like it was an overwhelming defeat.

It was not long after their failure in Vietnam before Nixon and Kissinger adopted détente as the core concept underpinning US foreign policy towards the Soviet Union, especially in Europe. Détente would be the prevailing theory on how to 'manage' the Soviet Union—until Ronald Reagan became president in 1981.

Détente was welcomed by Moscow which immediately saw that it could be used to manipulate the good intentions of Western nations to the USSR's benefit. As Vladimir Bukovsky explains in his book *Judgment in Moscow*, one immediate benefit of détente and the agreements signed under its aegis

---

23. Jessica Pearce Rotondi. May 9, 2022. *Henry Kissinger's Controversial Role in the Vietnam War.* History.com.

(such as the 1975 Helsinki Accords on human rights) was the de facto recognition of Moscow's hegemony over east and central Europe.[24]

The US Failure in Afghanistan Encouraged Putin

The failure of containment and détente were not limited to Western relations with Communist states. They have also failed to prevent aggression by non-Communist states with authoritarian governments.

For example, in 2021 President Joe Biden precipitously ended the war in Afghanistan by withdrawing all US forces before US and other Western civilians and their Afghan allies had been evacuated, and Western military equipment sent home. There was no good reason for caving to the terror-loving Taliban who overran the country in a matter of days. The regime they established in Kabul soon looked exactly like the one ousted by American forces 20 years earlier.

The war in Afghanistan caused close to 2,500 US deaths and over 20,000 US soldiers injured. And it cost America some $2.3 trillion. There were also an estimated 70,000 Afghan civilian deaths that resulted from the fighting.

The reason for American intervention in Afghanistan was pretty straightforward: the terrorists who bombed the World Trade Center and Pentagon on September 11, 2001, had been trained by Al Qaeda in camps on Afghanistan's territory.

However, once the Taliban government was first defeated by America and its allies, the reasons for staying in Afghanistan—and the end goal for being there—became increasingly murky. The Taliban was largely contained, but it was never thoroughly beaten and forced to surrender. Thus as soon as the US pulled out, the Taliban returned to power.

America's enemies took note of the 2021 collapse of the American presence in Afghanistan, which echoed the disastrous American exit from Vietnam in 1975. The Afghanistan debacle was no doubt an encouraging development for Putin, who must have calculated that—based on Biden's

---

24. Vladimir Bukovsky. 2019. *Judgment in Moscow: Soviet Crimes and Western Complicity.* p312.

performance in Afghanistan—Russia could seize pieces if not all of Ukraine without expecting a robust response from America or the rest of NATO.

Reagan Was Right: Containment and Détente Had Not Worked

The uneasy and ultimately false peace of containment and détente was finally challenged by President Ronald Reagan. He had extensive knowledge of the Soviet Union and the suffering of people under Communism, and he was determined to treat the USSR as the enemy of freedom that it was. He did not accept Soviet hegemony over its European satellites or its international provocation and support for Marxist revolutionary wars and regimes around the world.

His clear articulation of a US policy aimed at defeating the Soviet Union and loosening its grip on Communist allies and dependents, shook up relations between the two superpowers. With the ideological and diplomatic support of Great Britain under Prime Minister Margaret Thatcher and the Vatican under anti-Communist Polish Pope John Paul II, Reagan's challenge to Moscow would mark the beginning of the end of the Soviet Empire.

The USSR's centrally planned socialist economy simply did not work. Moscow could no longer feed its people, let alone support its satellites and other dependents. Only continuous supplies of Western aid could save it, and Reagan was not interested in saving it.

As Aleksandr Solzhenitsyn's great book *The Gulag Archipelago* set out clearly, the Soviet Union fully deserved Reagan's label for it: the Evil Empire. It is worth quoting more from the speech in which Reagan first used the term:

> Yes, let us pray for the salvation of all of those who live in that total-itarian darkness—pray they will discover the joy of knowing God. But until they do, let us be aware that while they preach the suprem-acy of the State, declare its omnipotence over individual man, and predict its eventual domination of all peoples on the earth, they are the focus of evil in the modern world .... So, in your discussions of the nuclear freeze proposals, I urge you to beware the temptation of

pride—the temptation of blithely declaring yourselves above it all and label both sides equally at fault, to ignore the facts of history and the aggressive impulses of an evil empire, to simply call the arms race a giant misunderstanding and thereby remove yourself from the struggle between right and wrong and good and evil.[25]

Reagan recognized the fallacy of containment and détente because they normalized evil. He was determined to help the victims of Communism by remaining resolutely committed to their liberation from totalitarian oppression.

As the history of the post-WWII era demonstrates all too clearly, there can be no compromise with evil. All attempts at containment end in signaling weakness to the bad actors who would destroy our civilization and impose their rule over us. Whenever we do make concessions to evil in the name of peace, the fix is always inconclusive and we are forced to deal again with a renewed and reinvigorated enemy. And the price we have to pay is always higher the second or third time around.

---

25. Ronald Reagan. March 8, 1983. *Address to the National Association of Evangelicals*.

Chapter 3

Putin's Russia Becomes a Fascist State

The Soviet Empire Collapses

We have already referred to Vladimir Bukovsky's book, *Judgment in Moscow*. Bukovsky was allowed by President Boris Yeltsin for a brief period in the early 1990s to go through the archives of the Central Committee of the Communist Party of the Soviet Union, and its top decision-making body, the Politburo. He copied the minutes of many of these meetings which reveal the economic crisis in the USSR that steadily worsened until Moscow was no longer able to maintain its hold on satellite countries or provide significant support for Communist parties around the world.

The Soviet invasion of Afghanistan, initiated by Leonid Brezhnev in December 1979, followed by a disastrous eight-year occupation, would drain Moscow's precious resources and push the USSR to the brink of collapse. A succession of Russian leaders in the 80s (Brezhnev, Yuri Andropov, Konstantin Chernenko and Mikhail Gorbachev) clung to an increasingly hopeless belief that their regime would survive—although you would never have thought the mighty Soviet Union was on the verge of collapse if you listened to the propaganda bluster that flowed ceaselessly from Moscow's state media organs.

Foreign aid to encourage Gorbachev's programs of *glasnost* (openness) and *perestroika* (reform) helped prop up the crumbling economy for a while, but as unrest spread through Moscow's satellites, beginning with Poland, there simply was not enough money to sustain the puppet regimes in these countries.

Bukovsky points out that Gorbachev himself was a dedicated Communist, but that he and the other Central Committee members calculated that if they allowed a measure of independence in their European dependencies the economic burden on Moscow would be lightened while political control could be maintained through a new breed of socialist leaders. Military intervention (as in the Hungarian uprising of 1956 and the Prague Spring of 1968) was off the table. It was no longer militarily or financially feasible.

Like Communist China today, the Soviet Union had always spent a huge slice of its budget on its military as well as on its security services—such as the KGB and GRU. This is because its agenda was never the wellbeing of its population (despite its endless propaganda claiming compassion for the proletariat and the downtrodden of the world), but only and always for its acquisition, retention and expansion of power—with the ultimate goal of creating a Communist world, led by Moscow.

Unlike Communist China, the USSR never came to terms with the obvious fact that centrally planned socialist economies simply don't work. Belatedly, it did allow families to cultivate small plots of land and keep or trade the produce they were able to grow, but this was far too little too late to save their decrepit economy from collapse.

With Moscow's European satellites seeking independence from Moscow in the last years of the 1980s, the Communist Party of the Soviet Union (CPSU) was confronted with the inevitable: It could no longer hold on to power even within Russia itself, let alone keep control of other countries.

Meanwhile, Boris Yeltsin, who presented himself as an advocate of multiparty democracy under an elected president, became a popular alternative to Mikhail Gorbachev, and was elected the first president of the Russian Federation on June 12, 1991.

The USSR is Replaced with the CIS

Despite the remarkable success of Reagan's policy towards the Soviet Union, leading to its final collapse in 1991, there are elements of the transition to a post-Communist Russia that have resulted in it now becoming an aggressive nation that is once more seeking to create an empire.

On the positive side, the constituent states of the Soviet Union gained their freedom when, under the leadership of Yeltsin, on December 8, 1991 the USSR was replaced with the Commonwealth of Independent States (CIS). Moscow was no longer the seat of a federation of 15 separate socialist states, but the capital of the Russia Federation which included many small autonomous sub-states within Russia's territory, such as Chechnya, Dagestan, Tatarstan, etc.

The three Baltic States (Lithuania, Latvia and Estonia) wanted a complete break with their former Soviet masters, and did not join the CIS. This left 12 former members of the Soviet Union (Armenia, Azerbaijan, Belarus, Georgia, Kazakhstan, Kyrgyzstan, Moldova, Russia, Tajikistan, Turkmenistan, Ukraine, and Uzbekistan) to join the CIS. All dropped "socialist" from their names as they were transformed into independent republics. The CIS would prove to be a rather weak association of countries, and members would enter into additional agreements for economic and military alliances—such as The Collective Security Treaty Organization (CSTO).

Nevertheless, Russia emerged from the USSR as the largest country in the world, stretching across 11 time zones—from Kaliningrad on the Baltic Sea in the west to the Bering Sea in the east. This vast territory with its massive natural resources makes Russia a potential global threat so long as it is being led by expansionist despots.

Without exception, it was Communist leaders of the Soviet states who became the first leaders of the newly independent CIS republics. Thirty years on, the degree of independence from Russia of these countries varies considerably, from Belarus under Alexander Lukashenko being little more than a Russian sub-state, to Ukraine fighting to the death to assert its permanent independence.

No Nuremberg for the Soviet Leaders

When Hitler was forced to surrender unconditionally to the Allies in 1945, many of the Nazi leaders were brought to trial for war crimes in the city that had been the center of their cult and the scene of massive Nazi rallies—Nuremberg. Most of these trials ended in execution or very long prison terms for the leaders of the Reich.

To prevent a possible resurgence of German militarism, the country was occupied by the armies of four of the main WWII Allies: the United Kingdom, the United States, France and the Soviet Union. The capital, Berlin, was surrounded by Russian-controlled territory when the fighting stopped, so it was separately divided into four sectors with each under the control of one of these four Allies.

The great difference between the Soviet Union and its Western WWII Allies was revealed in their behavior after the Nazi surrender. The three Western allies, and in particular the United States through its Marshall Plan, helped Germany get back on its feet, albeit as a country that now was shorn of its army. By contrast, the Soviets, who at Yalta had insisted on extracting at least $10 billion in reparations from Germany after the war, proceeded to create a satellite Communist state in East Germany, a pawn it occupied until 1994.

When the Soviet Union collapsed, there was no Nuremberg-like mechanism that enabled the victims of decades of Communist aggression to bring those responsible to justice. There were no Allied armies to impose a new order, and the United Nations was so thoroughly compromised by Soviet influence that it made no effort on behalf of the victims of Soviet oppression.

Plus, most importantly, Moscow was one of the five permanent Security Council members, who had veto power over this key decision-making body.

Within the former USSR itself, despite the political changes sweeping through the erstwhile Soviet empire, the Russian Federation and other CIS members were all run by ex-Communists who (obviously!) had no interest in supporting a process of establishing accountability for past Soviet crimes.

Thus the world has moved on, leaving the victims of Communism to suffer yet another injustice. Those still alive have had to make new lives the best they can under post-Soviet regimes that are preoccupied with their own survival, or find new homes in places that offer true freedom.

The CPSU Elite and KGB Have Created a Fascist State

More seriously for the world, elements of the CPSU and its security agencies, especially the KGB, lived on after the public collapse of their regime. Without the Communist Party in power, the people who ran the Soviet state soon adapted their totalitarian methods to the post-Soviet environment.

There were two main changes. First, making money was unquestionably a prime objective of power. This led to the creation of a Mafia-like state. Second, instead of crushing the church, as Communist states have always done, Putin and his allies co-opted the Russian Orthodox Church into serving the state's interests. (It was recently revealed that Patriarch Kirill had himself been a KGB operative.[1])

Taken together, these two changes meant that the Soviet Union became a fascist state that features crony capitalism and exploitation of the church. Added to this mix is the ever-present nationalism that has fueled Russian imperialism for centuries. Thus Russia today is similar to Hitler's Germany. This is hardly progress from its hardcore Communist past!

On August 26, 1991, five days after the CPSU failed in an attempted coup to depose Gorbachev (still the Soviet Secretary General and President at this time), Nikolay Kruchina—a man largely unknown to the world—fell to his death from his 7th-floor Moscow apartment.[2]

---

1. Originally from two Swiss publications: Le Martin Dimanche and Sonntagszeitung. *Patriarch Kirill worked for the KGB in the 1970s, Swiss media report.* Euronews.

2. James O. Jackson. September 9, 1991. *The Party Is Over.* Time; Paul Klebnikov. 2000. *Godfather of the Kremlin: Boris Berezovsky and the Looting of Russia.* Harcourt, 2000. p76.

Kruchina was a key player in the Communist Party who since 1983 had been responsible for the management of its assets. These included gold, cash, bank deposits and real estate, in Russia and abroad, with an estimated value of $9 billion.[3] His sudden death did not occur in isolation. His suicide was followed by dozens of other mysterious deaths in the organization he headed, and included his predecessor, Georgy Pavlov.[4]

Other 'suicides' immediately after the failed coup were Boris Pugo, Minister of Interior, who knew the secrets of the security services and died on August 22, and Marshall Sergey Akhromeyev, a senior military leader who had also supported the coup and died on August 24. These people knew too much, and the real powers behind the coup could not allow them to remain on earth. Who were these powers? Almost certainly elements of the Central Committee with control over the security services—the people skilled at arranging 'suicides'.

Apparently a lot of money had been transferred from the accounts managed by Kruchina to newly formed entities in the period leading up to the coup. Whatever happened to these CPSU-held 'off the books' assets, none were ever recovered by the Russian state.

Clearly, some Soviet deep state actors not only survived the end of the Soviet Union, but left office rich, and are therefore dangerous still.

Enter Putin, Russia's New Dictator

Vladimir Putin established himself in the Soviet government through 16 years of service in the KGB. In 1990 he left the world of espionage to take up political posts in Leningrad (later St. Petersburg) and then, in 1996, he moved to Moscow.

Putin became the protégé of President Yeltsin, who appointed him in 1998 to head the newly-formed FSB—which replaced the FSK and KGB

---

3. Associated Press. August 27, 1991. *Soviet Turmoil; New Suicide: Budget Director.* The New York Times, Section A, p6.

4. Konstantin Samoilov. January 25, 2023. *Inside Russia.* https://www.youtube. com/watch?v=0Qw3Tb98VUk&t=565s

before it. In 1999, Putin was made one of three first deputy prime ministers, and then acting prime minister. When Yeltsin resigned on December 31, 1999, Putin became acting president. On March 26, 2000 he was elected president on the first round of a general election.

During the Soviet era, the CPSU was firmly in control of all government organs, including the KGB. So Putin's rise through the Soviet ranks indicates that he was a 'good' Communist, someone who fit well into the Soviet system. This background also prepared him to run the FSB.

Kamil Galeev, a very knowledgeable observer of Russian politics, recently pointed out that Putin's rapid rise to power was accompanied by another very significant change in Russia that he was instrumental in effecting: the ascendancy of the FSB until it supplanted the Communist Party as the dominant force in the country:

> Indeed, the domination of State Security "the new nobility" over all other institutions is a particular feature of Putin's regime. Which hadn't been the case in the USSR. State security rule is the major innovation of Putin.[5]

Putin seems to be someone who understands Russian chauvinism well, and he exploited this knowledge to get elected to the presidency in 2000. He is widely believed to have engineered a series of deadly terror attacks on Moscow residential buildings in September 1999, which he promptly blamed on the Chechens and then used as a pretext to launch an all-out war against them.

The Russian voters were apparently not particularly concerned by Putin's rigged terror attacks and they were impressed with this bloody crackdown on a Muslim minority. He rode this macho persona to victory at the polls.

As Galeev notes, the FSB was found to be responsible for a terror attack that was averted when residents discovered the bomb it had planted—clear-

---

5. Kamil Galeev. February 23, 2022. Twitter. https://twitter.com/kamilkazani/status/1496506490202513413.

ly pointing to Putin's culpability. Nevertheless, he was rewarded with the presidency:

> [Putin's ridiculous explanation for the planned bombing] sounded shady, but the military planes were already razing Grozny to the ground. The successful invasion that followed changed the electoral balance completely. In August 1999 2% of voters would have voted for Putin; in 2000, 53% did. Russian people love victorious wars.[6]

A Mafia-Like Operation

Once in office, Putin managed to circumvent constitutional term limits and stay in power by switching positions with his prime minister, Dmitry Medvedev for the 2008 to 2012 term. Once this four-year term was over, they switched again so that Putin could return to the presidency for another two terms. A June 2020 referendum secured two additional terms for him

Meanwhile, he has steadily crushed independent media, bringing all but a handful of peripheral outlets under state control. In 2005 he launched RT as a global propaganda channel, which broadcasts state produced content in five languages.

He has also eliminated political critics and opponents through Mafia-like means, including imprisonment, poisonings, stabbings, accidents and (a new favorite) people plunging to their deaths from windows in hotels and other high-rise buildings.

Could Putin have had a hand in all those strange 'suicides' in 1991? If not him, it was likely some other deep state operatives who continue to work in the shadows to exert a lethal grip on Russia.

Galeev points out that a big difference between the Soviet Union and today's Russia is that the FSB is not similarly ideological. Its functionaries are obsessed with power and wealth, not Communist revolution. The Soviets believed they really were changing the world. The FSB is focused on creating the best pipeline and transport systems possible (rail, road and ports)

---

6. Kamil Galeev. February 24, 2022. https://twitter.com/kamilkazani/status/1496724106716274690.

to facilitate the export of Russian commodities—first among which are, of course, oil and gas—so that it can benefit the FSB.

Putin himself has become fantastically rich while in office. No one knows the extent of his fortune, but it is estimated to be in the tens of billions of dollars. In a January 2022 edition of *Forbes*, the distinguished Swedish economist Anders Åslund, who in 2019 published the book *Russia's Crony Capitalism*, estimated that Putin's fortune was between $100 billion and $130 billion.[7]

Putin uses his political clout and FSB influence to control oligarchs who try to be independent. If they dabble in politics, they are crushed. An early example of Putin's unsavory methods was the arrest, prosecution for tax evasion and imprisonment for 10 years of Mikhail Khodorkovsky, once Russia's richest man as owner of the major oil company, Yukos.

Khodorkovsky got into trouble when he became increasingly critical of Putin, and was jailed in 2003. Adding insult to injury, in 2004 Khodorkovsky was forced to offer for sale his ownership share in Yukos to meet a purported tax bill. In 2006 the company went bankrupt anyway, and its assets were seized by the Russian state.

The rise of billion-dollar oligarchs in Russia is part of the dismal post-Soviet landscape, since much of the country continues to be impoverished, as it was in Soviet times. According to World Bank data, in 2021 the GDP per capita was estimated at $12,195, putting Russia on a par with Bulgaria and Costa Rica. This ranking places Russia at the global average for GDP per capita.[8]

Putin's hunger for power and wealth (he loves gilded palaces), his imprisonment and murder of opposition figures, his control of media and projection of state propaganda around the world—all while many Russians live in poverty—is reminiscent of the Soviet Union ruled by the CPSU's

---

7. Forbes Wealth Team. January 27, 2022. *As Biden Mulls Sanctions, Three Theories On How Putin Makes His Millions*, Forbes.

8. World Bank, GDP per capita, 2021. https://data.worldbank.org/indicator/ NY.GDP.PCAP.CD

Nomenklatura. There is more wealth than before, but it continues to be very unevenly distributed.

Back in the USSR

The war in Ukraine can be understood as Putin trying to refresh his credentials as a modern-day Tsar, repeating a formula that first brought him to power on the heels of his victory in Chechnya. He has reverted to that formula several times since—notably in Georgia in 2008 and in Ukraine's Crimea and the Donbas in 2014.

Now that it is all too clear that he has made a terrible miscalculation in Ukraine, he is having to return to his roots as a good Communist. Short of any real international friends, Putin has had to look to the few Communist states still in business to replenish his army's dwindling arsenal. Thus he has sought weapons from Beijing and Pyongyang (of all places!). He has other allies of sorts in the Communist regimes of Cuba, Venezuela and Nicaragua, although these countries can offer little to help his war effort.

And, in a new twist of resurrected fraternity, Putin has become a loving brother to Ayatollah Khamenei, the Islamist dictator of Iran, who has provided hundreds of bomb-bearing drones to Moscow. The man is desperate.

Nevertheless, Putin still sits atop a vast country with massive resources. Finding himself diminished by the wretched performance of his army, he is a dangerous dictator who must be prevented from undertaking further reckless and murderous adventures abroad.

Chapter 4

Putin's History of Unjustified Invasions

A Small Man With Giant Ambitions

Like many other totalitarians before him, Putin seems to suffer from a short-man complex. His climb to the top of power and wealth in Russia has gone to his head. On the way up he has developed an ability to manipulate world powers with a combination of threats and entreaties. He's been getting what he wants far too easily.

At heart, he is a would-be Russian Tsar, an emperor ruling over vast lands with tens of millions of people looking at him with awe and fear. Blessed with the riches of Russia's abundant resources of fossil fuels and various other valuable minerals, as well as wheat and other crops, he apparently sees the world as a place that he can bend to his will.

No moral principles stand in his way; no human ties hold him back. Nevertheless, like Russian rulers before him (think Stalin), he is obsessed with his own security, viewing all around him with suspicion and trepidation. Despots never seem to learn that their despotism and greed always put their own lives at risk.

A Would-be Tsar Justifies His Bloody Conquests

On February 21, three days before the invasion, Putin made a televised address to the nation in which he revealed his real motives for his 'special military operation'. (See Appendix 1 for the full text.) The real issue was not

NATO expansion or Nazis influence in Ukraine, as he so often claims, but his personal ambition to reconstitute the Russian Empire.

In an April 25, 2005 address to the nation, Putin had revealed this thinking when he lamented the collapse of the Soviet Union as the "greatest geopolitical catastrophe of the century," a disaster that had forced millions of fellow citizens to live outside the Russian Federation:

> …it should be acknowledged, and I have spoken of this before, that the collapse of the Soviet Union was the greatest geopolitical catastrophe of the century. And for the Russian people, it was a real drama. Tens of millions of our citizens and fellow-countrymen found themselves outside the Russian Federation.[1]

In his February 21 speech, he picked up this theme by claiming that Ukraine historically belongs to Russia:

> I would like to emphasize again that Ukraine is not just a neighboring country for us. It is an inalienable part of our own history, culture and spiritual space. These are our comrades, those dearest to us-not only colleagues, friends and people who once served together, but also relatives, people bound by blood, by family ties.

Putin made it clear that in his opinion even the structure of the Soviet Union itself had been faulty insofar as it granted limited autonomy to its constituent states, the blame for which he laid at the feet of Vladimir Lenin and the Bolsheviks when they created the USSR in 1922, after five years of civil war and conquest:

> So, I will start with the fact that modern Ukraine was entirely created by Russia or, to be more precise, by Bolshevik, Communist Russia. This process started practically right after the 1917 revolution, and Lenin and his associates did it in a way that was extremely harsh on Russia—by separating, severing what is historically Russian land. Nobody asked the millions of people living there what they thought.

---

1. Vladimir Putin. April 25, 2005. *Russian President Putin Delivers State of the Nation Address*, RTR Russia TV, via BBC Monitoring.

He added:

> When it comes to the historical destiny of Russia and its peoples, Lenin's principles of state development were not just a mistake; they were worse than a mistake, as the saying goes. This became patently clear after the dissolution of the Soviet Union in 1991.

Putin goes on to list what he calls crimes against Russia committed by Ukraine, and claims that Kyiv was planning to build nuclear weapons as part of a program of military integration with the West. He concludes with this rationalization for the invasion:

> We want those who seized and continue to hold power in Kiev to immediately stop hostilities. Otherwise, the responsibility for the possible continuation of the bloodshed will lie entirely on the conscience of Ukraine's ruling regime.

The behavior of Vladimir Putin since he became Russia's president in 2000 confirms that he is above all else a believer in the Russian Empire and that he sees himself as a historical, Tsar-like figure who will reverse the mistakes of the Soviet Union by re-integrating its now independent descendants into a restored Russian Empire.

Crushing Chechnya and invading Georgia were the first small steps; invading Ukraine in 2014 initiated a much bigger step, which was launched in earnest in 2022. There is no indication that he will stop short of his goal.

Putin the Conqueror: First, Georgia

On August 8, 2008, Putin launched an invasion of Georgia, ostensibly to protect Russian minorities in the country, in particular the regions of South Ossetia and Abkhazia. Both had claimed the status of independent republics after the collapse of the Soviet Union, but the international community still recognized them as part of Georgia.

The Georgian army was unable to prevent this invasion, and a ceasefire was negotiated on August 12, just four days after the fighting began. Meanwhile, the Russians living in these areas conducted ethnic cleansing operations against Georgian residents, forcing them to flee to areas controlled by Tbilisi. (Today there are some 20,000 Georgian refugees from these areas who have not been able to return to their homes.)

Russian forces did withdraw from several Georgian cities they had occupied in the war, but they have continued to occupy the two breakaway regions. To this day only a handful of countries recognize the regions as independent republics: Nauru, Nicaragua, Russia and Syria. (It seems Moscow has fewer 'friends' than ever under Putin.)

Some fairly stern scolding of Russia by the international community followed this invasion, but Putin faced little meaningful international censure, let alone punitive measures with real teeth. The Russian dictator must have smiled when—a decade after his aggression in Georgia—the US National Security Advisor John Bolton in 2018 claimed that the United States had imposed all necessary sanctions on Russia for its 2008 invasion.[2]

If Bolton was correct, the Russian army would be in Georgia no longer and Putin would not have contemplated undertaking his next move—the annexation of Crimea in 2014.

In hindsight, it is clear that Putin believed he had pulled off the invasion of Georgia with no lasting negative consequences. The limp international response signaled a weakness that he would continue to exploit on behalf of his ambition to restore Russia to its former imperial glory.

Putin the Conqueror: Second, Crimea

In February 2014, there were massive demonstrations in Kyiv against the Putin-backed president, Viktor Yanukovych, as part of what became known as the Revolution of Dignity, or the Maidan Revolution (named after Kyiv's central square where crowds gathered for days of anti-government demonstrations).

The political base for Yanukovych and his Regions Party was in eastern and southern Ukraine, where the Russian-speaking populations were dom-

---

2. Staff Report. October 26, 2018. *U.S. has put all necessary sanctions on Russia over 2008 Georgia war—Trump adviser*. Reuters.

inant. Long an ally of Putin, Yanukovych had in November 2013 refused to sign an association and free trade agreement with the European Union, something that Putin did not want but the majority of Ukrainians did, especially those in the Western regions of the country.

On February 20, a police crackdown against the demonstrators resulted in the death of at least 21 protesters and one policeman, the BBC reported.[3] Two days later, the Ukrainian Rada (parliament) impeached Yanukovych, removing him from office.

The same BBC story noted that before the Rada vote Yanukovych broadcast a statement in which he complained of being the victim of a coup: "He insisted he was the 'lawfully elected president' and compared the actions of the opposition to the rise to power of the Nazis in 1930s Germany."

Meanwhile, with Ukraine and much of the world distracted by the dramatic developments in Kyiv, Putin made a move of his own, exploiting this opportunity to pull the trigger on a project he had long prepared for—the occupation and annexation of Crimea as the first step towards the conquest of all Ukraine.

Putin could not have engineered the chaos that led to Yanukovych's ouster, although that clearly did provide him with a pretext to occupy Crimea—to protect its Russian-speaking population, of course. However, seeing that his man was about to be ousted, he judged this to be an opportune moment to implement his plan to invade Ukraine before an anti-Russian government could take power in Kyiv.

On February 20 Putin's army occupied Ukraine's Crimean Peninsula, where the large Russian-speaking population had been heavily infiltrated by Putin's agents in preparation for this move. A March 16 referendum on the peninsula—conducted under the watchful eyes and loaded guns of Russian soldiers—resulted in Crimea being annexed into the Russian Federation.

The timing of this invasion is significant because it reveals just how

---

3. February 22, 2014. *Ukrainian MPs vote to oust President Yanukovych.* BBC News.

important to Putin his 'operation Crimea' was. It should be remembered that under Putin's leadership Russia had just poured an astronomical $51 billion into hosting the 2014 Winter Olympics in Sochi, a resort town on the Black Sea.[4] The Games—which ran from February 7 to 23—were supposed to enhance Russia's image and elevate Putin as a world leader. However, Putin risked destroying all that expensive branding when he ordered his army to take Crimea three days before the Games were over.

Disturbingly, despite the sheer criminality of this annexation, the response of the international community was muted. Sanctions were imposed on Russia, but these had limited effect and Putin could see that he was once more getting away with a massive violation of international law.

Despite this being his second illegal annexation of a neighbor's territory, Putin himself was not ostracized by the world. He continued to be treated as any other world leader—attending summits and conducting meetings with other heads of state and senior officials.

As if to confirm the lack of a serious international response to Russia's Crimea operation, Moscow remained one of the five members of the UN Security Council and Foreign Minister Sergey Lavrov continued to travel the world to lecture other countries on Russia's virtues while complaining about its mistreatment by the international community. Poor Russia!

Putin the Conqueror: Third, The Donbas

The Russian dictator not only was interested in Crimea. The whole of southern and eastern Ukraine represented a rich target for him. He focused first on the Donbas, a region that includes two major Ukrainian oblasts (states): Donetsk and Luhansk (or Lugansk).

As in South Ossetia, Abkhazia and Crimea, Putin's agents long agitated for the people of these oblasts to seek independence from Kyiv. In the wake of Yanukovych's ouster and the referendum in Crimea, Russian-backed separatists in the Donbas in April of 2014 created the Donetsk People's Repub-

---

4. Owen Gibson. October 9, 2013. *Sochi 2014: the costliest Olympics yet but where has all the money gone?* The Guardian.

lic and Luhansk People's Republic. (Both the DPR and LPR were formally annexed by Moscow—along with the Kherson and Zaporizhzhia oblasts—on September 30, 2022, following Russian-run referenda in all four regions.)

In August 2014, Ukraine's government forces pushed the rebels almost all the way back to the border with Russia, but on August 24 Putin sent units of the Russian army into Ukraine to assist the separatists. That this amounted to a Russian invasion of Ukraine was denied by Moscow, which claimed that the soldiers who participated in this operation were on leave from the army and fighting as volunteers—they did not wear regular uniforms, but their weapons were provided by Moscow.

This Russian operation and its strategic objectives were analyzed by the Centre for Eastern Studies (CES), a Polish think tank, in an article published on September 3, 2014.[5] According to its analysis, there were an estimated 45,000 Russian soldiers engaged in the operation, making Moscow's claim of non-involvement ludicrous.

Russia's participation in the fighting would prove decisive, as the Ukrainian army was soon pushed out of the cities of Donetsk and Luhansk and other territories it had recently re-captured from the rebels. Kyiv was forced to sign a ceasefire agreement with the DPR and LPR in Minsk on September 5, 2014.

CES identified Moscow's strategy at the time—a strategy that we are all familiar with now. It is worth reprinting the key elements here since they confirm that the war now raging in Ukraine is not something Putin cooked up in a moment of anger, but part of his long-term strategy to destroy Ukrainian independence.

This is how CES described Moscow's three strategic objectives:

> The Kremlin's political decision to launch a limited, direct military intervention in Eastern Ukraine was apparently a reaction to the threat of the effective collapse of the so-called Donetsk and Lugansk

---

5. Piotr Zochowski, Rafat Sadowski and Marek Menkiszak. September 3 2014. *The Russian military intervention in eastern Ukraine.* Center for Eastern Studies.

People's Republics, which in the Kremlin's perception would hinder and postpone the opportunity to implement Russia's plans for the political subordination of Ukraine. Moreover, it would draw accusations from nationalist circles in Russia that the authorities of the Russian Federation had left the population of the Donbas to their fate, and betrayed Russia's national interests.

Secondly, Russia has demonstrated to the leaders of Western countries (especially Germany) that it is ready to lay bare their ineffectiveness in the face of Russian military aggression. Russia has also pre-emptively warned Western countries against making any attempts to assist the military in Ukraine (President Putin warned against this on 29 August, noting that Russia is a nuclear power). In this way, Russia is suggesting that the only way for the leaders of the West to save face and credibility is to exert effective pressure on Kyiv to agree to a ceasefire, i.e. a de facto freezing of the conflict, which would give room for the separatists to consolidate their forces, and for Kyiv to seek a modus vivendi with Russia.

Thirdly, by escalating the military action, Russia wants to show that the theses and proposals formulated by President Putin on the political and geopolitical status of Ukraine should be taken seriously, and should be adopted as the subject of talks with Moscow. It is no coincidence that the Russian military offensive took place simultaneously with the meeting at the summit made up of the Eurasian Union (Russia, Belarus and Kazakhstan), Ukraine and the European Union on 26 August in Minsk. In his speech there, President Putin firmly restated the basis of his concept: that Ukraine is part of the historically shaped, natural sphere of influence of Russia; and of the area of the process of economic integration (controlled by Russia); that the states which are part of the area have only limited sovereignty, which means that they cannot make any choices in domestic, foreign, economic and security policies which would conflict with the interests of the Russian Federation (as defined by Moscow).

A Deafening Chorus of Western Crickets

Putin's 2014 invasion of Ukraine (in Crimea and the Donbas) took place at the halfway point of the presidency of Barak Obama. The Russian president rightly judged that Obama's response to Moscow's aggression would be tepid and definitely not threaten his master plan for making Ukraine part of the Russian Federation.

Obama was not exactly a man of decisive action on the international stage, and apparently his administration took seriously Putin's warnings that Washington should not arm Ukraine. It only sent non-military aid to Kyiv and did nothing to reverse Russia's illegal occupation of Crimea and the Donbas. (To his credit, Donald Trump as president sent anti-tank Javelins and some other military equipment to help Kyiv.)

But the sad truth is that Washington and NATO did little to nothing to reverse Russia's aggression and prevent its repetition—despite Moscow's disturbing ethnic cleansing in Crimea and the Donbas and its continued support for illegal separatist states in Georgia and Ukraine.

Thus not only did the West foolishly heed Putin's threats of retaliation in 2014, it continued and even expanded its economic ties with Moscow. European countries which had grown to depend on Russian oil and gas were especially guilty of failing to recognize and respond to the obvious danger this dependence posed to their own security. Suffering from a dangerous myopia induced by commercial greed, they actually expanded their Russian energy dependency while failing to help Ukraine protect itself against Putin's continued military and economic aggression.

Multinational Western corporations continued to invest in Russia, not only in strategic industries such as mineral extraction and distribution, but also in joint ventures offering industrial and consumer goods and services. It was as if Russia was like any other capitalist society that could be trusted to choose financial success and security over ideological interests or territorial ambitions.

European leaders like Chancellor Angela Merkel in Germany and President Emmanuel Macron in France considered themselves statesmanlike for maintaining good relations with Putin, even while the would-be Russian emperor tightened his grip on power, poisoned his political enemies, shut down almost all credible opposition media, and prepared to expand his hold on Ukraine.

No wonder Putin came to believe that he was invincible, that he could shrug off any blowback from decisions he made or actions he took. He was given little reason to believe the West would do anything beyond making statements of protest and imposing sanctions that Russia could circumvent.

Putin the Conqueror: Fourth, All Ukraine

The trajectory of Russian troops that entered Ukraine on February 24, 2022 reveals that Putin's ambition was to conquer the rest of Ukraine in one fell swoop. Russian forces crossed the Ukrainian border from the north, south and east. They also entered from Belarus where the distance from Ukraine's border to the capital Kyiv is shortest.

Putin no doubt calculated that the United States and NATO would respond with more words but little to no action. President Joe Biden was now in office in Washington, and he had already shown a mind-boggling incompetence, cold-heartedness and lack of strategic sense in yanking the American military out of Afghanistan in the summer of 2022.

Not only had 13 US servicemen died in the chaos at the airport in Kabul, but hundreds of American and other western civilians, plus thousands of Afghans who had supported the United States and other NATO allies in Afghanistan, were left behind to face the ruthless punishment of the Taliban.

Meanwhile, in an act of gross negligence and strategic foolishness the US armed forces destroyed or left behind tens of billions of dollars of the latest armaments and ammunition at the strategically important Bagram Air Base—which they abandoned overnight.

The exact value of this mountain of arms is disputed, especially since the Biden administration stopped publicizing data on the scope of the disaster so as to limit the political recriminations from angry Republicans and the American public in general. What is not disputed, however, is that the US provided Afghanistan somewhere in the neighborhood of $83 billion in weapons over the course of the war, and that the remaining arsenal was left behind when Washington pulled out.[6]

Putin must have concluded that he was dealing with a weakling in the White House. And, as he had demonstrated in his previous acts of aggression, as a predator he knew how to exploit any signs of weakness in his Western opponents.

Russia's 2022 invasion made clear that it was Moscow's intent to capture Ukraine's capital and other major population centers in one swift blow. Thus its forces aimed for Kyiv, Kharkiv, Kherson, Zaporizhzhia, Dnipropetrovsk and Odessa. Fortunately, the Russians were stopped short of all of these objectives, except for Kherson—which fell without a real fight.

Ukraine was in great peril during the first days of the invasion. The rapid Russian advances at the beginning of the war were the result of inadequate preparations by Ukraine—which had wrongly figured that Russia was posturing and did not actually plan to invade once more. Furthermore, Russia was greatly aided by an army of collaborators in Ukraine who 'opened gates' for them as they advanced.[7]

Russia's attempt to conquer Ukraine in one rapid operation proved to be a costly strategic and tactical mistake since the Russian army was simply unable to surmount the resistance put up by Ukraine's army in many areas along the line. And, from the first day, Russia's use of Soviet-era command structures and tactics—combined with armaments whose quantity and effectiveness had been vastly overstated by Russia's own corrupt military establishment. This led to a military debacle and a staggered Russian retreat from the Kyiv, Kharkiv and Kherson oblasts after several months.

The dream of Russia taking all Ukraine is slowly receding into the dis-

---

6. Adam Andrzejewski. August 23, 2021. *Staggering Costs—U.S. Military Equipment Left Behind In Afghanistan.* Forbes.

7. Stefanie Glinski. January 17, 2023. *Russia's Fifth Column in Ukraine Is Alive and Well.* Foreign Policy.

tance. Moscow lacks the army and equipment to overwhelm its neighbor. Fortunately, this time most of the world has finally awakened to the real evil Putin is perpetrating against his victims, and now recognize him for the Satanic figure he really is. Only the naïve and those duped by Russian propaganda still believe a word Putin says.

Putin Keeps Elaborating Specious Arguments for His Invasion

Meanwhile, a stunned Putin continues to scramble for justifications for this war, justifications that can keep Russian nationalists on his side and anti-war critics from trying to oust him. It is unlikely that he still thinks he can pull the wool over the eyes of the rest of the world, but he is trapped in a world of lies of his own making—and his propaganda machine continues to have some success, both inside and outside Russia.

He initially told a national TV audience in Russia that he had no option but to mount a "special military operation" in response to NATO expansion and to "protect Russia and her people," including the ethnic Russians in Ukraine. He claimed his purpose was the "demilitarization and denazification of Ukraine" and that he had no intention of occupying Ukraine.[8]

Here are some key excerpts from this speech, starting with his opening:

> Today, I again consider it necessary to come back to the tragic events taking place in the Donbas and the key issue of ensuring Russian security. Let me start with what I said in my address of February 21. I am referring to what causes us particular concern and anxiety — those fundamental threats against our country that year after year, step by step, are offensively and unceremoniously created by irresponsible politicians in the West.
>
> I am referring to the expansion of NATO to the east, moving its military infrastructure closer to Russian borders. It is well known that for 30 years we have persistently and patiently tried to reach an agreement with the leading NATO countries on the principles of

---

8. Staff Report. February 24, 2022. *'No other option': Excerpts of Putin's speech declaring war.* Al Jazeera.

equal and inviolable security in Europe. In response to our proposals, we constantly faced either cynical deception and lies, or attempts to pressure and blackmail, while NATO, despite all our protests and concerns, continued to steadily expand. The war machine is moving and, I repeat, it is coming close to our borders.

After reeling off a long list of grievances against the West, he came to the point:

The course of events and the incoming information show that Russia's clash with these forces is inevitable. It is only a matter of time: they are getting ready, they are waiting for the right time. Now they also claim to acquire nuclear weapons. We will not allow this to happen.

We have been left no other option to protect Russia and our people, but for the one that we will be forced to use today. The situation requires us to take decisive and immediate action. The people's republics of Donbas turned to Russia with a request for help.

In this regard, in accordance with Article 51 of Part 7 of the UN Charter, with the approval of the Federation Council of Russia and in pursuance of the treaties of friendship and mutual assistance ratified by the Duma on February 22 with the Donetsk People's Republic and the Luhansk People's Republic, I decided to launch a special military operation.

Its goal is to protect people who have been subjected to abuse and genocide by the regime in Kyiv for eight years. And for this we will pursue the demilitarization and denazification of Ukraine, as well as bringing to justice those who committed numerous bloody crimes against civilians, including citizens of the Russian Federation.

Our plans do not include the occupation of Ukrainian territories. We are not going to impose anything on anyone by force. At the same time, we hear that recently in the West there is talk that the documents signed by the Soviet totalitarian regime, securing the outcome of World War II, should no longer be upheld. Well, what is the answer to this?

In Chapter 7 we address many of the bogus claims of threats against Russia that Putin uses here to justify his invasion. But any student of history will know that tyrants of all stripes will almost always claim to be victims of aggression by others as a justification for their own aggression. (For example, Saddam Hussein claimed Iraq was a victim of Iranian aggression as his justification for invading Iran, and, later, that Iraq was the victim of Kuwaiti aggression as his justification for invading his tiny neighbor!)

In the light of Putin's aggressive actions against neighbors that we have documented in this chapter, his arguments for invading Ukraine are clearly based on an imaginary world that the Russian president has dreamed up to justify his evil behavior. Despite the setbacks he has encountered in Ukraine, he has not backed down, and he and his army of propagandists continue to put out one theory after the other as to why Russia really does need to crush Ukraine. (We will address the propaganda aspect of Putin's program in the next chapter.)

In the meantime, Putin continues to refine his core accusation that the West is threatening Russia as the main justification for his own aggression. As *Bloomberg News* reported on March 31, 2023:

> President Vladimir Putin approved a new Russian foreign policy concept that set out to confront the US and its allies, claiming an "era of revolutionary changes" was under way in international relations.
>
> The US is "the source of fundamental risks to the security of the Russian Federation" and most European states are pursuing an "aggressive policy" aimed at undermining Russia's sovereignty, according to the 42-page document signed by the president on [March 31].[9]

Unfortunately, there still are those in the West and elsewhere who take him at his word. However, increasingly news of the barbarity of his army in Ukraine has undermined his credibility for all but the willfully blind.

---

9. Staff Report. March 31, 2023. *Putin Signs New Russia Foreign Policy Against 'Hostile' West.* Bloomberg News.

Putin as a New Macbeth

Putin now is the victim of his own ambitions. He is like Shakespeare's Macbeth, a ruler so mired in corruption and blood that he can see no alternative to his self-destructive path:

> I am in blood stepp'd in so far that, should I wade no more, returning were as tedious as go o'er.[10]

And, like all tyrants facing imminent failure, Putin increasingly hides behind officials he blames for his own mistakes, all the while desperately mobilizing wave after wave of conscripts to fight this war for him. This mobilization started formally in September, 2022, and appears to be continuing, although many if not most able-bodied young Russian men are leaving their homeland if they have the means to do so. The mobilized men are used to soften up the Ukrainian side in preparation for regular army troops to advance. In other words, as cannon fodder.

In desperation, Putin has also resorted to hiring mercenaries and prisoners, whose sentences are commuted in exchange for serving with the private Wagner Group or the regular army. He also uses Chechen fighters loyal to the Kremlin.

Estimates of Russian and Ukrainian casualties in the war vary greatly, but it is likely that after a year of fighting the Russians had lost some 200,000 soldiers (killed or wounded) while Ukraine had lost half that number.[11] (Ukraine estimated Russian deaths alone reached 183,000 in mid-April, 2023.) These staggering casualty figures, combined with Russian losses of thousands of tanks and other armored vehicles as well as hundreds of helicopters and fighter jets, confirm just how costly this war has already been for Russia.

And for what?

---

10. William Shakespeare. *Macbeth*. Act III, Scene 4.

11. Helene Cooper, Eric Schmitt and Thomas Gibbons-Neff. February 2, 2023. *Soaring Death Toll Give Grim Insight Into Russian Tactics*. The New York Times.

Putin's Grave Miscalculations

Putin's success in flouting the international, rules-based order before February 24, 2022 gave him an unwarranted confidence that he would meet with success in Ukraine. It is now all too apparent that he made a number of huge miscalculations.

He underestimated the political resolve of Ukraine's leaders; he underestimated the resolve of the Ukrainian people to fight for their land; he underestimated the capabilities of Ukraine's revamped military; he underestimated the strength of the reaction from NATO members; he underestimated the reaction of Sweden and Finland, who decided to join NATO after decades of staying out of the alliance; he underestimated the severity of Western sanctions imposed on Russia; and he underestimated the determination of Ukraine's supporters, especially in Europe and North America, to continue providing assistance until Russia is driven from all of Ukraine.

Frankly, given the current European Union preoccupation with transgender rights and other burning social issues, it is pleasantly surprising that a group of countries obsessed with political correctness has been able to respond fairly forcefully to a threat to their way of life unlike any since WWII. Putin appears to have awakened a sleeping giant. The NATO behemoth is still fairly dazed, but it is getting increasingly focused and effective in opposing Russian aggression.

Chapter 5

Putin is Conducting a Brutal War of Genocide

Putin Indicted as an International Criminal

On March 17, 2023 the International Criminal Court (ICC) issued international arrest warrants for Vladimir Putin and Maria Lvova-Belova (Russia's Commissioner for Children's Rights), charging them with personal responsibility for the illegal deportation of Ukrainian children to Russian territory. The Ukrainian government estimates that at least 16,000 of these children had been abducted by March 2023, but the number is likely much higher, as we will discuss later in this chapter.[1]

The ICC ruling obliges the court's 123 member countries to arrest Putin should he enter their territory, in effect turning the Russian president into an international pariah.

It is good that the ICC has identified Putin as an international criminal, but we would contend that the charges brought against him represent only a small fraction of the crimes he has committed against the people of Ukraine, crimes that amount to genocide.

As if to confirm this, in late March, 2023 secret emails leaked by a whistleblower in Russia's FSB (the post-Soviet reincarnation of the KGB) to a Russian human rights activist associated with the website Gulagu.net

---

1. Anthony Deutsch and Toby Sterling. March 17, 2023. *ICC judges issue arrest warrant for Putin over war crimes in Ukraine*. Reuters.

revealed that the security agency—under direct instructions from former KGB officer Putin—had developed a plan for the "total cleansing" of Ukraine's resistance to Moscow's takeover.[2]

The plan called for the use of excessive violence to suppress demonstrations of dissent and thereby terrorize the population into passivity; house-to-house searches to root out any Ukrainians trying to escape Russia's program of transforming Ukraine into an integral part of Russia; and the removal of dissidents to concentration camps for re-education.

Such a draconian plan of ethnic cleansing and genocide would have likely been dismissed as a hoax if it had come to light a couple of years ago. Not anymore. It explains perfectly the brutality of the Russians—the indiscriminate bombing of civilian targets, the torture chambers and the forcible deportation of hundreds of thousands of Ukrainians to Russia.

What is Genocide?

In the aftermath of WWII, the United Nations General Assembly on December 9, 1948 adopted the *Convention on the Prevention and Punishment of the Crime of Genocide.*[3] Article II defines genocide in this way:

> In the present Convention, genocide means any of the following acts committed with intent to destroy, in whole or in part, a national, ethnical, racial or religious group, as such:
>
> (a) Killing members of the group;
>
> (b) Causing serious bodily or mental harm to members of the group;
>
> (c) Deliberately inflicting on the group conditions of life calculated to bring about its physical destruction in whole or in part;
>
> (d) Imposing measures intended to prevent births within the group;

---

2. Tariq Tahir. March 25, 2023. *Putin planned 'total cleansing' of Ukraine with 'house-to-house' terror & victims dragged off to camps, leaked docs show.* The US Sun.

3. For an explanation of Genocide and a copy of the full text of the Convention, see: https://www.un.org/en/genocideprevention/genocide.shtml

(e) Forcibly transferring children of the group to another group.

The immediate impetus for formulating this Convention was the Nazi campaign to exterminate the Jews that Hitler had pursued throughout WWII. But the Convention also addressed a history of atrocities aimed at destroying a particular group of people.

Its purpose was to warn any regime responsible for any of these inhuman practices that it would be punished by the international community. This is stated in Article I:

> The Contracting Parties confirm that genocide, whether committed in time of peace or in time of war, is a crime under international law which they undertake to prevent and to punish.

So far 150 countries have joined this convention, including all those directly or indirectly involved in the current war in Ukraine.

Is Putin Committing Genocide in Ukraine?

Almost all major media outlets have for over a year now been showing evidence of Russia's brutality in Ukraine. The first grisly images of Russian atrocities were seen by the world when the invaders were forced to retreat from Bucha and Irpin, two towns that stood in the way of them reaching the capital, Kyiv—the capture of which was Putin's primary objective for the invasion.

Amidst the wreckage of burned-out residential towers and shops, and streets littered with the carcasses of armored vehicles and tanks, there lay the bodies of civilians who had been shot by Russian soldiers. Many had their hands tied and showed signs of having been tortured. Soon eyewitnesses shared horrific tales of torture in interrogation chambers, summary executions and rape on a massive scale.

The suffering of the people of Bucha and Irpin would prove to be typical for Ukrainians victimized by Russia's invasion and occupation. Once Ukraine liberated large areas of the Kharkiv and Kherson oblasts, the evidence of Russian atrocities became overwhelming. Many residents of liberated cities and towns were discovered to have suffered vicious genocidal torment at the hands of the Russians. Many had been murdered while others had been forced into exile in Russia.

Investigators have already gathered masses of this evidence, which will ultimately be used to prosecute those responsible for acts of genocide in the field, but also Vladimir Putin himself. After all, he is responsible for launching the invasion with the purpose of destroying Ukraine's independence and nationhood.

The investigative process and the charging and conviction of those guilty of genocide in Ukraine will take years, possibly decades. In this chapter we will simply point to some of the evidence that is already available to the world, making denial of the genocide underway in Ukraine untenable.

Putin is Determined to Destroy Ukraine's National Identity

As the Convention states, at the heart of genocide lies the intent to eliminate a group of people based on their race, ethnicity, nationality or religion. If we examine Putin's statements, his preparation for the invasion through a series of smaller occupations, and the manner in which he is conducting this war, there can be little doubt as to his intention to eliminate Ukraine as a separate nation by destroying the sense of national identity enjoyed by Ukrainians.

But Putin is not stupid and he recognizes that he needs to offer reasons for the invasion that disguise his real motives and enable him to avoid full censure by the international community. As we have noted, when he announced the launch of his "special military operation" on February 24, 2022, Putin claimed that the reason for this military action was to "denazify and disarm" Ukraine.[4] However, from the outset this was a patently ludicrous claim, given that Ukraine has a Jewish president and only a handful of fringe neo-Nazi elements—similar to those in several other European countries and the United States.

Thus, from its outset the Russian invasion has been justified by griev-

---

4. Andrew Osborn and Polina Nikolskaya. February 24, 2022. *Russia's Putin authorizes 'special military operation' against Ukraine.* Reuters.

ances fabricated by Putin and his circle of nationalists. The real reason has always been Putin's personal ambition to restore Russia to (what he believes) was the greatness of the Soviet Empire by reintegrating into Russia the former Soviet socialist states—beginning with Belarus and Ukraine.

Putin has always hated the independence of Ukraine and has constantly meddled in Ukrainian politics to keep Kyiv in Russia's orbit. The 2022 invasion was intended to be his permanent solution to the problem of Ukrainian independence. As Olesya Khromeychuk wrote in an opinion piece for *The New York Times*, Putin insists that Ukraine does not exist as an independent country. And, since it clearly won't abandon its independence, he believes he has the right to destroy it as a nation and integrate what remains into Russia.[5]

Russian Propaganda Reveals Putin's Animus Towards Ukraine

Putin originally expected the invasion to be over in a matter of weeks—or months at most.[6] As the situation in Ukraine has worsened for Russia, Putin's regime has had to scramble to amplify its justifications for the war—including the repeated claim that Russia is defending itself against US and NATO aggression.[7]

But Putin's propaganda apparatus also has continued to spew arguments that align with Putin's original denazification pretext for the invasion. For example, an April 3, 2022 article in *RIA Novosti* by Timofei Sergeitsev specifically builds on Putin's February 24, 2022 speech by arguing that Ukraine's elite "must be liquidated as re-education is impossible" and claiming that a "significant part of the masses… are passive Nazis and accomplices."[8]

---

5. Olesya Khromeychuk, November 1, 2022. *Putin Says Ukraine Doesn't Exist. That's Why He's Trying to Destroy It*. The New York Times.

6. This is the contention of many Western analysts. It is reflected in this article, for example: Holly Ellyatt. November 29. *'Losing is not an option': Putin is 'desperate' to avoid defeat in Ukraine as anxiety rises in Moscow*. CNBC.

7. Staff Report. February 21, 2023. *Putin falsely claims it was West that "started the war" in Ukraine almost a year after he ordered the invasion*. CBS News.

8. Chris Brown. April 5, 2022. *A Kremlin paper justifies erasing the Ukrainian identity, as Russia is accused of war crimes*. CBC News.

Indeed, although Russia must face a lot of difficulties finding authentic Nazis to denazify in Ukraine, the denazification theme does provide a pretext for the ethnic cleansing Moscow's army has embarked on in Ukraine and it does appeal to some in Russia—which suffered greatly from the Nazi invasion in WWII.

Putin's original announcement of his reasons for the invasion naturally did not include mention of his plans to conduct ethnic cleansing, although his army has been doing exactly that in Ukraine ever since. Nevertheless, when his propagandists repeat his Nazi accusation in state-controlled media—necessarily with the approval of Putin—they confirm the Russian president's true animus towards the people of Ukraine and the lengths to which he is willing to go in order to demonize and destroy their independent identity.

Meanwhile, Putin can always deny responsibility for the statements of his propagandists while he is actually both feeding the propaganda machine and using it to bolster his justifications for the invasion. The result has been one insane argument for the war after another appearing in Russian media. A case in point: Putin's top propagandist, Vladimir Solovyov, recently claimed that Russia is actually engaged in a "holy war" against "Satanism."[9]Anything to justify genocide, however preposterous the claim.

Nevertheless, despite the seeming irrationality of many Russian propaganda claims, there is an evil method to this apparent madness. Dehumanization and demonization of a target was a tactic employed by the Nazis to excuse the murder of six million Jews in the Holocaust, and Stalin used it for his pogroms, such as the starvation of Ukraine's six million kulaks in the 1930s. It is a standard excuse for genocide and it has been used extensively by Putin in this war.

Putin's War Crimes Meet All Genocide Criteria

Ultimately, genocide cannot be hidden, and all the propaganda in the world

---

9. Isabel Van Brugen. January 19, 2023. *Russian Troops Given Pep Talk with LGBTQ Attacks and Warnings of Satanism.* Newsweek.

cannot disguise Putin's real motivations for the war as they are revealed in his rape, murder and pillage of Ukraine.

Following are the five types of crime that the Convention identifies as genocide, with evidence that these crimes are being committed by Russia in Ukraine:

A. Killing members of the group

There is no evidence that any of the Ukrainians killed by the Russian army were indeed Nazis. Yet Russian troops have killed a large number of Ukrainian civilians, both through indiscriminate bombings of residential areas, and through bombings apparently targeting concentrations of Ukrainian civilians—such as the theater in Mariupol where families were seeking shelter from the fighting. The word "CHILDREN" had been written outside the theater to warn off Russian bombers. To no avail. An estimated 600 innocents were killed in one horrific attack.[10] Russia is killing Ukrainians simply because they are Ukrainians.

The full death toll of civilians killed in this war will probably never be known, but the number runs into tens of thousands. There is no military justification for these deaths, only hatred of an 'enemy' fabricated in the mind of Putin and his circle of Russian chauvinists and murderers.

B. Causing serious bodily or mental harm to members of the group

The Russian invaders are known to practice intimidation and torture on Ukrainians they capture, whether members of the Ukrainian military or ordinary civilians. These atrocities have come to light after Ukraine recaptured cities like Bucha, Izyum and Kherson.

In Kherson, for example, investigators have identified 20 sites used as torture centers by Russia. They have noted that these were not random operations but part of the Russian state's "calculated plan to terrorize" locals. Over 1,000 survivors have given their testimonies of being tortured in the

---

10. Lori Hinnant, Mstyslav Chernov and Vasilisa Stepanenko. May 4, 2022. *AP evidence points to 600 dead in Mariupol theater airstrike.* AP.

Kherson region. At least 400 people from the area have disappeared altogether, and are assumed to have been killed by the Russians.[11]

In April, 2023, gruesome videos appeared on Russian social media sites showing Russian soldiers beheading captured Ukrainian soldiers. This evil behavior echoed the barbarism of the Islamic State, which killed its prisoners through beheadings, burning prisoners alive in cages and other horrific acts of cruelty.[12]

C. Deliberately inflicting on the group conditions of life calculated to bring about its physical destruction in whole or in part

This is a perfect description of Russia's relentless bombing of infrastructure and destruction of whole cities, designed to make living in the country nigh impossible. These bombings have been carried out to inflict maximum misery on the Ukrainian people, especially through the destruction of electricity generating and distribution infrastructure, plunging whole regions and cities into darkness while depriving residents of the means to heat their homes and access drinking water in the midst of bitter winter weather.

Meanwhile, many cities and towns have been reduced to rubble, and are unlivable. The first of these was Mariupol, but many others have suffered the same fate, as many journalistic reports confirm. The city destroyed most recently is Bakhmut, where the Russians have been trying to drive the Ukrainians out for many months—in the process turning the city into a wasteland.

D. Imposing measures intended to prevent births within the group

In addition to torture, Russian soldiers have been found guilty of raping women and girls on a massive scale. For many victims, these assaults have meant the ruin of their lives and ability to bear children, and for some rape has been a prelude to death.

---

11 Isobel Koshiw. March 1, 2023. *Kherson torture centers were planned by Russian state, say lawyers.* The Guardian.

12. Vasco Cotovio, Andrew Carey, Josh Pennington and Yulia Kesaieva. April 12, 2023. *Zelensky slams 'beasts' who purportedly beheaded Ukrainian soldiers after video emerges.* CNN.

This behavior came to light early in the invasion, when eyewitnesses in Bucha testified that Russian soldiers had raped dozens of women in the town. In one instance alone, 25 teenage girls were kept in a basement where they were gang raped. Nine became pregnant.[13] This is in no way an isolated phenomenon, as witnesses recount in one liberated city after another.[14] As many have noted, the widespread rape of Ukrainian men, women and children by Russian soldiers has been an instrument of war designed to force the Ukrainian people into accepting Russian rule.

E. Forcibly transferring children of the group to another group

As we mention at the beginning of this chapter, the practice of forcibly relocating Ukrainian children to Russia has become so pronounced that the ICC has now indicted Vladimir Putin and Maria Lvova-Belova for instigating this crime. The children taken to Russia are often forcibly removed from their families and placed in Russian orphanages or with Russian families. Meanwhile, both these children and those trapped in occupied areas of Ukraine are forced to abandon Ukrainian and use Russian instead, and are subjected to Russian propaganda.[15]

The Special Evil of Rape

Rape is a special kind of evil because it is a violation of a person's integrity and dignity that can stain its victims forever. It can cause severe mental harm and destroy a person's plans for life. On a practical level, it can result in severe medical injuries, psychological trauma or death. And unwanted pregnancies can mean a dismal future for the children born to rape victims.

---

13. Amie Ferris-Rotman. April 20, 2022. *Ukrainians Are Speaking Up About Rape as a War Crime to Ensure the World Holds Russia Accountable.* Time.

14. Lisa Bjurwald. April 19, 2022. *Russian rape in Ukraine: "You can tell from their eyes."* EUobserver.

15. Darren Boyle. March 23, 2023. *Freed—the kidnapped kids Putin 'tried to beat the Ukrainian out of': Overjoyed children embrace family as they finally get back home after months in brutal Kremlin 'camps'—but thousands remain missing as war crimes warrant awaits Russian President.* MailOnline and AFP.

Rape is part and parcel of the dehumanization of a population group, making it a core feature of genocide. As we have indicated, in Ukraine it has been used as a weapon of war to intimidate and terrorize the Ukrainian people.

As first lady Olena Zelenska told an international conference in London:

> Sexual violence is the most cruel, most animalistic way to prove mastership over someone. And for victims of this kind of violence, it is difficult to testify in war times because nobody feels safe.
>
> This is another instrument that they (Russian forces) are using as their weaponry. This is another weapon in their arsenal in this war and conflict. That's why they're using this systematically and openly.[16]

There is something particularly grotesque about Russia's use of rape in this war. It has to do with the widespread rape culture in its prisons and its use against young conscripts in the military. Remember, the Wagner Group has employed tens of thousands of Russian convicts to fill its ranks, including those who have been victims of rape in prison.[17]

Rape was also known to be a common war crime committed by Soviet troops in WWII.[18]

In Ukraine, the victims of Russian rape range in age from four to 82, and include both males and females.[19] The individual stories are heart-breaking. For example, in some of the most despicable cases that have come to light, family members have been forced to watch their children, siblings or parents being raped by Russians.

---

16 Olena Zelenska. November 29, 2022. Quoted in: *Wives of Russian troops 'encourage' them to rape Ukrainian women, Ukraine's first lady says.* Sky News.

17. Anna Nemtsova. October 25, 2022. *Now Putin's Sending Prison Rape Victims to Die on the Front Line.* Daily Beast.

18. Andrew Salmon. August 11, 2020. *Red Storm on Rising Sun.* Asia Times.

19. Niamh Lynch. February 24, 2023. *'They took turns raping me': Ukrainian survivors reveal how Russian soldiers use sex attacks 'as a weapon of war.'* Sky News.

The Human Toll of the Invasion

The issue of genocide must also be viewed in the larger picture of the enormous human toll in death, injury, dislocation and displacement that Russia's invasion has inflicted on Ukraine. There is no reliable data on these human losses, but there must be tens of thousands of Ukrainian civilians who have been killed or injured in the war, in addition to tens of thousands of Ukrainian soldiers killed or injured in the fighting. (Not to mention the huge human losses suffered by Russia's army, losses that Putin is directly responsible for.)

Furthermore, there is the matter of private property losses suffered by the Ukrainians and the damage done to the nation's infrastructure. These material losses have an enormous impact on the quality of life for all the people.

There is reasonably reliable data on the Ukrainians displaced by the war. According to the United Nations Refugee Agency (UNHCR), by March 2023 there were over eight million Ukrainians who had been uprooted from their homes and were living as refugees across Europe. Of these, almost three million (2,852,395) were in Russia.[20] UNHCR has also estimated that there were another five million Ukrainians who had been displaced from their homes but were still living within Ukraine.[21]

Furthermore, the forcible deportation of children the ICC addressed, is just the tip of the iceberg when it comes to Russia's program of forcible transport of Ukrainians into its territory. As early as July, 2022, the US State Department estimated that as many as 1.6 million Ukrainians were victims of Russia's abductions:

> Estimates from a variety of sources, including the Russian government, indicate that Russian authorities have interrogated, detained,

---

20. UNHCR Operational Portal, March 13, 2023. https://data.unhcr.org/en/situations/ukraine.

21. United Nations High Commissioner for Refugees. February 23, 2023. *UNHCR: One year after the Russian invasion, insecurity clouds return intentions of displaced Ukrainians.* UNHCR, USA.

and forcibly deported between 900,000 and 1.6 million Ukrainian citizens, including 260,000 children, from their homes to Russia—often to isolated regions in the Far East. Moscow's actions appear pre-meditated and draw immediate historical comparisons to Russian "filtration" operations in Chechnya and other areas. President Putin's "filtration" operations are separating families, confiscating Ukrainian passports, and issuing Russian passports in an apparent effort to change the demographic makeup of parts of Ukraine.[22]

The World Must Prosecute Putin and Russia for Genocide

Upon a Ukrainian victory, Russia must be made to provide a full accounting of the crimes it has committed in Ukraine, including the identity of all its victims. This will be the basis for prosecuting those responsible, starting with Vladimir Putin who undoubtedly bears the greatest responsibility for this catalogue of evils.

Unfortunately, Putin is not able to pay for even a tiny fraction of the myriad crimes against humanity he is responsible for in this war. Thus it will fall to the Russian people to pay. Those clearly responsible for agitating for the war and supporting Putin must shoulder the main burden of these consequences. But having kept Putin in power through a series of elections, the Russian population as a whole will also be forced to pay for their leader's crimes. (In Chapter 13 we discuss what some of the reparations Russia must pay should look like.)

---

22. Press Statement of Antony J. Blinken, Secretary of State. July 13, 2022. *Russia's "Filtration" Operations, Forced Disappearances, and Mass Deportations of Ukrainian Citizens.* US State Department.

Chapter 6

Why Ukraine Must Achieve Total Victory

We Must Learn the Lessons of the Post-WWII Era

In the years since the end of WWII, the West, led by the United States, has assumed a defeatist, containment posture. Thus the knee-jerk response to Russia's invasion by many of the wise men of foreign policy has been to immediately call for peace talks and a settlement.

This reaction is very much in concert with the late George Kennan's own views on Ukrainian independence, which he believed would anger the Russians and provoke them into retaliatory action. He set out this view in a secret 1948 State Department policy paper, and repeated it after the fall of the Soviet Union. As a recent article in *Foreign Affairs* explains:

> George Kennan, the remarkable U.S. diplomat and probing observer of international relations, is famous for forecasting the collapse of the Soviet Union. Less well known is his warning in 1948 that no Russian government would ever accept Ukrainian independence. Foreseeing a deadlocked struggle between Moscow and Kyiv, Kennan made detailed suggestions at the time about how Washington should deal with a conflict that pitted an independent Ukraine against Russia. He returned to this subject half a century later. Kennan, then in his 90s, cautioned that the eastward expansion of NATO would doom democracy in Russia and ignite another Cold War.[1]

---

1. Frank Costigliola. January 27, 2023. *Kennan's Warning on Ukraine: Ambition,*

In his 1948 policy paper, Kennan expressed the opinion that Ukraine was not really a nation and could not become one:

> Ukrainians have been an important and specific element in the Russian empire, they have shown no signs of being a "nation" capable of bearing successfully the responsibilities of independence in the face of great Russian opposition. The Ukraine is not a clearly defined ethnical or geographic concept... There is no clear dividing line between Russia and the Ukraine, and it would be impossible to establish one.[2]

In the same passage, Kennan dismissed Ukrainian independence aspirations with these words:

> The real basis of "Ukrainianism" is the feeling of "difference" produced by a specific peasant dialect and by minor differences of custom and folklore throughout the country districts. The political agitation on the surface is largely the work of a few romantic intellectuals, who have little concept of the responsibilities of government.

Kennan continued this argument by stating that the economies of Russia and Ukraine were so intertwined that they could not be separated:

> The economy of the Ukraine is inextricably intertwined with that of Russia as a whole... To attempt to carve it out of the Russian economy and to set it up as something separate would be as artificial and as destructive as an attempt to separate the Corn Belt, including the Great Lakes industrial area, from the economy of the United States.

This is a pretty extreme statement—comparing Ukraine's relationship with Russia to the relationship of a group of contiguous US states to the United States as a whole!

Perhaps we should remember at this point in discussing Kennan's advice,

---

Insecurity, and the Perils of Independence. Foreign Affairs.

2. George F. Kennan. 1948. *United States Objectives with Respect to Russia.* The State Department Policy Planning Staff Papers 1948, Vol. II. Garland Publishing, p406.

that at Yalta, in 1945, Stalin insisted to FDR and Churchill that Ukraine and Belarus should be accepted as separate and independent member states when the United Nations was established. He got his way (especially since he had earlier demanded that all 16 constituent states of the USSR should become members of the UN and was now demanding 'only' three), and thus Moscow always controlled at least three votes in the UN: Russia, Ukraine and Belarus.[3]

And in a prefect articulation of containment's fundamental blindness to the actual evil of Communism, Kennan invoked the "feelings of the Great Russians":

> Finally, we cannot be indifferent to the feelings of the Great Russians themselves. They were the strongest national element in the Russian Empire, as they now are in the Soviet Union. They will continue to be the strongest national element in that general area, under any status. Any long-term U.S. policy must be based on their acceptance and their cooperation. The Ukrainian territory is as much a part of their national heritage as the Middle West is of ours, and they are conscious of that fact. A solution which attempts to separate the Ukraine entirely from the rest of Russia is bound to incur their resentment and opposition, and can be maintained, in the last analysis, only by force.

Kennan did admit later in this piece that if Ukraine succeeded in gaining independence his analysis would have been proved wrong. However, in the event of this occurring, he recommends that Washington should advocate for a "reasonable federalism":

> And only if it became clear that an undesirable deadlock was developing [between Russia and Ukraine], we would encourage a composing of the differences along the lines of a reasonable federalism.

In other words, Washington should respond to Ukrainian aspirations for

---

3. Stephen Schlesinger. May 10, 2022. *To Stalin, Ukraine Was an Independent Country*. PassBlue.

independence by advocating that Russia allow Ukraine a degree of autonomy within a Moscow-led federation.

Despite the terrible truth about the Soviet Union revealed in Khrushchev's 1956 speech on Stalin, Solzhenitsyn's *Gulag Archipelago*, and a host of other exposés of the evils of Russia's USSR, Kennan made no reference to the evils of Soviet Communism in his analysis.

A fluent Russian speaker who spent years in Moscow during the WWII era, Kennan simply offers suggestions to Washington that are intended to be the least troublesome for Moscow. In other words, Russian propaganda.

His views did not change significantly, even after the collapse of the Soviet Union and the subsequent emergence of 16 independent states. In a 1997 opinion piece for *The New York Times*, Kennan said he thought NATO's expansion eastward was "the greatest mistake of Western policy in the entire post-Cold War era" because it would "inflame the nationalistic, anti-Western and militaristic tendencies in Russian opinion." In other words, it would upset the Russians! Here are two key paragraphs:

> But something of the highest importance is at stake here. And perhaps it is not too late to advance a view that, I believe, is not only mine alone but is shared by a number of others with extensive and in most instances more recent experience in Russian matters. The view, bluntly stated, is that expanding NATO would be the most fateful error of American policy in the entire post-cold-war era.

> Such a decision may be expected to inflame the nationalistic, anti-Western and militaristic tendencies in Russian opinion; to have an adverse effect on the development of Russian democracy; to restore the atmosphere of the cold war to East-West relations, and to impel Russian foreign policy in directions decidedly not to our liking. And, last but not least, it might make it much more difficult, if not impossible, to secure the Russian Duma's ratification of the Start II agreement and to achieve further reductions of nuclear weaponry.[4]

---

4. George F. Kennan. February 15, 1997. *A Fateful Error.* The New York Times.

Well, there you have it—George Kennan in the 1990s advocating for the same Western sensitivity to Russian feelings that he considered so important in 1948. He showed no consideration for the feelings and hopes of the countries that had just escaped from the grip of the Russian bear after decades of oppressive Soviet rule—the Baltic States, non-Russian CIS members and the former Soviet satellite states.

For Kennan, the immediate danger would soon become joint NATO-Ukrainian naval exercises in the Black Sea, a concern he elaborated on in an alarmed letter to Strobe Talbott, at the time deputy secretary of state. In it, he pointed out that any foreign naval vessel in the Black Sea would invoke for Russia "...painful memories of... the entry of British and French fleets into the Black Sea, and their attacks on the Crimea and Sevastopol in particular, in the Crimean War."[5]

The Crimean War was fought from 1853 to 1856, 140 years before Kennan wrote this letter in 1997, by which time the whole of Crimea, including the strategic port at Sevastopol, had been part of Ukrainian sovereign territory for six years. Kyiv had every right to conduct naval exercises in the Black Sea, yet Kennan was only concerned for Russia's hurt feelings incurred a century and a half earlier.

Kennan died in 2005, but his legacy lives on in the thinking of many in the foreign policy world. At the head of this venerable but hopelessly wrong group of 'experts'—which has been calling for negotiations while Russia still occupies much of Ukraine—is none other than Henry Kissinger, the chief architect of the failed détente policy.

In the December 17, 2022 edition of the *Spectator*, under the ominous title, "How to avoid another world war," Kissinger echoes Kennan's fears regarding Russian anger over Ukraine, and presents his most recent arguments for peace talks as soon as possible:

---

5. George F. Kennan. April 22, 1997. *Letter to Strobe Talbott*. The State Department.

Ukraine has become a major state in Central Europe for the first time in modern history. Aided by its allies and inspired by its President, Volodymyr Zelensky, Ukraine has stymied the Russian conventional forces which have been overhanging Europe since the second world war. And the international system — including China — is opposing Russia's threat or use of its nuclear weapons.

This process has mooted the original issues regarding Ukraine's membership in Nato. Ukraine has acquired one of the largest and most effective land armies in Europe, equipped by America and its allies. A peace process should link Ukraine to Nato, however expressed. The alternative of neutrality is no longer meaningful, especially after Finland and Sweden joined Nato. This is why, last May, I recommended establishing a ceasefire line along the borders existing where the war started on 24 February. Russia would disgorge its conquests thence, but not the territory it occupied nearly a decade ago, including Crimea. That territory could be the subject of a negotiation after a ceasefire.[6]

Negotiations after a ceasefire that will leave Russia in control of Crimea and much of the Luhansk and Donetsk oblasts! Nice for Russia. Disaster for Ukraine. No sir. You and those like you who constantly call for negotiations, for Ukraine to be 'realistic' in accepting that it must cede some of its territory in order to get peace with its unrepentant neighbor, are wrong.

Zelensky and the Ukrainians are absolutely right in insisting that Russia must exit all Ukrainian territory before negotiations can begin. Russia must not be rewarded for its brutal and totally unjustified invasion and its bloody occupation of Ukrainian territory. That would be the worst of all outcomes, cementing in place a reward for aggression, and undoubtedly fueling continued Russian ambitions to conquer the rest of Ukraine.

That Kissinger and other major figures of the post-WWII diplomatic landscape, such as John Mearsheimer at the University of Chicago, have

---

6. Henry Kissinger. December 17, 2022. *How to avoid another world war.* The Spectator.

still not recognized the fallacy of containment and détente is sobering. It is a sure sign that the foreign policy 'experts' housed in international relations departments at prestigious universities and think tanks, or entrenched in senior policy positions at the State Department and other foreign ministries in major Western countries, are lost. They cling to failed and outdated theories—based on fear and weakness—that have already proved their fatal inadequacies.

Among those in government who has pushed for negotiations as soon as possible is US Chairman of the Joint Chiefs of Staff Mark Milley. He is joined by all the political leaders around the world aligned with Moscow.

And, of course, leading this chorus is Vladimir Putin and his nationalist leadership group, including Foreign Minister Sergey Lavrov. These corrupt and dishonest people speak about the war in Ukraine as if they had nothing to do with its inception. They constantly complain that Russia is being attacked by the United States and NATO, and call for negotiations to find a peaceful settlement!

Never Forget Who Invaded Whom

Fortunately, most leaders in the West continue to hold firm in support of Ukraine, recognizing the one salient issue in this conflict: Russia is the aggressor and Ukraine the victim of aggression.

From its outset, Putin and Lavrov have lied about the invasion, initially claiming that they had no intention of proceeding with it, and then, once their tanks started rolling towards Kyiv and other major population centers, claiming they were saving Ukraine from Nazism in a "special military operation."

At this point, Putin's credibility beyond Russia's borders is about zero. His actions reveal his real policies much better than do his words. We know what he really thinks by observing his foreign adventures over the past few years, when he used his army to take territory from Georgia and Ukraine.

Even before he ventured abroad, Putin first showed his true colors as Russia's leader when he oversaw the destruction of Chechnya with a brutal military operation that destroyed the capital, Grozny, and resulted in an estimated death toll of 200,000 Chechen civilians, as well as 40,000 soldiers from both sides.

It is telling that Putin's tough stance on Chechnya was a reason for him winning the presidency in 2000. One is reminded of an earlier demonstration of Russian infatuation with powerful dictators: their outpouring of grief over the death of Stalin in 1953. Stalin was a monster who had sent some 20 million Russians to their death and millions more to prison camps in Siberia, yet they wept at his passing.

What is wrong with Russian society that it honors mass murderers?

When Putin calls for negotiations it is certain that he is not seeking peace, but rather trying to gain an advantage on the battlefield, where his army has been doing so poorly. He needs time to regroup and resupply his battered forces, so that they can renew their push to conquer Ukraine.

As we have demonstrated, Western humanitarian sensibilities and restraint in wars past have all too often resulted in compromising with evil regimes in the name of preserving peace and saving lives. This has inevitably lead to the prolongation of conflicts and more suffering inflicted by despots who only use negotiations to prevaricate while preparing the further expansion of their aggression. (Think of Hitler before WWII or Saddam Hussein after the First Gulf War in Iraq.)

Putin and today's Russia are no exception. They cannot be allowed to remain on Ukraine's territory under any circumstances. Theirs is a completely illegitimate military action of naked aggression, coupled with duplicitous and illegal referenda to annex territory from Ukraine. Putin must not be allowed to retain any of his ill-gotten gains from this war. He must be made to pay for the suffering he has inflicted on Ukraine.

Ukraine Must Win as Quickly as Possible

As General George Patton liked to point out, the best defense and the least costly posture on a battlefield is the most aggressive offense possible:

71

In war the only sure defense is offense, and the efficiency of the offense depends on the warlike souls of those conducting it.[7]

This view was echoed by General Douglas MacArthur when he gave a farewell address to the US Congress in April 1951. Speaking about the rise of a predatory Communist China in Asia and the dangers of appeasement, he said this about the need to respond forcefully to aggression:

> But once war is forced upon us, there is no other alternative than to apply every available means to bring it to a swift end.
>
> War's very object is victory, not prolonged indecision.
>
> In war there is no substitute for victory.[8]

Increasing aid to Ukraine only after it suffers a setback is wrongheaded. Our goal must be victory at the earliest possible time, not a settlement that leaves Russia in control of some Ukrainian territory. The battle has been engaged. The Allies must do whatever they can to see that it is won as soon as possible.

The Sooner Ukraine Achieves Victory, the Less the Suffering

Both Patton and MacArthur pointed out that weakness and hesitation in war only increase its casualties, whereas the earliest possible victories have the opposite effect. As we see Russia grinding down Ukraine through one bombardment after another, this lesson is all too relevant. To limit human losses Ukraine must win as soon as possible. It must break out of its defensive positions and drive the Russians from its land.

And, by the way, this will also limit the loss of life and suffering of Russians—many of whom have been pressed into military service against their will.

---

7. George S. Patton. 1947. *War as I knew It*. Haughton Mifflin.

8. Douglas MacArthur. April 19, 1951. *Farewell Address to Congress*.

Chapter 7

Bogus Arguments Against Supporting Ukraine

Don't Be Deceived by Russian Propaganda

The propaganda put out by totalitarian regimes always seeks to achieve through deception and intimidation what likely cannot be achieved through legitimate means. In the bad old days of the Soviet Union, Moscow employed this stratagem constantly. Aware of the internal conflicts in the West over how it should deal with the Communist Bloc, the USSR played on Western fears of war with Russia—and in particular a nuclear attack—to press the West into abandoning its defense programs.

This fear-mongering was typically couched in terms of the danger of escalation to a nuclear conflict posed by Western defense initiatives, such as deploying US missile systems and the Neutron Bomb in Europe, and the development of 'Star Wars' technologies for anti-missile defense. The louder the Soviets protested, the more certain was it that Moscow saw the defense programs as a threat to its plan to conquer the world for Communism.

After all, the Soviet leaders knew full well that NATO was a defensive alliance that was effective in blocking their ambition to spread Communism. It was not intended—and had never been used—to advance an aggressive or expansionist agenda.

The Soviet protests spread through disinformation networks were often successful, as when European countries were cowed into refusing to allow

Neutron Bombs to be deployed on their territories. In the case of Star Wars—the Strategic Defense Initiative (SDI)—Reagan simply refused to back down when Gorbachev insisted that this defense program threatened Russia and had to be stopped if an agreement on nuclear arms was to be made.

The American president knew who he was dealing with and chose to walk away from the Iceland summit with the Soviet leader rather than compromise on the right of America to defend itself.

This would prove a great example of how to call the bluff of a bully, because in fact the Soviet Union did not have the resources to counter SDI. In the end, Gorbachev simply caved and signed a deal to limit both side's arsenals of nuclear weapons.

Listen to the Countries That Know Russia Best

The countries that suffered the most from Soviet deception and aggression, such as Finland, Poland and the Baltic States, are now some of Russia's most vocal and effective critics. They can see right through Russian bluster and bullying, and they are not ready to be intimidated into giving up their hard-won freedom. These are the voices to listen to.

Some of them have offered up to half of their own annual defense spending to support Ukraine in the war, and they are the most persistent and compelling in calling on Western nations to unite in support of Ukraine, and to provide Kyiv with the weapons it needs to defeat Russia.[1] For them, Russia continues to be a real threat, and they know that if Russia gets its way in Ukraine, the threat to them will increase dramatically.

As Sanna Marin, the prime minister of Russia's neighbor Finland, put it:

> We don't know when the war will end, but we have to make sure it will end the Ukrainians' way [a Ukrainian victory]. I don't think there is any other choice. If Russia would win the war, then we would only see a decade of this kind of behavior ahead of us. I think other coun-

---

1. W. J. Hennigan. February 16, 2023. *'Don't Play With Us.' Estonia Sends Message to Russia With Ukraine Aid.* Time Magazine. https://time.com/6256280/estonia-aid-russia-ukraine/

tries are looking very closely at what is happening now in Ukraine, and if Russia would win it would send a message that you can invade another country, you can attack another country, and you can gain from that.[2]

Don't Be Fooled by Bogus Arguments

Nevertheless, despite the warnings of these countries that know Russia best, and despite the unsavory history of Soviet imperialism and Putin's expansionism, there are still many strident voices in the West who say that helping Ukraine is not in American's national interest or of critical importance to NATO, and therefore not deserving of Western military and other support.

These voices bring a wide range of arguments to the table, but rarely offer proof for their claims, and somehow seem to forget the most important fact about this conflict: Russia invaded Ukraine, a peaceful neighbor of like people and culture that has never threatened Russia.

Below are some of the bogus arguments being made against the West supporting Ukraine. There is overlap among them, of course, but it's worth discussing them in some detail.

Russia is Threatened by NATO Expansion

This is a favorite but totally invalid argument for not supporting Ukraine. How often does it have to be said that NATO is a defensive rather than offensive treaty organization? Is there any evidence to the contrary from its decades-long history?

It is precisely because NATO is a defensive alliance that the former Soviet Baltic States and satellite countries were all determined to join it as soon as they gained their freedom from Moscow, anticipating that Russia might once more want to expand its empire.

NATO members get the protection of Article 5, which guarantees that any member attacked by a third party will be assisted in its defense by all the other members. In exchange for this protection, all members agree to adopt common standards for weapons, share responsibilities for maintaining secu-

2. Sanna Marin. January 17, 2023. *As reported by Business Ukraine Magazine.*

rity in the NATO sphere, and pledge to spend a certain percentage of GDP on defense (currently two percent).

NATO was founded in the post-WWII era to deter aggression in the Euro-Atlantic space, and to put in place the necessary military capabilities to deal effectively with threats to stability and peace in that space.

NATO has never mounted a war to expand the territory of its members. Indeed, many of its members have all too often been reluctant to take significant action against aggressors when it has been justified.

Ukraine is a potential member of NATO, and this is said to have provoked Putin into his aggression against his neighbor. But why? How would Ukraine joining a mutual defense pact threaten Russia in any way? The answer is that Ukraine in NATO would stymie Putin's territorial ambitions, which include absorbing Ukraine into the Russian Federation.

Putin's arguments are not legitimate. He may be frustrated by Ukraine joining NATO, but Ukraine is an independent country and has the right to join any international security structure that invites it to join.

Ironically, if Putin does have a legitimate fear of NATO expanding on Russia's border—a fear that we are to believe prompted him to invade Ukraine—he clearly made a very bad miscalculation. His invasion and saber-rattling have had the opposite effect. Sweden and Finland—the former facing Russia across the Baltic Sea; the latter with a long land border with Russia—were prompted by Putin's aggression to end their neutrality and apply for membership in NATO. This is a remarkable development, and it underscores the fact that northern Europe has seen no similar danger from Russia since WWII.

Additionally, many members of the Western alliance are now expressing a conviction that Ukraine should indeed join NATO, to prevent future Russian military adventures towards Europe. Before the invasion, many of these countries hesitated to endorse Ukraine's membership, simply because of Putin's nuclear threats.

Ukraine is Better Off as a Buffer State

How can this possibly be a good idea? Surely any state with the ill fortune to be located between two belligerents is in great danger of being used as a battleground between them. In other words, it will pay the price for the aggression of its neighbors. In the case of Ukraine, why on earth would it be a good idea to make this its permanent status in Europe? Much better for Ukraine to belong to one side or the other. Kyiv certainly does not want to be allied with Russia against NATO, so it should be allowed to join NATO.

The argument that Ukraine should be a buffer state is foolish. It is an ill-conceived proposal coming from those who say that Ukraine joining NATO will inflame the Russians and provoke them to attack. This is a position that echoes George Kennan's thinking on Ukraine, and in particular the importance of recognizing de facto Russian hegemony over that part of the world (see Chapters 2 and 6). As with the rest of Kennan's analysis, this view only addresses the interests of Russia while dismissing the authentic right to self-determination of Ukraine.

Furthermore, Kennan was writing long before the Baltic States joined NATO, and, of course, long before the current war prompted Sweden and Finland to join NATO as well. Thus, with Finland a member, there already is a border of some 1,000 miles between Russia and NATO, a status quo that poses no threat at all to Russia—voiding the 'don't make Russia angry' argument.

Thus the buffer argument also holds no water. Worse still, it ignores the interests of the Ukrainians who are determined to leave Russia's orbit permanently.

It's All the Fault of America and the West

There are a number of 'experts' on Russia who have long argued that Putin's aggression is entirely the result of unwise US policies. Among leading academics in this field is the late Princeton historian, Dr. Stephen F. Cohen, who consistently explained Putin's aggression as a reasonable response to American and NATO foreign policy mistakes.

In 2014, Cohen defended Putin's annexation of Crimea, as *The Washington Post* reported in its obituary:

> When Russia annexed Crimea — part of the country of Ukraine — in 2014, then instigated an armed uprising in Ukraine, Dr. Cohen said the actions were justified as a response to "surreptitious NATO expansion."

> The purpose of the aggressive stance, he said on WABC radio's "The John Batchelor Show," was to "restore Russia's traditional zones of national security on its borders, [and] that means Ukraine as well."

> On CNN, he declared, "Putin is not a thug. He's not a neo-Soviet imperialist who's trying to re-create the Soviet Union. He's not even anti-American."[3]

Really?

Another Putin apologist who loves to blame America and the West for the Russian dictator's actions, is international relations scholar and Chicago University professor John J. Mearsheimer. The headline of a piece he wrote in 2014 for the September/October edition of the distinguished *Foreign Affairs Magazine* summarizes his views perfectly: *Why the Ukraine Crisis Is the West's Fault: The Liberal Delusions That Provoked Putin.*[4]

Have Mearsheimer's sympathies for Putin's annexation of Crimea and proxy war in the Donbas been affected by Russia's massive 2022 invasion and destruction of much of Ukraine? Apparently not. He believes Russia has been doing what could only be expected from Moscow given Ukraine's growing closeness to America and the West.

In a recent interview with *New Yorker Magazine*, Mearsheimer updat-

---

3. Matt Schudel. September 22, 2020. *Stephen F. Cohen, historian of Soviet Union whose revisionist views influenced Gorbachev, dies at 81.* The Washington Post.

4. John J. Mearsheimer. September/October 2014. *Why the Ukraine Crisis is the West's Fault: The Liberal Delusions That Provoked Putin.* Foreign Affairs Magazine.

ed his analysis to include reflections on Russia's current invasion, given Ukraine's deepening ties with the West:

> The Ukrainians have a vested interest in paying serious attention to what the Russians want from them. They run a grave risk if they alienate the Russians in a fundamental way. If Russia thinks that Ukraine presents an existential threat to Russia because it is aligning with the United States and its West European allies, this is going to cause an enormous amount of damage to Ukraine. That of course is exactly what's happening now. So my argument is: the strategically wise strategy for Ukraine is to break off its close relations with the West, especially with the United States, and try to accommodate the Russians. If there had been no decision to move NATO eastward to include Ukraine, Crimea and the Donbass would be part of Ukraine today, and there would be no war in Ukraine.[5]

Could we translate? Since America and the West have foolishly promoted Ukraine's accession to NATO and the European Union, Ukraine has justifiably been invaded by Russia and would do well to ditch its close ties with America in particular. It should wise up and do what Putin wants it to do.

This is exactly the type of upside down thinking that prolonged the Cold War and fueled the many hot wars that erupted around the world in the post-WWII era. As we point out several times in this book, when Allied policies favored coming to terms with evil aggressors rather than working to defeat them, conflicts always were prolonged. The Soviets loved these Western policies of appeasement, for obvious reasons.

Why on earth should Ukraine cut its ties to America and the West? Does it not have the sovereign right to choose what system of government it wants and which countries it chooses to associate with? And does Moscow have a right to dictate to Kyiv what policies it should pursue?

Nuts!

---

5. John J. Mearsheimer. March 1, 2022. In an interview with Isaac Chotiner: *Why John Mearsheimer Blames the U.S. for the Crisis in Ukraine*. The New Yorker Magazine.

We Must Not Escalate the War

This is the probably the most common argument for not supporting Ukraine. Again, as we have noted, there is no way to escalate the war in Ukraine with non-nuclear weapons, because Russia has already thrown everything in its arsenal short of nuclear weapons at its smaller neighbor. A full arsenal of Russian missiles and bombs has since the outset of the war been raining down on Ukrainian residential areas.

Illegal phosphorus bombs have also been used by Russia, with devastating effect on civilian populations. According to Human Rights Watch:

> White phosphorus can burn people to the bone, smolder inside the body, and reignite when bandages are removed. Toxic to humans, white phosphorus can seep into the bloodstream through the skin, poisoning the kidneys, liver, and heart and causing multiple organ failure. People can die simply from inhaling white phosphorus."[6]

So Russia has already unleashed its whole arsenal of lethal weapons, legal and illegal, and we are worried that we might escalate the fighting? How? Moscow's propaganda is aimed at getting the West to buy into the 'we must not escalate the conflict' argument, since this will delay—or prevent altogether—NATO's supply of the arms needed by Ukraine to win the war.

This Russian propaganda seems to work. Whenever the West is contemplating upgrading the weapons it is supplying to Ukraine, there are somber voices raised to tell us that this will likely result in escalation of the conflict. Again, Russia has already unleashed all the non-nuclear weapons at its disposal, so why are we asking Ukraine, our friend and ally, to fight with one hand tied behind its back?

In January 2023, the 'fear of escalation' issue that prompted the most Western hand-wringing was the supply of main battlefield tanks to Kyiv. Ukraine badly needs modern tanks to counter the armor arrayed against it by the Russians, and to drive them out of the country. Berlin in particular

---

6. Human Rights Watch. November 9, 2020. *"They Burn Through Everything"*. *The Human Cost of Incendiary Weapons and the Limits of International Law.*

saw a great deal of tortured debate. However, as global pressure mounted for Germany to provide its prized Leopard 2 tanks to Ukraine, after months of dithering the German government finally relented.

NATO has long-since rightly determined that Russia must not be allowed to overrun and occupy Ukraine, but its leaders are still conflicted over providing Ukraine with the weapons it needs to end the conflict successfully and as soon as possible. This lack of resolve to act expeditiously to stop the clearly evil actions of Russia in Ukraine reeks of Western Cold War equivocation in the face of Soviet aggression.

(It should be noted that Germany has come a long way since it's initial aid to Ukraine was 100,000 helmets! It has now supplied a wide range of military equipment and ammunition, as well as assistance for the civilian population. See more on German ambivalence in Chapter 10.)

The next issue up is fighter jets, and once more we are hearing concerns about escalation of the war.

When will they ever learn?

Putin May Use Nukes

With his armies being destroyed on the ground, Putin has resorted to using the old Soviet trick of threatening a nuclear attack on the West. This worked for the Soviets and it has worked in part for Putin. It forces all sensible commentators and policy experts in the West to acknowledge that a nuclear attack has been threatened and must be taken into account when deciding policies on Ukraine. Obviously, a nuclear attack by Russia would be a catastrophe. But it is very unlikely.

Putin's real aim is transparent. He wants to intimidate Ukraine's supporters into backing down from their morally just positions. He wants them to support his calls for negotiations. If he wins in this, he will have won the war, since any negotiations at this point would undoubtedly leave Moscow in control of at least some of Ukraine's territory.

Many military observers of this conflict have pointed out that if Putin did use so-called tactical nuclear weapons against Ukraine, the result would not likely deliver significant advantages on the battlefield. And (luckily!) Washington and other NATO leaders have made it clear to Putin that if he does anything of the sort, NATO's gloves will come off and Russia's Black Sea fleet will join the Moskva now resting on the seabed in the shadows of a damaged Kerch bridge—Putin's pet project that binds Crimea to Russia.

(For more on Russia's threat of a nuclear WWIII, see the following chapter.)

Ukraine is a Corrupt Country

This has got to be the most insubstantial reason among many to argue against supporting Kyiv. Not that there is no corruption in Ukraine. Of course there is. Ukraine—like all the other CIS states—inherited a maximally corrupt system from the Soviet Union. Like most ex-Soviet countries, Ukraine's economy is dominated by billionaire oligarchs, and even some Washington politicians—notably the Bidens—have been caught up in unsavory deals tied to some of them.

However, anyone who has any knowledge of post-Soviet Russia and the governments led by Putin will recognize that Russia is a far more corrupt system than Ukraine ever was. And since when was the invasion of a corrupt country by another corrupt country a justified action? Does Russia enjoy some special qualifications to purify Ukraine of its corruption?

Ironically, Zelensky himself was elected president in a landslide based largely on his promise to clean up corruption in his country. Even during this war he has been taking on corrupt officials, and especially those profiteering from the war. Wouldn't this be a good reason to support him now?

And, by the way, when will Russia come under greater international pressure to clean up its massive corruption?

Some conservatives in America have claimed that $100-$120 billion in US aid to Ukraine has been misused by members of the Ukrainian government. For example, popular *Fox News* host Tucker Carlson has expressed his disdain for Ukraine and its president, going so far as to claim that Zelensky is more like Lenin than George Washington, and that he has stolen $100 billion of US taxpayer funds to build a police state:

> Whatever you think of the war in Ukraine, it is pretty clear that Zelensky has no interest in freedom and democracy. In fact, Zelensky is far closer to Lenin than to George Washington. He is a dictator. He is a dangerous authoritarian who has used a hundred billion in U.S. tax dollars to erect a one-party police state in Ukraine. And that's not an overstatement.[7]

(For a more detailed discussion of Carlson's theories on Ukraine, see the section on the US baiting Russia into the conflict later in this chapter, and see Chapter 9 for a more thorough discussion of the wrongheaded positions on Ukraine being promoted by a faction of conservatives in America.)

No evidence of massive corruption has been provided, and there are some obvious flaws in this theory. First, Western aid to Ukraine is primarily in the form of weapons systems and ammunition. According to the US Department of Defense, in the first year of the conflict Washington provided over $30 billion worth of military supplies to Ukraine.[8] It's not easy to slip tanks and howitzers into your pocket or deposit them in your bank account. And many of these weapons are very expensive, as is the ammunition they use, which explains the very high costs.

There is also budget support assistance being provided by Washington, the EU and others, in the billions of dollars, and this likely is subject to some illegal diversion of funds. All foreign aid should of course be closely monitored to make sure it is spent as intended.

However, it should be noted that on January 31, 2023, Treasury Depart-

---

7. Tucker Carlson. December 7, 2022. *Tucker Carlson: This is the reality about Ukraine's Zelenskyy*. Fox News.

8. Jim Garamone. March 3, 2023. *U.S. Sends Ukraine $400 Million in Military Equipment*. DOD News.

ment spokesperson Megan Apper told Reuters: "We have no indication that U.S. funds have been misused in Ukraine."[9]

But the existence of corruption in Ukraine is not a reason to leave an important and strategic friend to fend for itself against Russian aggression. After all, is there no corruption in the US government? Is there no corruption in the German government? In the French government?

There Really are Nazis Lurking in Ukraine

In WWII, the Nazis did recruit some Ukrainians to support their side against Stalin's regime in Moscow. At the time, this was an option for Ukraine to get free of the Communist yoke. (Remember, Stalin, in the early 1930s had starved to death some six million Ukrainian kulak farmers in the name of collectivizing the country's rich agriculture under Communist Party control, in what is called the Holodomor.)

The claim that there is a real Nazi threat in Ukraine today is, frankly, ridiculous. There are no Nazi parties in the Rada (the Ukrainian parliament), and any evidence of a lingering Nazi influence from decades ago is slim indeed.

To wit, a March 19, 2018 Reuters commentary by Josh Cohen, under this tantalizing heading: *Ukraine's neo-Nazi Problem*, had the following to say:

> A January 28 demonstration, in Kiev, by 600 members of the so-called "National Militia," a newly-formed ultranationalist group that vows "to use force to establish order," illustrates this threat. While the group's Kiev launch was peaceful, National Militia members in bala-clavas stormed a city council meeting in the central Ukrainian town of Cherkasy the following day, skirmishing with deputies and forcing them to pass a new budget.
>
> Many of the National Militia's members come from the Azov move-ment, one of the 30-odd privately-funded "volunteer battalions"

---

9. Andrea Shalal. January 31, 2023. *U.S. funds not misused in Ukraine, U.S. Trea-sury says amid corruption crackdown*. Reuters.

that, in the early days of the war, helped the regular army to defend Ukrainian territory against Russia's separatist proxies. Although Azov uses Nazi-era symbolism and recruits neo-Nazis into its ranks, a recent article in *Foreign Affairs* downplayed any risks the group might pose, pointing out that, like other volunteer militias, Azov has been "reined in" through its integration into Ukraine's armed forces. While it's true that private militias no longer rule the battlefront, it's the home front that Kiev needs to worry about now.

When Russian President Vladimir Putin's seizure of Crimea four years ago first exposed the decrepit condition of Ukraine's armed forces, right-wing militias such as Azov and Right Sector stepped into the breach, fending off the Russian-backed separatists while Ukraine's regular military regrouped. Though, as a result, many Ukrainians continue to regard the militias with gratitude and admiration, the more extreme among these groups promote an intolerant and illiberal ideology that will endanger Ukraine in the long term. Since the Crimean crisis, the militias have been formally integrated into Ukraine's armed forces, but some have resisted full integration: Azov, for example, runs its own children's training camp, and the careers section instructs recruits who wish to transfer to Azov from a regular military unit.[10]

Well this is shocking. Some 600 suspected neo-Nazi demonstrators gathered peacefully in Ukraine, while others forced passage of a new budget in a small Ukrainian town.

Isn't it more important that after Putin annexed Crimea in 2014, Azov militias (who are accused of using Nazi insignia) stepped into the fight in the east—where Putin's proxy armies were seizing territory—standing in for poorly trained and equipped regular Ukraine army troops?

In the current war, we all got to see the bravery of Azov fighters in Mariupol. They stayed to fight on when the city was surrounded and had been reduced to rubble by Russian artillery and air raids. In other words, they demonstrated for all the world to see that they are Ukrainian patri-

---

10. Josh Cohen. March 19, 2018. *Ukraine's neo-Nazi Problem*. Reuters.

ots who have long-since proved their courage in the fight for their country. And—as the article quoted above points out—the Azov fighters are now integrated into the Ukrainian army, as are other semi-autonomous groups fighting Russia.

Ukraine Baited Russia into Invading Ukraine

This twisted and far-too-clever idea is not as isolated a view as you may think. For example, in a primetime December 7, 2022 discussion with Glenn Greenwald on his *Tucker Carlson Tonight* program, America's number one news anchor on cable news, Tucker Carlson, referred to this theory as a likely explanation for the war in Ukraine.

Like other theories that blame the US for provoking Russia, this one appears to be sympathetic to Russia's cause. It is certainly a popular theme used in Russian propaganda. Carlson and Greenwald see no American interest to be upheld in this war. However, they do see America using the proffer of NATO membership to Ukraine as Washington's strategy to lure Putin into this invasion.

Here is their conversation:

> Carlson: What bothers me is not so much what Zelensky is doing, there is a lot of tyranny around the world. I don't brood on it. But the fact that, A, we are paying for it and, B, our leaders are defending it... I think every American should be upset about that.
>
> Greenwald: I think in general Americans should be very skeptical when the US government says, "We are going to fight in wars on the other side of the world, we're sending tens of billions of dollars in military aid in order to spread democracy." The US government doesn't actually care about spreading democracy. Many of its closest allies in the world have been and still are some of the world's most despotic regimes, like Saudi Arabia, Egypt. All the US cares about is that governments serve American interests, not whether they are democratic or not.
>
> If you want to believe the fairy tale that the US government goes to

war to spread democracy, Ukraine is not the place for you. You mentioned this argument: "Well, Zelensky's at war. He has to curb liberty." Go back to 2021, a year before Russia invaded and you can find articles (just Google it) where he shut down opposition, television stations. He has now shut down opposition parties. Every hallmark of what a despot and tyrant—not a democrat—does, is shaping the Zelensky government, and that was true well before Russia invaded.

Carlson: I wonder two things. One, how can Republicans on the Hill continue to defend this, and, B, what's it really about. I think you are right. Our foreign policy is almost always about defending our interests. I think it should be, actually. But I don't see a critical interest at stake here, so what is this about?

Greenwald: Right. I think the first point is: If the US government was honest, it would get rid of this whole script about, "Oh we have to go and defend democracy." That's a fairy tale that's trying to get Americans to feel better about the fact that we are involved in many, many countries all over the world. That's not the real reason. The only reason is to do it for vital US interests. The line in Washington for decades was the US has no vital interests in Ukraine. That was Obama's view, that was the bipartisan view. Why did that change? The only reason is because we saw an opportunity to trap Russia inside Ukraine all based on the view that Russia is our enemy, something only Democrats could believe, because they think Russia is to blame for the 2016 election and Hilary's win [he meant loss]. But why would Republicans want confrontation with Russia? What Americans does that benefit besides arms manufacturers?

Carlson: Well, that's a really good question. I haven't quite unraveled it. It seems pretty clear that the Biden administration baited Russia into this invasion. You have the vice president of the United States in Western Europe days before telling Zelensky to join NATO, which of course they knew it was a red line. They wanted this invasion. That's my view. It's very obvious. You think this was all about preparing for a war with Russia?

Greenwald: If you think that Russia is a grave enemy of the United States, then it makes sense to try and lure them into a war that they can't win. Like we got lured into one with Afghanistan for 20 years, and we lured the Soviet Union into a war in Afghanistan back in the 70s because it does deplete your enemies. The question is: Why should Russia be seen as our enemy? Both Obama and Trump said there is no reason to see Russia that way. It has 1/15th the size of our military budget, its not threatening American borders. Why are we so obsessed with spending tens of millions of dollars to weaken Russia which we could be using here at home to benefit the lives of American citizens, when Russia is not doing anything against the United States unless you are a crazy resistance person who believes there is a reason Donald Trump won. But if you don't believe that, what is the rationale for this? There is none.

Carlson: I know. And as usual they have hijacked the best instincts of Americans, their compassion, and turned that against them.[11]

This is Nuts!

Carlson usually has a good nose for US government policies and programs that are harmful to America. In this case, he appears to largely miss the broader strategic issues in Ukraine, and to be cynically uninterested in Ukraine's suffering at the hand of Putin's army.

If—as the Carlson-Greenwald theory holds—Washington really believed the offer of NATO membership to Ukraine would lure Russia into a conflict that would significantly reduce the potency of Moscow's military, how come most of the wise men of the US administration—as well as most other Western military and strategic experts—believed that Ukraine could not resist a Russian invasion for more than a few days or weeks?

If these Western calculations were right, surely such a swift Russian victory would have meant that instead of Ukraine joining NATO and strengthening the alliance against Russia and other potential enemies, it would have

---

11. Tucker Carlson and Glenn Greenwald. December 7, 2021. *Tucker Carlson Tonight.* Fox News Channel. https://video.foxnews.com/v/6316782340112.

been absorbed into Russia, making Russia a greater threat to NATO than it already was. In other words, it is the fact of sustained and effective Ukrainian resistance to the invasion that has resulted in Russia's military strength being degraded. This is NOT what Washington expected.

To remind our readers of the conventional wisdom in Western capitals on the eve of the invasion: According to *Fox News*, a few weeks prior to the invasion, US Chairman of the Joint Chiefs of Staff Mark Milley testified to Congress that Kyiv would likely fall to Russia in just three days:

> Milley told lawmakers during closed-door briefings on Feb. 2 and 3 that a full-scale Russian invasion of Ukraine could result in the fall of Kyiv within 72-hours, and could come at a cost of 15,000 Ukrainian troop deaths and 4,000 Russian troop deaths.[12]

Again, if America's top military commander believed Ukraine would collapse under the weight of a full-scale Russian invasion in a matter of days, how could it have been a US strategy to bait Russia into invading Ukraine in order for Ukraine to deplete the Russian military since Russia was expected to lose only 4,000 soldiers? Only if Ukraine put up a fierce and prolonged resistance could its army make a dent in Russia's military capabilities, and this is precisely what Milley did not anticipate.

As evidence for his theory, Greenwald suggests that the US lured the Soviet Union into invading Afghanistan in December, 1979. If that is true, President Jimmy Carter must not have been aware of American strategy, since he was exceptionally surprised and angry at Soviet leader Leonid Brezhnev for breaking his promise not to invade.[13]

Furthermore, it should be remembered that Moscow launched its invasion of Afghanistan with a purge of that country's Communist rulers (the president was a blood-drenched Communist called Hafizullah Amin, whom

---

12. Jacqui Heinrich and Adam Sabes. February 5, 2022. *Gen. Milley says Kyiv could fall within 72 hours if Russia decides to invade Ukraine: sources.* Fox News.

13. Editors. July 27, 2019. *Carter reacts to Soviet intervention in Afghanistan.* History.com.

the Russians killed on the first day of the invasion), followed immediately by the installation of their own pro-Moscow Communist, Babrak Kamal. This clearly was an attempt by Moscow to gain more control over Afghanistan through a more pliant communist regime in Kabul. Washington had nothing to do with it.

The several Communist governments in Afghanistan had been fighting Mujahedeen for years as they tried to impose a Marxist-Leninist regime on an understandably resistant conservative Muslim population. But Washington under Carter did not begin providing assistance to these Muslim groups until July, 1979, just a few months before the Russian invasion—and then only $500,000.[14]

What exactly was the tempting American bait that induced the Soviet Union to engage in a decade-long occupation of Afghanistan at a cost it could not afford?

At the time of the Soviet invasion, Leonid Brezhnev was the paramount leader in Moscow. His "Brezhnev Doctrine" called for members of the Soviet Bloc to defend one another. What this really meant was that the Soviet Union should have the permanent right to use military force to intervene in fellow Communist countries to impose its will, as it had done in the Hungarian uprising of 1956 and the Prague Spring of 1968. In this way it could prevent Communist countries breaking away from Moscow's control.[15]

Brezhnev at the time was declining in health, and his decision to commit dwindling Soviet resources to what would become an eight-year conflict proved to be a catastrophic mistake that triggered the collapse of Russia's Communist empire. This was not because the Soviet military was degraded, but because the Soviet Union was no longer economically viable.

And who was the cunning party that engineered the US invasion of Afghanistan after 9/11? According to Greenwald's theory, it must have been

---

14. Kai Bird. September 1, 2021. *How Jimmy Carter Started America's Afghanistan Folly*. Washington Monthly.

15. Suzanne McGee. March 4, 2022. *Why the Soviet Union Invaded Afghanistan*. History.com.

a pretty devious bad actor bent on bringing America to its knees through a long war of attrition. Is there evidence it was Russia or China manipulating the Taliban into helping Al Qaeda launch an attack on 9/11? Or was it the Taliban itself that wanted to take on and degrade the US army? Neither is likely. The more plausible explanation is the obvious one—America wanted to punish the Taliban for its role in the terror attacks.

To call Zelensky a tyrant and despot is pretty strong stuff, given the supposed evidence referenced for this accusation. Greenwald seems to forget that Russia first invaded Crimea and the Donbas in 2014, not 2022. Thus Ukraine had been fighting the Russians and their proxies to regain its territory for six years, not one.

To save Ukraine, Zelensky has had to purge it of Russia's fifth column actors while revamping Ukraine's outdated military to make it capable of meeting the Russian military threat. Taking such measures is not tyranny, as Carlson implies, but what any sane leader must do to protect his country in times of war. Would Greenwald and Carlson have Zelensky leave Russian agents and provocateurs in place? If so, Ukraine is lucky these pundits are not its leaders.

The fifth column problem is particularly dangerous in Ukraine because so much of the population is ethnically and linguistically tied to Russia. Furthermore, it was some of these pro-Moscow Ukrainian citizens and military commanders who practically handed Crimea to Putin in 2014, thanks to Russian active measures that prepared the groundwork for the annexation.

Zelensky has had to take action against pro-Russian media companies and political organizations, as well as the Ukrainian branch of the Russian Orthodox Church, which was found to be working for Moscow.[16]

Again, any country at war would take such precautions, especially with evidence of subversion by fifth columnists, as in Ukraine's case. Ukraine is fighting for its life, and simply cannot afford to give its arch-enemy any more

---

16. Andrew E. Kramer. December 31, 2022. *Clergymen or Spies? Churches Become Tools of War in Ukraine*. The New York Times.

advantages than it has already exploited through turning Russian-speakers in Ukraine into traitors.

And, yes, America does have an interest in Ukraine prevailing in this war, just as much as it had an interest in supporting the Allies in WWI and WWII. Russia may seem far from US borders, but Putin's aggressive behavior—which has been on display since at least 2008—is the most serious threat to European and global peace and security since WWII, with the possible exception of Communist China's global subversion.

And, yes, there is an implicit warning for a dangerous Communist China in the increasingly robust Allied support for Ukraine, which sends a long-overdue message to Beijing: the West will no longer turn a blind eye to Communist China's subversion, intimidation and threats of invasion against other states.

Finally, there is something cynical about this discussion. To conclude that Russia's brutal invasion is nothing more than the result of ill-advised US foreign policy decisions, is to ignore the great suffering of the Ukrainian people and their remarkable cohesion and courage in the face of Russian aggression. Beginning with Zelensky, they have proved their valor and righteousness.

What About Our Own Border?

This argument is used to criticize the Biden administration for its failure to secure America's border with Mexico. This is a perfectly valid criticism of that failure, but what does it have to do with Ukraine? Shouldn't we both secure our own border and help Ukraine resist Russia's invasion? Aren't those logically consistent purposes?

A slightly different version of the border argument is the infrastructure argument: Why should America send billions of dollars to help Ukraine defend itself when our roads and bridges are in such need of repair? Again, need it be either/or? Shouldn't we work to fix our infrastructure and help Ukraine?

The War in Ukraine Does Not Serve America's National Interests

As the Carlson-Greenwald discussion quoted above shows, the essence of this argument is that there is no obvious American national interest at stake in Ukraine. This is a truly myopic and hence dangerous view. It echoes the position of the very active peace movement in America that tried hard to keep the United States out of WWII at a time when England was hanging on for dear life against an onslaught of Hitler's *Luftwaffe*. In that case, this argument was only set aside in December 1941 once Hitler's ally Japan bombed Pearl Harbor, drawing America into the war to defend itself against the aggression of the Axis Powers.

Do we really have to see massive destruction of our friends and allies before we feel justified to help them? And are we not able to recognize international threats to ourselves and our friends before they materialize in wars? Finally, is not a key purpose of NATO to deter countries like Russia from even contemplating aggression?

Consider this: If NATO and other countries did not support Ukraine, the chances of a Russian victory would loom large. Would it really be of no national interest to us if some of our NATO allies had Moscow's victorious army poised to invade on their border? Could we trust that Putin's adventurism would not entice him to go after other former Soviet states and satellites that are now our NATO allies?

The spirit that inspired America's founding continues to compel Americans to fight for liberty and against injustice at home and abroad. Like a good person, America cannot ignore the suffering of others inflicted by tyrants, and it must live up to its treaty commitments.

Our experience with the growth of Nazism and Communism in the last century proved that we stood by for too long while totalitarian states prepared for war. This encouraged their aggression, again and again. In WWII, the consequences of America trying to remain neutral would catch up with us when imperial Japanese Zeros appeared in the morning skies of a peaceful Hawaii and started bombing the US Navy.

Ukraine is the country standing between Russian aggression and the West right now. As such, it is serving the interests of all Western nations, including the United States. It is imperative to recognize this, and to avoid the moral equivalency arguments that proved so wrongheaded during the Cold War.

The Budapest Memorandum is Not Binding

There is another argument for America to support Ukraine that is often overlooked by those who would have us remain on the sidelines. Under President Bill Clinton, on December 5, 1994 the United States joined Ukraine, Britain and Russia in signing The Budapest Memorandum, which opened the way for Ukraine to join the Treaty on the Non-Proliferation of Nuclear Weapons (NPT).

The signing of the Memorandum concluded the negotiations for Ukraine to give up all the Soviet-era nuclear weapons on its territory (they were so substantial that Ukraine in the early 1990s was the third largest nuclear power in the world). Kyiv had already in 1993 signed an agreement with Moscow to transfer these weapons and the Black Sea Fleet at Sevastopol to Russia in exchange for forgiveness of a $2.5 billion debt for oil and gas.[17]

As we mentioned in the Introduction, the Memorandum was designed to give Ukraine security assurances that would protect it from aggression once it had completed the transfer of its nukes to Russia. In the second paragraph, the signatories "reaffirm their obligation to refrain from the threat or use of force against the territorial integrity or political independence of Ukraine."[18]

Russia has clearly been in violation of its commitments to respect Ukraine's territorial integrity and sovereign rights since it first invaded Crimea in 2014.

What about our obligations under this agreement? True, the Memoran-

---

17. Fred Hiatt. September 4, 1993. *Ukraine and Russa Reach Accord.* The Washington Post.

18. Full Text: *The Budapest Memorandum of 1994.* Harvard Kennedy School. https://policymemos.hks.harvard.edu/links/ukraine-budapest-memorandum-1994

dum does not provide the security guarantees that Ukraine wanted, but it does provide assurances. Kyiv acted in good faith in response to Washington urging it to join the NPT, and clearly trusted the United States to come to its defense in case Russia violated the agreement. Is it not important to honor this obligation in the face of Moscow's blatant violations of the agreement?

Chapter 8

Are We on the Brink of World War III?

Russia Threatens a Nuclear WWIII

Perhaps the most alarmist of all reasons suggested for not supporting Ukraine is that this support is driving Putin to escalate the war into a global conflict, a nuclear Third World War. As with so many of these widely repeated fears, the origin of this truly terrifying scenario is the Kremlin, which has repeatedly claimed that Ukraine seeking membership in NATO, and the alliance supporting Kyiv in the current war, are tantamount to acts of aggression against Russia, which Moscow might have to respond to with a nuclear attack.

Here is one of many such threats from Moscow, as reported by the *New York Post:*

> Russia bluntly warned Thursday [October 13, 2022] that further meddling by Western powers in Ukraine would spark World War III — this time a nuclear one that "will be catastrophic for all mankind."

> A top Kremlin official specifically threatened worldwide carnage if NATO approves Ukraine's bid to join its alliance.

> "Kyiv is well aware that such a step would mean a guaranteed escalation to a World War III," the deputy secretary of Russia's Security Council, Alexander Venediktov, told the state TASS news agency.

The warning came a day after a senior NATO official said a Russian nuclear strike would almost certainly trigger a "physical response" from Ukraine's allies — and Defense Secretary Lloyd Austin said the US was "committed to defending every inch of NATO's territory."[1]

Russia Claims NATO is Threatening to Use Nukes

The Russian threats of a nuclear WWIII are all couched in terms of a necessary Russian response to threats from the West, as if Western leaders have suggested that NATO itself might resort to using nuclear weapons to defeat Russia. However, NATO has never threatened to use nuclear weapons in defense of Ukraine. Nuclear saber-rattling is coming exclusively from the Russian side and, as we have mentioned, it echoes the threats made by the Soviet Union when it wanted to deter the West from taking necessary defensive measures.

As usual, the Russians simply lie when making threats. For example, in the *New York Post* article quoted above, Venediktov is reported making this unfounded claim:

> "Meanwhile in Europe, some politicians openly call for such actions … Even a number of politicians in the EU do not conceal and do not rule out the possibility of using weapons of mass destruction against Russia," he claimed, without evidence.

And, in case anyone on earth thought they might escape such a global nuclear war, Venediktov added:

> "We must remember: A nuclear conflict will affect absolutely the whole world—and not only Russia and the collective West, but in general any country on this planet. Its consequences will be catastrophic for all mankind," he warned ominously, days after President Biden conceded fears of impending Armageddon.

As this article points out, President Joe Biden himself had only days

---

1. Lee Brown. October 13, 2022. *Kremlin warns of nuclear World War III that 'will be catastrophic'*. New York Post.

earlier raised the specter of a nuclear "Armageddon"—referring to a Biblical war that will see much of the world destroyed.

As NBC reported:

> President Joe Biden said Thursday [October 6] the risk of nuclear "Armageddon" is the highest it has been for 60 years after Russian President Vladimir Putin renewed his threats as his military retreats in Ukraine.
>
> In remarks at a reception for the Democratic Senatorial Campaign Committee, Biden said it was the first time since the 1962 Cuban Missile Crisis that there has been a "direct threat" of nuclear weapons' being used, "if, in fact, things continue down the path they are going."
>
> "We have not faced the prospect of Armageddon since Kennedy and the Cuban Missile Crisis," he said, offering his bluntest comments about the use of nuclear weapons since Russia invaded Ukraine in February.[2]

The NBC article quotes the nuclear threat Putin had made in a televised address on September 21, 2022, a few days before Biden responded. This was by no means the first time Putin had made this threat, but this time the Russian president tried to make his threat more believable by claiming that he was not bluffing:

> "If the territorial integrity of our country is threatened, we will certainly use all the means at our disposal to protect Russia and our people," the Russian leader said in a televised national address.
>
> "This is not a bluff," he added.[3]

The concerns expressed by Biden in response to Putin's speech echoed

---

2. Zoe Richards and Patrick Smith. October 6, 2022. *Biden warns risk of nuclear 'Armageddon' is highest since Cuban Missile Crisis.* NBC News.

3. Guy Faulconbridge. September 21, 2022. *Putin escalates Ukraine war, issues nuclear threat to West.* Reuters.

those of Former President Donald Trump from a week earlier. Asked by interviewer John Catsimatides on WABC radio in late September 2022 what kept him awake at night, Trump responded in this way:

> I think more than anything else, I think we can end up in World War III. All of the horrible things that took place in Ukraine, looks like it's going to happen in China with Taiwan. What's happened in Ukraine should've never, ever happened, and now the word "nuclear" is being discussed, and I think that's one of the most dangerous things, I think we're at the most dangerous time maybe in many, many years, maybe ever, because of the power of nuclear. For a major nation that's equal with us on nuclear power to be throwing around the word cavalierly like nuclear is a very bad time, a very bad time for this country, and a very bad and very dangerous time for the world.[4]

Even Pope Francis had earlier in September warned of a new world war, indicating that it was already underway. As *Fox News* reported:

> "But unfortunately, Europe and the entire world are convulsed by a war of particular gravity, in terms of the violation of international law, the risks of nuclear escalation, and the grave economic and social consequences," Pope Francis continued. "It is a 'piecemeal' third world war, to which you bear witness in the places where you carry out your mission."[5]

This article notes that the pope made a similar comment during his August 31 general audience, where he acknowledged the anniversary of World War II's dramatic beginnings:

> "Tomorrow you will remember the anniversary of the outbreak of World War II, which so painfully marked the Polish nation," the pope said before referencing the current era as the "third World War" and

---

4. Joe Silverstein. September 28, 2022. *Trump warns World War 3 can be accidentally sparked over Ukraine, Taiwan conflict.* Fox News.

5. Timothy H. J. Nerozzi. September 9, 2022. *Pope Francis repeats warning of 'third world war'.* Fox News.

saying the overarching conflict will most likely play out piecemeal, unlike previous global wars, according to Vatican media.

With leaders talking about WWIII, it is no wonder that people everywhere are becoming concerned. A mid-2022 survey of 17,000 people from various parts of the world found that in America and a handful of other countries, over 80 percent of those surveyed agreed with this statement: "I fear we are moving closer to World War III." Among respondents worldwide aged 25-35, some 76 percent agreed with that statement.[6]

NATO Makes the Right Response to Putin's Nuclear Threats

It is a credit to the United States and the rest of NATO that their collective commitment to Ukraine has only strengthened as the threats from Russia and its brutalization of Ukraine have continued. More specifically, Putin's nuclear saber-rattling in September 2022 elicited some of the strongest responses yet from the West.

On Sunday, September 25, 2022 *The New York Times* reported that during appearances on that day's talk shows, President Biden's National Security Advisor Jake Sullivan said that there would be "catastrophic consequences" should Russia use a nuclear weapon in the Ukraine war. What's more, Sullivan said that Washington had "spelled out" to Moscow what those consequences would be.[7]

The same article pointed out that in May that year, Biden had written an essay in the Times that said essentially the same thing: "…any use of nuclear weapons in this conflict on any scale would be completely unacceptable to us as well as the rest of the world and would entail severe consequences."

What those consequences would be has not been made public. However, consistent with the US policy of maintaining strategic ambiguity regarding the use of military options—including nuclear weapons—such details

---

6. Elliott Davis Jr. September 29, 2022. *Fears About WWIII Are Growing Amid Russia-Ukraine War, Survey Finds.* US News and World Report.

7. David E. Sanger and Jim Tankersley. September 25, 2022. *U.S. Warns Russia of 'Catastrophic Consequences' if It Uses Nuclear Weapons.* The New York Times.

are typically not provided. In this case, however, it is widely assumed that NATO's response to Russian use of a tactical nuclear weapon would not be nuclear.

However, there have been a number of predictions regarding what those non-nuclear consequences might include. Perhaps the most authoritative have come from former CENTCOM commander and CIA director, General David Petraeus. As *The Guardian* reported on October 2, 2022, Petraeus told ABC what he thought would likely be the response:

> Just to give you a hypothetical, we would respond by leading a NATO—a collective—effort that would take out every Russian conventional force that we can see and identify on the battlefield in Ukraine and also in Crimea, and every ship in the Black Sea.[8]

Petraeus addressed the possibility that a frustrated and angry Putin might respond to his losses in Ukraine by resorting to the use of a tactical nuclear weapon by pointing out that such a strike would not give Moscow a military advantage on the battlefield:

> It can still get worse for Putin and for Russia. And even the use of tactical nuclear weapons on the battlefield won't change this at all.

Nevertheless, while NATO is not about to use nuclear weapons of its own in retaliation, "You have to take the threat seriously." And it is important for Russia to know that using nukes is truly unacceptable:

> You don't want to, again, get into a nuclear escalation here. But you have to show that this cannot be accepted in any way.

Putin Backs Down on His Nuclear Threats

NATO's stern warnings regarding its likely response to Russia using nukes seems to have registered with Putin. As AP reported:

---

8. Edward Helmore. October 2, 2022. *Petraeus: US would destroy Russia's troops if Putin uses nuclear weapons in Ukraine*. The Guardian reporting on an ABC News interview.

Russian President Vladimir Putin on Thursday [September 29, 2022] denied having any intentions of using nuclear weapons in Ukraine but described the conflict there as part of alleged efforts by the West to secure its global domination, which he insisted are doomed to fail.

Speaking at a conference of international foreign policy experts, Putin said it's pointless for Russia to strike Ukraine with nuclear weapons.

"We see no need for that," Putin said. "There is no point in that, neither political, nor military."

Putin said an earlier warning of his readiness to use "all means available to protect Russia" didn't amount to nuclear saber-rattling but was merely a response to Western statements about their possible use of nuclear weapons.[9]

But Russian government officials and regime-friendly commentators on state-controlled media continue to beat the nuclear drum, perhaps suggesting that while Putin said he would not use nukes in Ukraine, he did not rule out using them on NATO members.

One of the most vitriolic of these voices in Russia is that of former prime minister and president Dmitry Medvedev. In January 2023 he made the following threat:

"It never occurs to any of the lowlifes to draw an elementary conclusion from this: The defeat of a nuclear power in a conventional war can trigger a nuclear war," former Russian President Dmitry Medvedev, a top Putin ally who now serves as deputy chairman of the Security Council, said in a post on Telegram.

"Nuclear powers have not lost major conflicts on which their fate depended," added Medvedev, whose rhetoric has grown increasingly bellicose over the course of the nearly a year-long war.[10]

---

9. Staff Report. October 27, 2022. *Russia's Putin says he won't use nuclear weapons in Ukraine.* AP.

10. Staff Report. January 19, 2023. *As U.S. and allies arm Ukraine, Russia warns that losing a conventional war "can trigger a nuclear war".* CBS News.

Remember What's at Stake in Ukraine

Nuclear weapons are indeed terrifyingly lethal, as the world witnessed in Hiroshima and Nagasaki in 1945—although today's weapons are much more powerful. However the real danger to civilization lies not in the power of the weapons themselves but in the evil that exists in the hearts and minds of totalitarian leaders who wield them.

Free people cannot live in a world where the threat of nuclear weapons controlled by bad actors can result in paralysis of the good. Yes, the threat of nuclear war is extremely disturbing, but the loss of liberty is worse yet.

Fortunately, although America was the first to develop nuclear weapons, it has not used them since WWII—including the period when it was the sole nuclear power in the world. Fortunately too, Western leaders have consistently recognized that as unpleasant as the thought of nuclear war is, they must maintain an arsenal to deter any and all nations who would use their own nukes in service of evil ambitions.

There have always been tyrants, and there has always been a need for brave men and women to resist tyranny. When the American colonies chaffed under the rule of the mighty British Empire, they were inspired to take up arms against their oppressors by Thomas Paine, who wrote in 1776:

> These are the times that try men's souls. The summer soldier and the sunshine patriot will, in this crisis, shrink from the service of their country; but he that stands it now, deserves the love and thanks of man and woman. Tyranny, like hell, is not easily conquered; yet we have this consolation with us, that the harder the conflict, the more glorious the triumph.[11]

Will free men and women today have the resolve to risk their lives for the sake of freedom? Will Western governments stand firm in supporting Ukraine's freedom despite the nuclear threats from Russia?

Another American patriot, Patrick Henry, in 1775 pleaded with his coun-

---

11. Thomas Paine. 1776. *The American Crisis.*

trymen to recognize that they had no alternative but to confront and fight the British, even at the cost of their lives:

> It is in vain, sir, to extenuate the matter. Gentlemen may cry, Peace, Peace but there is no peace. The war is actually begun! The next gale that sweeps from the north will bring to our ears the clash of resounding arms! Our brethren are already in the field! Why stand we here idle? What is it that gentlemen wish? What would they have? Is life so dear, or peace so sweet, as to be purchased at the price of chains and slavery? Forbid it, Almighty God! I know not what course others may take; but as for me, give me liberty or give me death![12]

It is this willingness to sacrifice one's life for liberty that gives an individual or a nation the resolve needed to confront evil. For Henry, the lethal threat to overcome was an impending British invasion. For the world today, it is the ongoing Russian invasion of Ukraine.

If Russia is allowed to use the threat of nuclear weapons in a new world war to intimidate the West into accepting Russia's rules for this war and its illegal annexation of Ukrainian territory, then what is to prevent Russia using this ploy again, or for any other nation that acquires nukes to imitate the Russian threats to get what it wants?

Finally, it should not be forgotten that Russia itself has good cause to fear the West. The economic and military power of NATO is vastly greater than Russia's own, and this imbalance is not likely to change in the foreseeable future. Russia knows that NATO has no intension of attacking it with nuclear weapons, but even a conventional weapons response to any type of nuclear attack by Russia would likely be devastating. The regime in Moscow would undoubtedly be in jeopardy, as would the future of the whole country.

The Good Lessons the West is Learning

Threatening a nuclear WWIII is the best Russia can do. It is losing on the

---

12. William Wirt. 1836. *Sketches of the Life and Character of Patrick Henry.* Reproduced in *The World's Great Speeches* edited by Lewis Copeland and Lawrence W. Lamm.

battlefield and it's propaganda aimed at deterring NATO from supporting Ukraine is not working. In the meantime, Ukraine is receiving ever more of the weapons it needs to win this war, and continues to build the competency of its military to use those weapons effectively.

Leaders in the West should not encourage Russia by echoing Kremlin propaganda and spreading fear of a nuclear WWIII. Rather, NATO members and other allies should strengthen the unity of the West in support of Ukraine. This will also give hope to Russians wanting to oust Putin and Taiwanese being called to stand up to Communist China—as well as all other people suffering under totalitarianism.

And whatever Russia threatens, the West must not lose sight of what is at stake in Ukraine. Russia cannot be allowed to succeed in its illegitimate attempt to seize Ukrainian territory. This is a moment when the West must hold strong. It would do well to remember that it was Reagan's resolve to see the evil Soviet Empire defeated that led to its demise.

Today the people of Ukraine are on the front line fighting tyranny. They are shedding their blood and suffering the loss of their homes and possessions in the cause of defeating Russian aggression. The West must stand with them, come what may. We cannot be intimidated into passivity by the threat of nuclear weapons and WWIII.

And the West must understand that weakness, disunity and equivocation only encourage more aggression from predators like Putin. As we have pointed out, there is little doubt that Putin launched his invasion in 2022 because his earlier aggressive actions in Georgia and Crimea had met with so little pushback from the West. And he must have been further encouraged at America's precipitous exit from Afghanistan, in the summer of 2021.

Also, just a month before the invasion, when well over 100,000 Russian troops massed on Ukraine's border, President Biden showed a lack of seriousness and resolve when he responded to a question from *Bloomberg's* Jen Epstein during a White House press conference. She wanted to know what the likely US reaction would be to a Russian invasion of Ukraine. Biden responded:

I think what you're going to see is that Russia will be held account-able if it invades. And it depends on what it does. It's one thing if it's a minor incursion and then we end up having a fight about what to do and not do, et cetera.[13]

In other words, a "minor incursion" would only engender a dispute among Western allies as to what their response should be and not a forceful reaction spelling out severe consequences for any military incursion. This was hardly a statement to make Putin think twice before invading. Weakness and equivocation in the face of evil is likely to be fatal.

In the Introduction to this book we referred to a speech by Ronald Reagan in which he articulated the policy that guided his own thinking—and should guide the West in its response to Russia today. This was in 1964. It was at the height of the Cold War when Soviet domination of the world under the cover of a nuclear threat seemed a real possibility. Here again are Reagan's words, which resonate perfectly with those of Thomas Paine, quoted above:

You and I have the courage to say to our enemies, "There is a price we will not pay. There is a point beyond which they must not advance." … Winston Churchill said, "The destiny of man is not measured by material computations. When great forces are on the move in the world, we learn we're spirits — not animals." And he said, "There's something going on in time and space, and beyond time and space, which, whether we like it or not, spells duty."[14]

Yes, the West has a duty to stop Russia, not just for the sake of Ukraine but for the sake of the civilizational values upon which our societies are built and therefore upon which our future as free people depends. These values cannot be surrendered in the name of peace but at the cost of liberty.

Nevertheless, true to its own values, the West should offer an olive branch

---

13. Joe Biden. January 19, 2022. *Remarks by President Biden in Press Confer-ence.* The White House.

14. Ronald Reagan. October 27, 1964. *A Time for Choosing.* Ronald Reagan Pres-idential Library and Museum.

to Russia, a path to its redemption—but only with clear conditions. The West will help Russia recover from the war only after 1. Putin's regime is replaced by a democratic government that is committed to upholding international rules and standards of behavior; 2. Russia withdraws completely from all Ukrainian territory; and 3. Russia compensates Ukraine and its people for all the damage it has done to them in this war.

Chapter 9

Wrongheaded Conservative Support for Russia

Why Some American Conservatives Don't Support Ukraine

In chapter 7 we discussed a range of bogus arguments for not supporting Ukraine in the war now raging there. For those who identify with the traditional values of faith, family and patriotism, some of the most disturbing voices raised in the chorus of opposition to supporting Ukraine are those of a group of America's most capable and influential conservatives.

We quoted extensively from a discussion between the *Fox News* host, Tucker Carlson, and his guest, Glenn Greenwald, a prominent investigative journalist. They agreed that Washington's strategy in Ukraine was to lure Russia into invading its neighbor by inviting Kyiv to join NATO. In other words it was American provocation that was responsible for Putin's aggression and not Putin's own imperial ambitions. The Carlson-Greenwald theory is that Washington was using this provocation so that the Russian military could be degraded through a war in Ukraine.

Where does a theory like this come from? And why do otherwise dependable conservative leaders like Carlson, Congressman Matt Gaetz and Congresswoman Marjorie Taylor Greene all rail against American support for Ukraine?

Gaetz and Greene are two of the staunchest social and fiscal conservatives in America today. They are close to former President Donald Trump and thus, with Carlson, stand to influence America's policy on Ukraine in the presidential race, and more so if Trump were to regain the presidency in 2024.

A Justified Suspicion of Washington and the Biden Administration

One thing these strong conservatives share in common is a justified suspicion of the real motivations of the Biden administration for its support of Ukraine, and in particular of President Biden himself. As a mountain of incriminating evidence regarding his family's history of corruption continues to grow, it has become clear that the Bidens have received (primarily through his son Hunter) large bribes from America's enemies, including China[1] and Russia, as well as from other countries run by leaders with a Soviet-era habit of buying influence by bribing officials. Two of these countries with ties to the Bidens are Ukraine and Kazakhstan.[2]

What these murky relationships and illicit transactions signify is that Joe Biden has been willing to use his influence as an official in the top echelon of the US government (especially as Vice President under Barak Obama) to enrich himself and his family at the cost of his country's interests and security.

This brazen behavior has been protected by the heavily pro-Democratic Party bias of the Washington establishment, and in particular the Department of Justice and its enablers in the so-called mainstream media. So conservatives have good reason to suspect the president of harboring ulterior motives for his resolute support of Ukraine, and for his DOJ and other agencies for being complicit in hiding this corruption.

Then there is the wider and deeper issue of 'deep state' influence in Washington. This is not limited to the DOJ, but can be found wherever federal bureaucracies operate. It is not new, but a feature of virtually all gov-

---

1. Press Release. March 16, 2023. *Comer Reveals Biden Family Members Receiving Payments from Chinese Energy Company*. Congressional Committee on Oversight and Accountability.

2. Jessica Chasmar. March 31, 2022. *Hunter Biden's foreign business dealings: 4 countries with financial links to president's son*. Fox News.

ernment agencies that have enormous powers that can easily be misused to target political opponents. Hence the unelected forces of government that operate from the shadows have been called 'the Swamp' for good reason.

In recent years the government agencies that should be the most trusted, such as Homeland Security and the DOJ, have established a dismal record of political activism. Consequently, they have violated the very purpose for their existence by failing to protect the rights of all Americans. They have failed to secure America's borders and thereby devalued citizenship for all Americans, all the while encouraging crime; they have failed to secure elections against abuse and thereby deprived citizens of the value of their votes; and they have failed to bring to justice radical Leftist groups like Antifa and BLM that have attacked innocents and destroyed whole city neighborhoods.

Worse still, instead of carrying out their obligations to protect Americans from the predations of criminals they have misused the law to prosecute patriotic and law-abiding Americans whom they disfavor. These abuses are of greatest concern in the realm of social activism, since the Biden administration is pushing anti-faith and anti-family policies by embracing the woke agenda while censoring free speech through cancel culture.

Why would you not be suspicious of the motives of a government this corrupt and unjust?

The Subtle Influence of Russian Propaganda
Russian propaganda is aimed at exploiting this suspicion while presenting Russia as a paragon of Christian values and traditional families. This Moscow messaging has targeted a wide range of audiences and it has been diabolically effective particularly with some conservative Christians. As we showed in Chapter 9, taking a pro-Christian stand often appeals to the righteous minds of Americans who are justifiably outraged at what their government is doing to destroy America's moral foundations.

Whatever Western virtue a specific line of Russian propaganda seeks to exploit, the conclusion Moscow would like you to draw is that the Biden administration is corrupt and that its motives for being in Ukraine are an extension of this corruption. Second, Russia would also like you to believe that Ukraine joining NATO would indeed be a real threat to Moscow's sovereignty, and that Russia is therefore justified in its invasion of Ukraine to prevent that from happening. Finally, Russian propaganda is aimed at convincing people and governments in the West that Moscow might actually use nukes against Ukraine and/or NATO countries if it is not allowed to reach its objective in Ukraine.

The conservatives who echo these Russian talking points would never concede that they are merely parroting Moscow's propaganda. But they nevertheless appear to be getting information and opinions about the war from an array of news and social media sites that are being used to spread Russian disinformation that is disseminated by an army of pro-Russian writers and podcasters operating under the cover of credible media channels.

We are not talking about the dissemination of the rants of pro-Putin pundits on Russia's state-owned channels—which are obviously designed to encourage domestic support for Putin—but rather the subtle shaping of the news to justify Russia's invasion while questioning the value of the West continuing its support for Ukraine. The sources may not be political in nature—they may even be tech blogs or financial news outlets.

It is this clever Russian disinformation campaign that has proved so insidious and effective in shaping the arguments of conservatives who believe they are upholding America's real interests by opposing a suspect US administration's massive support for Ukraine.

A case in point. On April 20, 2023 a group of Republican lawmakers made up of three senators and 16 congressmen sent a letter to President Biden asking him to stop sending aid to Ukraine. Here are key extracts that must be cause for cheer in the Kremlin:

> We write to express concern regarding the U.S. response to Ukraine. Over a year ago, Russia launched an invasion that has upended decades of peace in Europe. We are deeply concerned that the trajectory of U.S. aid to the Ukrainian war effort threatens further escalation and lacks much-needed strategic clarity.

With every new aid package and every new weapon provided to Ukraine, the risk of direct conflict with Russia climbs.

There are appropriate ways in which the U.S. can support the Ukrainian people, but unlimited arms supplies in support of an endless war is not one of them. Our national interests, and those of the Ukrainian people, are best served by incentivizing the negotiations that are urgently needed to bring this conflict to a resolution. We strongly urge you to advocate for a negotiated peace between the two sides, bringing this awful conflict to a close.[3]

These political leaders are calling for Biden to stop sending weapons to Ukraine and to start "incentivizing the negotiations that are urgently needed" to end the conflict. The letter makes no reference at all to the strategic and humanitarian importance of defending Ukraine, or the need to make sure that Ukraine wins this war.

And once public figures buy into the Moscow line—probably unwittingly—they can be expected to continue looking for evidence that they deem confirmation for their opposition to continued US and NATO support for Ukraine.

Moscow So Loves This Tune

We don't mean to pick on Tucker Carlson, but he is the most visible and vocal critic of the West's fulsome support of Ukraine, and recently he has increasingly echoed Moscow's warning that the war in Ukraine is actually a proxy war between Russia and NATO, and that by supporting Ukraine we are risking a new world war.

In an April 13, 2023 monologue on his daily *Fox News* program, Carlson referred to the recent publication of secret documents about the war in Ukraine—originally posted on the Discord social media platform by a young airman, Jack Teixeira—as proof that he had been right on the war all along, since he believes the documents prove that the American people are being

---

3. See the full text of this letter in Appendix 4.

told two major lies about the war. Here is a transcript of relevant parts of Carlson's monologue:

> For the past 14 months, you have heard two main things about the war in Ukraine. The first is that the war in Ukraine is a war of national sovereignty. It is not a proxy battle between superpowers. Russia invaded Ukraine. That was immoral. The United States supports Ukraine because the United States supports democracy, but the United States itself is not at war with Russia. This is Ukraine's war to fight. The second thing we have heard over and over again is that Ukraine is winning that war. Ukrainian troops are brave and noble. Russian troops are evil and incompetent.
>
> The Ukrainians are beating the Russians. In the end, their victory is inevitable. Now, you're very familiar with these points because you have heard them every day since last February. You've heard them repeated by every power center in the United States, the Pentagon, the White House, the leaders of both parties in Congress, CEOs and celebrities and most insistently of all, you've heard them from virtually every single outlet along the entire spectrum of our national news media. These are the two essential themes of the war in Ukraine and both of them are lies. We know that they're lies because late last week, leaked intelligence about the war in Ukraine began to appear on social media. Briefing slides prepared by the U.S. government begin to show up, among other places, on Twitter, and the slide show that this is in fact not Ukraine's war. It's our war. The United States is a direct combatant in a war against Russia. As we speak, American soldiers are fighting Russian soldiers. So, this is not a regional conflict in Eastern Europe. This is a hot war between the two primary nuclear superpowers on Earth and yet this war has never been formally declared
>
> It has not been authorized by Congress and for that reason, this war is a violation of American law. It is a crime. The second thing we learn from these slides is that despite direct U.S. involvement, Ukraine is in fact losing the war. Seven Ukrainians are being killed for every Russian. Ukrainian air defenses have been utterly degraded. Ukraine

is losing. The Biden administration is perfectly aware of this. They're panicked about it, but they have lied about this fact to the public. Just two weeks ago, for example, Secretary of Defense Lloyd Austin told the U.S. Senate that Russian military power is "waning." In other words, Russia is losing the war. That was a lie. He knew it was when he said it, but he repeated it in congressional testimony. That is a crime, but Lloyd Austin has not been arrested for committing that crime. Instead, the only man who has been taken into custody or likely ever will be is a 21-year-old Massachusetts Air National Guardsman who leaked the slides that showed that Lloyd Austin was lying. He revealed the crimes, therefore he's the criminal.[4]

In other words, everything we know about the war in Ukraine and its causes—including Putin's deceptiveness, aggression and brutality—is false. Ukraine is not valiantly defending its sovereignty against barbaric invaders, but simply being used as a pawn in a proxy war between NATO and Russia.

Carlson's piece is titled: *Telling the truth is the only real sin in Washington*. This headline is clever, but it also reveals the misdirection of this so-called conservative position. The issue in Ukraine is not fundamentally one of Washington intrigue and corruption but of real flesh and blood suffering in a country that has been victimized by Russia.

Furthermore, it should be remembered that Moscow is far more guilty of the sin of lying than Washington ever was. Lying is an art form in Communist countries and was a pillar of Soviet statecraft. It is a pillar of Putin's regime as well. The real issue, however, is not whether Washington or Moscow are lying, but what the objective truth is from the standpoint of human rights, international justice and the preservation of security in the Euro-Atlantic region.

But This Too Was Russian Propaganda

The revelations from the leaked secret documents that were the basis for Carlson's monologue would soon be exposed as doctored versions of the

---

4. Tucker Carlson. April 13, 2023. *Telling the Truth is the Only Real Sin in Washington*. Fox News.

original. As an April 16 expose by *The Wall Street Journal* explained, the originals had been 'edited' for a pro-Russia network of social media outlets and YouTube channels called *Donbass Devushka* (Donbas Girl). As the WSJ explained:

> A social-media account overseen by a former U.S. Navy noncommissioned officer—a prominent online voice supporting Russia's war on Ukraine—played a key role in the spread of intelligence documents allegedly leaked by Airman First Class Jack Teixeira...

> On April 5, the Donbass Devushka Telegram account posted four of the allegedly leaked classified documents to its 65,000 followers, according to a screenshot seen by *The Wall Street Journal*. That led several large Russian social-media accounts to pick up on the documents, after which the Pentagon launched an investigation...

> Airman Teixeira's posts had languished online for months, shared among a small circle of fellow war and computer-game enthusiasts who had joined his invitation—only server on the Discord platform. Even after another member reposted the files to a larger Discord server, they remained unnoticed by the broader public. It was only after the posting of some of the files on Donbass Devushka's account that they turned into fodder for military enthusiasts and Russia supporters across the internet...

> The Donbass Devushka Telegram account that Ms. Bils oversees describes itself as engaging in "Russian-style information warfare..."

> Linked accounts using the same name on other platforms also promoted the Russian agenda after Moscow's invasion of Ukraine in February 2022. The Donbass Devushka network hawked merchandise featuring Wagner and the Russian military, promising to send proceeds for the "freedom of Donbass" and to help "our men on the front..."

> "Some very interesting potential intel," the Donbass Devushka Telegram account posted on April 5, attaching images of four files that Airman Teixeira allegedly stole from the U.S. military. "The authen-

ticity cannot be confirmed but looks to be very damning nato information." The post remained online for several days…

Some of the slides reposted on the Telegram account overseen by Ms. Bils had been altered from the otherwise identical photographs allegedly posted by Airman Teixeira on Discord—changed to inflate Ukrainian losses and play down Russian casualties. A subsequent post on the Donbass Devushka Telegram channel, on April 12, denied that the image had been doctored by the administrators.[5]

According to the *New York Post*, Donbass Devushka was run by 37-year-old Sarah Bils, a Navy veteran originally from New Jersey, who claimed she was a Russian speaker who had been born in Ukraine's Luhansk Oblast. A pro-Ukrainian outfit called North Atlantic Fella Organization (NAFO)—which researches media operations using open intelligence sources—first identified Bils as the online personality Donbass Devushka, and passed the information to *Malcontent News*.

From the *New York Post*:

Sarah Bils, 37, a veteran who served at [the Naval Air Station on] Whidbey Island in Washington state, was outed as "Donbass Devushka," which translates to Donbas Girl, an online personality behind a vast network of pro-Kremlin blogs, podcasts and fundraising accounts.

While Bils touted herself online as a Ukraine-born woman backing Russia's invasion and spreading misinformation against Kyiv, she was actually born in New Jersey and now lives in Oak Harbor, Washington, *Malcontent News* first reported with information from the pro-Ukraine North Atlantic Fella Organization (NAFO).[6]

The *Malcontent News* article points out that Carlson had used the doc-

5. Yaroslav Trofimov and Bob Mackin. April 16, 2023. *Former Navy Noncommissioned Officer Helped Spread Secrets*. The Wall Street Journal.

6. Ronney Reyes. April 17, 2023. *Pro-Russian propagandist ID'd as US Navy vet who helped spread Pentagon intelligence leak*. New York Post.

tored versions of the secret documents as the basis for claiming that the American people had been lied to about Ukraine:

> An investigation by Bellingcat traced the spread of the documents from Teixeira's Discord to 4Chan, Telegram, and Twitter. Dueling versions of key documents were circulating, with one showing Russian losses far exceeded Ukrainian losses, and the other, poorly edited version showing the opposite. Bellingcat alleges the doctored versions originated on the Donbass Devushka Telegram channel, a claim Bils denies.

> Carlson… used the edited version distributed by her Telegram channel. On the April 13 broadcast of his Fox News show, "Tucker Carlson Tonight," he claimed that Ukraine was suffering a 7-1 troop loss ratio and was "losing the war."[7]

Indeed, as the transcript of his show, excerpted above, shows, he said: "The second thing we learn from these slides is that despite direct U.S. involvement, Ukraine is in fact losing the war. Seven Ukrainians are being killed for every Russian."

It would seem that Carlson was too eager to find evidence that supports his position on Ukraine, which the facts on the ground belie. His 'facts' were manufactured by Russia. He should have known better than to fall for this disinformation. After all, there are mountains of evidence that show Ukraine has done remarkably well in this war—pushing Russian forces from Kyiv, Kharkiv and Kherson—and now is readying itself for a major spring offensive.

A Lesson from Vietnam

It's worth remembering that it was Communist propaganda about a supposed Hanoi-backed Viet Cong victory in the Tet Offensive of 1968 that influenced Walter Cronkite to become a proponent of the United States getting out of

---

7. Staff Report. April 16, 2023. *A Russian Disinformation Empire in Oak Harbor, Washington.* Malcontent News.

the war in Vietnam without having first defeated Hanoi.[8] Cronkite was misinformed about the actual outcome of the fighting but he enjoyed the trust of a huge audience and he helped turn public opinion against continued American support for Vietnam.

In hindsight, you could only agree with Cronkite today if you believed the outcome of US involvement in Vietnam was either inevitable or acceptable. It was an outcome worse than that in Korea, where America at least managed to make sure the South remained free of Communist rule. In Vietnam the US eventually signed off on a phony peace deal that the North never planned to honor.

Hanoi's army overran the south and sent as many as a million prisoners to Gulag-type 'reeducation camps', where an estimated 165,000 died.[9] Those that survived were generally imprisoned for a minimum of three years. Another 2.5 million southerners risked their lives to escape the new Communist regime by boat, fleeing to any country that would accept them. No one knows the exact number of 'Boat People' who perished at sea, but estimates indicate it could have been as high as 50,000.[10]

As we discussed in Chapter 2, the outcome in Vietnam was determined more than anything else by the policies of several political leaders in Washington who, like Cronkite, believed that the war could not be won. Their half-hearted approach to the war and refusal to listen to the advice of their generals meant that tens of thousands of Americans died without achieving a victory.

Korea and Vietnam taught us just how important it is for America to have a clear interest in the outcome of a conflict before supporting or engaging in it, and then to use its great military strength to achieve a decisive

---

8. Kenneth T. Walsh. February 27, 2018. *50 Years Ago, Walter Cronkite Changed a Nation.* US News & World Report.

9. Patricia Nguyen. March 22, 2022. *Reeducation Camps & States of Suspension.* Amerasia Journal, Volume 47.

10. Dave Roos. September 1, 2021. *How the End of the Vietnam War Led to a Refugee Crisis.* History.com.

victory in the shortest time possible. Without this determination, any US engagement in wars will likely incur mounting losses of life and money without the objective being achieved.

American isolationists may never want the United States to engage in wars overseas. But, as the terror attack on September 11, 2021 demonstrated all too painfully, we live in an interconnected world that does not afford us the luxury of remaining aloof from all the inevitable international conflicts between forces of good and evil in the world. Some will always deserve our engagement.

The point is not to wash our hands of the problems of others, but to sustain a consistent policy for appropriate engagement in international conflicts. Because Washington was uncertain about its purpose in Korea and Vietnam, it was only partially successful in Korea and not at all in Vietnam. It was on the right side in both wars but its hesitations resulted in heavy casualties, high costs and unsatisfactory outcomes.

Conservatives Should Know Better

America's participation in NATO is of particular importance because the alliance was established with the clear purpose of deterring Soviet aggression against Europe and America, a purpose of undeniable relevance and importance to the United States. Since Russia has now inherited the Soviet mantle as the primary threat to Euro-Atlantic stability and peace—as Putin's aggressions have made clear—America has every good reason to block Moscow's expansion.

The benefit of a forceful European and American response to Putin's aggression should not be in question. Putin cannot be allowed to invade peaceful European countries, whether they are NATO members or not. This is not just true for non-member Ukraine, but also for other non-member European countries such as Finland (before it became a member on April 4, 2023), Sweden and Moldova.

Although there was a strong anti-war lobby in the United States at the outbreak of WWII, few Americans disagree that Washington's Lend-Lease support for Britain before Japan's attack at Pearl Harbor was the right thing to do. The moral issue in WWII was crystal clear—Germany, Japan and Italy were all aggressors against peaceful countries, and had to be stopped. Is the Russian invasion of Ukraine any less an aggression than Germany's WWII invasion of Belgium, Holland and France?

President Reagan was effective in ending the Cold War because he viewed that conflict as essentially moral in nature, as we have discussed in these pages. In the case of Ukraine, America does not have an Article 5 obligation to come to its defense—since Kyiv is not a member of NATO—but it does have a moral obligation under the Budapest Memorandum of 1994 to honor its commitment to protect Ukraine against any violations of its territorial integrity.

And there is the moral imperative to defend the victims of aggression wherever and whenever one can. This is a human obligation, and America has a proud tradition of coming to the aid of those in need, whether they are the victims of natural disasters, poverty, disease or war. This is not a foolish or naïve policy, but the natural behavior of a people endowed with a strong sense of justice and fairness.

It is particularly disturbing that Carlson et al seem to dismiss as insignificant the enormous suffering inflicted on the Ukrainian people by the Russian army, while dismissing out of hand their very real bravery in fighting an army many times the size of their own. Surely the whole point of maintaining a civilized international order is to prevent the sort of war crimes and human rights violations being perpetrated against the Ukrainians in this war?

Why are Carlson and similarly anti-Ukraine conservatives so unmoved by the aggression of Russia and the suffering of so many millions of Ukrainians who have been injured, killed, or forced to flee their homes and become refugees in other cities and countries?

In our view, this is an unseemly and cold-blooded attitude. It is also myopic. The consequences for the rest of the world if Putin has his way are undoubtedly disastrous. And America will likely have to pay a very high price for any further predations by an emboldened Putin who believes he can get America and the West to tolerate more of his aggressions.

Could this lack of any real empathy for the people of Ukraine be the result of limited experience of human suffering in the many countries that are less fortunate than America?

Providing Comfort for Putin is Dangerous

What we have not heard from Carlson, Gaetz, Greene and other conservative critics of US support for Ukraine is a credible justification for Russia's invasion. Which leaves us to conclude that they believe Russia's own arguments for invading Ukraine, and in particular that Ukraine wanting to join NATO was sufficient cause for Moscow to invade its neighbor and murder tens of thousands of Ukrainians while destroying the country's cities and infrastructure.

The implication is that this group of conservatives is fine with Russia occupying Ukraine for good—since that is clearly Putin's intension. However, according to recent surveys discussed in Chapter 14, the vast majority of Ukraine's 44 million people have become almost unanimous in wanting Putin driven from their land. This important point doesn't seem to register with Carlson.

If these Americans do not want to make sure Ukraine wins this war, aren't they in effect saying that Ukraine should be abandoned to its fate because it simply is not important enough for the West to defend?

It is no wonder that Russian state TV uses Carlson's programs to bolster its propaganda efforts, and has been doing so since the inception of Moscow's invasion. The Kremlin no doubt takes comfort from the support of such a high-profile pundit in Washington, and—according to an intercepted memo—it has instructed Russian state-owned media (which is virtually all major outlets) to use Carlson's programs to support Moscow's messaging.[11]

---

11. David Corn. March 13, 2022. *Leaked Kremlin Memo to Russian Media: It Is "Essential" to Feature Tucker Carlson.* Mother Jones.

America's Abiding Interest in a Peaceful Europe

NATO was established to prevent another world war erupting in Europe, and in particular as a counterweight to the rising power of the Soviet Union. As we have noted, both WWI and WWII proved that America could not stand aloof from major conflicts in Europe. The creation of NATO formalized recognition of the subsequent Cold War reality—Soviet aggression against European nations would necessarily lead to American involvement in their defense.

If we don't recognize Putin's invasion of Ukraine as a threat to Euro-Atlantic stability and peace, what on earth would ever constitute such a threat? Should we wait for Putin to invade Poland, the Baltic States, Moldova or some other nation before we take him seriously?

And if we continue to invest several hundred billions of dollars each year in defense spending, what purpose do these weapons have if we don't use them to deter Putin and his ilk? After all, US leadership in NATO is confirmation enough that Washington does have a very strong interest in the continued stability and peace of Europe. We cannot pretend—as we did initially in WWI and WWII—that we can just sit out major conflicts in Europe.

For conservatives, the foreign countries to take our cues from are not Russia, China or other aggressors, but the countries that share our cultural values and have already suffered greatly under foreign dictatorships. In this war, those countries are Poland, Finland and the Baltic States, as well as all the former Soviet republics that finally got their freedom in the late 1980s and early 1990s. Many are now NATO members themselves, and they know better than anyone in Washington what is at stake in this war.

A Lesson from Finland

Conservatives who say that NATO provoked Russia to invade Ukraine by inviting Kyiv to join the alliance, should listen to the words of Finland's president, Sauli Niinisto, who explained why this invasion finally pushed his country and Sweden to abandon their neutrality and join the alliance.

Speaking at a May 11, 2022 press conference to announce Finland's intention to join NATO, Niinisto recounted that Putin in 2021 had warned him of "contra steps" if Finland were to join NATO. "By stating that, Russia stated that we don't have our own will. That made a huge change."[12]

The invasion of Ukraine confirmed what those 'contra steps' might look like, even though Ukraine was invaded after only talking about joining NATO and not after actually starting down the path to accession. If Putin could invade Ukraine he could just as well invade Finland, Sweden or any other country he wanted to control. In other words, Putin was ready to invade Russia's neighbors at will.

"My response [to Putin] is that you caused this. Look in the mirror," an angry Niinisto said. Russian intimidation of Finland and its invasion of Ukraine had convinced Finland and Sweden to join the alliance after more than seven decades of post-WWII neutrality.

Doesn't the decision of Finland and Sweden validate Ukraine's contention that it is a victim of Russian aggression, and debunk the theory that Russia was justified in invading Ukraine to prevent it from joining NATO? Do conservatives believe that NATO would not be justified in defending Finland or Sweden's sovereignty if Russia attacked them, whether they were members or not?

Russia has no justification for its invasion of Ukraine, and it cannot be allowed to get away with the invasion. All but a handful of Americans and Europeans know this to be true. It's time the conservatives opposing support for Ukraine realized this too.

The Left's Peculiar Support for Ukraine

To see Leftist leaders stand up for Ukraine in the name of freedom and justice has been befuddling for many who long observed the Left's Cold War era policies of détente and appeasement towards the Soviet Union and, later, Communist China. Why this robust response to Putin's aggression now?

There could be several explanations, such as Biden needing to make

---

12. Thomas Harding. May 11, 2022. *'You caused this': Finland's president blames Russia for Nato alliance move*. The National.

up for his pathetic abandonment of Afghanistan, or even to draw attention away from his family's history of corrupt dealings with Ukraine, Russia and China. (Remember, in 1998 President Bill Clinton famously bombed a pharmaceutical factory in Sudan ostensibly targeting Osama Bin Laden in response to Al Qaeda terror attacks against US embassies in East Africa. However, many speculated that the president was mainly interested in distracting public attention away from the damaging fallout from his affair with Monica Lewinsky.[13])

Whatever the reason, the support of most Democratic Party leaders for Ukraine is justified and should be applauded. After all, while one may disagree with a rival's positions on most issues, it is a matter of integrity to applaud him when he is right on an issue. What's more, the moral issue in Ukraine is so black and white it should be recognized by everyone, regardless of party affiliation or political ideology.

You only have to look at Russia's allies today to know the nature of Putin's regime and why Russia must not be allowed to succeed in its aggression in Ukraine. Washington certainly does not belong on the side of Russia's backers in Beijing, Pyongyang and Tehran. They are all enemies of our values and pose threats to freedom and democracy.

In the final analysis, it is not important what motivates Joe Biden and others in his party and administration to support Ukraine. What is important is the bigger picture that we are laying out in this book. By standing up to tyrants we are protecting the innocent of the world and securing our own future in a peaceful world. We welcome all who join us in this fight.

Furthermore, as we discuss in the final chapter, it is a hopeful sign that a broad cross-section of American society and a large majority of countries around the world support Ukraine in this war. A successful outcome could make it a crucial turning point in the providence that is guiding humanity

---

13. Susan Baer. August 23, 1998. *Clinton's airstrike motives questioned. Many wonder if attack was meant to distract from Lewinsky matter.* The Baltimore Sun.

towards a future in which all people will benefit from living in a peaceful and prosperous world.

This is a fight America belongs in. This is a fight America should lead.

Chapter 10

The German Disease

The invasion of Ukraine has brought to light the inability of Germany to take a forceful, principled position in the face of evil. For decades this has been an issue that merely irritates many other countries, including the United States, but now the 'German disease' has become a very significant obstacle in the way of Europe moving decisively to address Russia's aggression.

With over 83 million people, Germany has the largest population of any West European country. And, according to the World Bank, its economy (with a GDP of $4.26 trillion in 2021) is also the largest in Europe—and over twice the size of Russia's $1.78 trillion economy.

But do you ever see Germany taking a leading role in world affairs?

A Lack of Moral Clarity Makes a Feckless Ally

Since being crushed in WWII, Germany has not succeeded in shaping a strong, constructive role for itself in Europe and the world. It has depended on the US-led NATO alliance to provide protection against aggressors—such as the Soviet Union during the Cold War—and in the post-Cold War era it has not met its NATO obligation to spend two percent of its GDP on defense.

There appears to be a faulty logic in Germany's post-WWII thinking. Instead of redirecting its nationalist energies—that were misused to build empires in WWI and WWII—into providing principled leadership for Europe and the world, Germany has pursued policies that incur a minimum risk for its own interests while contributing little to a good and peaceful world.

Behind the façade of its self-interested public policies there lurks the real driver of modern Germany—its powerful industrial companies with their global commercial interests. Thus instead of standing up to Russia under Putin, China under the Chinese Communist Party, or Iran under its clerical dictators, Berlin is forever trying to preserve its relationships with these despotic regimes on behalf of its business interests.

This approach makes Germany susceptible to manipulation by the world's bad actors, and compromises its ability to take principled stands on foreign policy issues. It is this German disease that now makes Berlin a feckless ally for the Western alliance.

A symptom of this disease was on display when the German delegation to the United Nations during the General Assembly in 2018 broke out in laughter when President Donald Trump warned that Germany's dependence on Russian gas was a dangerous policy that made it hostage to Moscow.[1]

In hindsight, Trump's words would prove prophetic:

> Reliance on a single foreign supplier can leave a nation vulnerable to extortion and intimidation. That is why we congratulate European states such as Poland for leading the construction of a Baltic pipeline so that nations are not dependent on Russia to meet their energy needs. Germany will become totally dependent on Russian energy if it does not immediately change course.[2]

The War in Ukraine has Exposed Germany's Weakness

German diplomats are laughing no more. Russia has indeed used its supply

---

1. German delegation laughs at Trump's UN warning. September 25. 2018. https://www.youtube.com/watch?v=FfJv9QYrlwg

2. Donald J. Trump. September 25, 2018. *Address to the United Nations General Assembly*. GB News. https://www.youtube.com/watch?v=D7Owe-MxNu8

of gas and oil to Germany for purposes of "extortion and intimidation"—to get Germany to back off from supporting Ukraine.

It took the invasion of Ukraine to finally awaken Germany from its *gemütlich* relationship with Russia, which was based on business opportunities for German companies in Russia in exchange for plentiful and inexpensive energy supplies for the German economy.

Suddenly Germany looks as foolish as Trump said it was. Berlin has had to scramble to find alternative suppliers of gas and oil, and to reopen coal mines to get fuel for its decommissioned coal-fueled power plants. Finally, faced with the prospect of a cold winter, the Leftist government of Olaf Scholz delayed the closure of Germany's last three nuclear plants from December 31, 2022 to April 15, 2023, when they were shut down.[3]

This was a triumph of unscientific ideology over science and reason. As France continues to demonstrate, nuclear power is a cheap, clean and reliable source of electricity. Given Germany's need for alternatives to Russian hydrocarbons, this move borders on insanity. (To its credit, Germany has moved rapidly to built out the infrastructure it needs to replace pipeline gas with LNG.)

The need for electricity, heat and water for a modern economy like Germany's is obvious, as is the fact that for now 'green energy'—wind, solar and hydro—is unable to meet those needs. Yet Germany has foolishly allowed itself to be pushed into a crisis of its own making.

On the one hand it has bowed to the commercial interests of its industrialists by building close ties with energy producer Russia, while on the other hand it has caved to pressure from the radical Left to do away with essential power generating capabilities that require fossil fuels or uranium. Nuts!

The irony of this short-sighted approach was brought home by the appearance of a grinning Greta Thunberg at demonstrations against coal in

---

3. Frank Jordans. April 15, 2023. *Over and out: Germany switches off its last nuclear plants*. AP.

January 2023.[4] Does that smile mean she knows where to find the energy Germany needs, but is just not telling?

However, while this energy comeuppance for Germany may seem somewhat humorous, Berlin's waffling on support for Ukraine is not. And it is here that we see the German disease on full display.

Instead of leading a robust European and NATO response to Russia's invasion, Germany has been exceptionally slow to respond. This changed somewhat when the evidence of Russia's many war crimes became obvious to all but the willfully blind. But decisive statements and actions by German leaders always seem too little too late.

In January 2023, the issue that most angered Ukraine's supporters was Germany's reluctance to provide Ukraine with the weapons it needs to win, and in particular its Leopard 2 tanks.

Germany's supply of heavy weapons to Ukraine was not a fresh issue, but something that has been discussed for many months. In mid-September 2022, Scholz gave an interview to *The New York Times* in which he explained his reservations about supplying certain German weapons to Ukraine:

> We are supporting Ukraine. We are doing it in a way that is not escalating to where it is becoming a war between Russia and NATO because this would be a catastrophe.[5]

The article points out that Scholz had so far refused to supply Ukraine with German tanks and infantry fighting vehicles:

> But Mr. Scholz has refused to provide Ukraine with Leopard battle tanks or Marder infantry fighting vehicles, which Ukrainian officials have repeatedly asked for. As they pivot from a defensive posture to an offensive one in the south, Ukrainian forces need tanks to break

---

4. Wolfgang Rattay, Riham Alkousaa and Victoria Waldersee. January 17, 2023. *Greta Thunberg released after brief detention at German mine protest, police say.* Reuters.

5. Katrin Bennhold. September 25, 2021. *Germany's Chancellor Has 'a Lot' for Ukraine. But No Battle Tanks.* The New York Times.

through defensive lines and recapture more territory before winter and, as Ukraine's foreign minister, Dmytro Kuleba, put it, "liberate people and save them from genocide."

Berlin's position is illogical. NATO is supplying Ukraine with weapons, as it should be. However, this makes NATO an ally, but not a belligerent in the war. The type of weapons has nothing to do with the principle of helping a friend and ally defend itself! The only way that NATO could become a belligerent would be if a NATO country initiated an attack against Russia directly, or—under Article 5—responded to a Russian attack against a NATO member.

One suspects that Germany is not in fact committed to a Ukrainian victory, but rather to some sort of settlement that would enable Berlin to preserve its commercial relations with Russia.

As if to remind Germany and other NATO members of Russia's intimidation modus operandi, on January 22, 2023—as the issue of tanks for Ukraine became a global priority—Russia's State Duma Chairman, Vyacheslav Volodin, made a new threat of retaliation against any countries that supplied offensive weapons to Ukraine:

> "Supplies of offensive weapons to the Kyiv regime would lead to a global catastrophe," said State Duma Chairman Vyacheslav Volodin, the speaker of Russia's parliament.

> "If Washington and NATO supply weapons that would be used for striking peaceful cities and making attempts to seize our territory as they threaten to do, it would trigger a retaliation with more powerful weapons," he said.[6]

So, apparently Scholz and Volodin agreed that providing heavy offensive weapons to Ukraine would be a "catastrophe." Instead of agreeing to Russian propaganda about the war, Scholz should be pointing out that any

---

6. Ellen Wulfhorst. January 22, 2023. *Russia warns of retaliation against West over providing Ukraine with powerful weapons.* Daily News.

"global catastrophe" would be entirely of Russia's making, since Moscow is clearly the aggressor in this war. It is not good policy to agree with the weaselly and dishonest propaganda of tyrants.

Dear Herr Scholz, the Russian invasion has already been a catastrophe for Ukraine! Equivocation by Germany over its support for Kyiv will only make that catastrophe worse, whereas unequivocal and timely support is the best way to lessen the suffering and damage being inflicted on Ukraine by Russia.

After coming under increased pressure from its NATO allies, Berlin finally approved both Marders and Leopard 2s for Ukraine. Russia, of course, responded by making new threats of 'catastrophic consequences', echoing Scholz's fears. Thus Russia's ambassador to Berlin, Sergei Nechaev, on January 25, 2023 called the German decision "extremely dangerous" since it would take the war in Ukraine "to a new level of confrontation."[7]

But, in fact, nothing has changed on the ground since Germany made its decision, except that Ukraine now has a better chance of winning the war soon.

The Cowardice of Coalitions

Scholz and his government repeatedly hide behind allies, refusing to take a stand on principle. Thus Scholz was only willing to send Marders and Leopards to Ukraine if the US first committed to sending Ukraine its Bradley fighting vehicles and M1 Abrams tanks.[8]

That is what happened when the US first sent its Bradleys and Germany followed with its Marders in early January 2023. Later, at the World Economic Forum in Davos, Scholz made it clear to an American delegation that the same formula would have to be followed for the tanks, knowing full well that Washington had already said it would not send the Abrams due to the

---

7. Rob Picheta. January 25, 2023. *Germany's decision to send tanks to Ukraine is a major moment in the war. Here's how it will change the conflict.* CNN.

8. Alexander Ward, Lara Seligman and Paul McLeary. January 19, 2023. *U.S., allies ramp up pressure on Germany to send tanks to Ukraine.* Politico.

logistical and maintenance requirements for that system—the Leopard 2 is said by military experts to be better suited to the war in Ukraine, but Scholz was looking for reasons not to have to supply them.

In the end, Washington did commit to sending Abrams, and thus Scholz had the cover he needed to free the Leopards. Now the German chancellor is going through the same routine regarding fighter jets. This is not leadership. It is cowardice.

Germany Should Want to Change its Poor Image

Several Deutsche Welle (DW) news programs about Germany's reluctance to support Ukraine, have featured a number of theories put forward to explain Scholz's foot-dragging. One expert suggested that the chancellor was afraid of resurrecting images of the Nazi hordes that invaded Russia in World War II, an invasion that cost millions of Russian lives. The main events of that invasion were massive tank battles, such as that at Kursk in July and August of 1943.

If this analysis is correct, it shows Germany's leaders occupying a very strange time warp. It is, after all, a very long time since anyone associated modern Germany with Nazi Germany under Hitler. But perhaps Germany's lingering fear that such an association might be made points to a real weakness in Berlin's foreign policy.

Specifically, what has Germany done to shake off its awful Nazi history? What values is Germany committed to, other than pan-European social conformity and a pro-business foreign policy? What does Berlin stand for? Apparently, as the invasion of Ukraine has shown, it stands for peace and prosperity for itself and the avoidance of problems that challenge the status quo.

Germany has played a very minor role in international conflicts since WWII ended. It is always cautious about being seen to take sides. This has created the image of a country that actually cares only about its own safety and prosperity, and not the wellbeing of other peoples and nations.

This is not good enough. This is not leadership. It reflects an unwillingness to risk your own peace and comfort to help those less fortunate. It is also short-sighted since inevitably the problems of others can come to hurt you.

The Miserable Legacy of the SPD

For much of its life, the Social Democratic Party (SPD) that Scholz leads was officially a Marxist party. As such, it was never an effective force to counter Soviet influence and empire-building. On the contrary, it was often manipulated by Moscow's propaganda aimed at the West.[9]

The conservative CDU (Christian Democratic Union) was the ruling party in Germany from 1949 to 1969, when the leader of the SPD, Willy Brandt, became chancellor. For the five years he remained in power he followed a foreign policy of seeking good relations with the East Bloc countries. This was called *Ostpolitik*, and it was similar in intent to détente. It did nothing to speed the end of the Cold War.

Later, Germany's SPD chancellor from 1998 to 2005, Gerhard Schröder, became an ally of Vladimir Putin and Moscow when he advocated for the construction of the Nord Stream pipelines to provide a direct supply of gas from Russia to Germany under the Baltic Sea. Just two weeks before leaving office in late 2005, Schröder arranged for Germany to provide a sovereign loan guarantee for the project and signed a $6 billion deal with Putin for the construction of the first pipeline.[10]

Almost immediately after leaving office, he was appointed to chair the shareholders committee of Nord Stream AG—a joint venture between Russia's Gazprom and Germany's E.ON and BASF, and the owner-operator of the Nord Stream pipelines. (A second pipeline, Nord Stream 2, was started in 2011, but canceled by Germany before becoming fully operational following Russia's 2022 invasion of Ukraine.)

---

9. For evidence of this, see for example several references here: Vladimir Bukovsky. 2019. *Judgment in Moscow: Soviet Crimes and Western Complicity.* Ninth of November Press.

10. Luke Harding. December 12, 2005. *Schröder faces growing scandal over job with Russian gas giant.* The Guardian.

Shortly after taking up this post, Schröder told journalists, "The pipeline is not aimed against anyone. It allows us to ensure the reliable supply of gas to Europe."[11] This attitude reflects perfectly the mindset of most of Germany's leaders, who treat foreign relations as purely transactional and without relevance to moral or even strategic considerations.

In 2017, Putin nominated Schröder to sit on the board of Rosneft,[12] Russia's largest oil producer, and on February 4, 2022, just 20 days before Russia's February 24 invasion, Schröder was nominated to sit on Gazprom's board.[13] In 2022 Schröder was estimated to be receiving close to $1 million a year from his positions with Russian energy companies.[14]

Given the harm caused other nations and peoples by the Nazi government, as well as the decades it has taken to diminish the dark Nazi stain on Germany's reputation, you would think that Berlin would be eager to take up the cause of nations suffering aggression now—to make amends for the suffering inflicted by Hitler's armies but also to shape a new national identity as a country committed to liberty for all.

In other words, shouldn't Germany be the first and boldest defender of Ukraine's freedom and independence instead of the hand-wringing and impotent giant it has been so far?

Much smaller Poland and the Baltic States have shown true leadership. On January 22, 2023 Polish Prime Minister Mateusz Morawiecki took Berlin to task:

> Almost a year has passed since the outbreak of war… Evidence of
> the Russian army's war crimes can be seen on television and on You-

---

11. Nick Paton Walsh. March 30, 2006. *Schröder defies critics over gas pipeline post*. The Guardian.

12. Staff Report. August 12, 2017. *Russia nominates German ex-chancellor Schroeder to Rosneft board*. Reuters.

13. Nastassia Astrasheuskaya. February 4, 2023. *Former German chancellor Gerhard Schröder nominated to join Gazprom's board*. Financial Times.

14. Katrin Bennhold. April 23, 2022. *The Former Chancellor Who Became Putin's Man in Germany*. The New York Times.

Tube. What more does Germany need to open its eyes and start to act in line with the potential of the German state?

He continued:

> The enemy is in the East and we're wasting time on discussions that yield nothing good... [Germany] hoped they would tame the Russian bear with generous contracts... to this day it has been hard for Germany to admit this error... I try to weigh my words, but I'll say it bluntly: Ukraine and Europe will win this war—with or without Germany.[15]

Germany Should Lead a European Defense Resurgence

Ukraine is bleeding while Berlin fiddles. This is a moment for Germany to finally come to terms with its post-WWII malaise. Germany should use this clear case of Russian aggression to let the world know that it is now on the side of good, and that—this time—it is willing to help if not lead the world in confronting the forces of evil with full determination and commitment.

The question is whether Germany's leaders can gain the moral courage to take this stand before the war is over. We hope so, for the sake of Germany and the future of the Euro-Atlantic system, and for the sake of the rest of the world which needs the most powerful nations to provide moral leadership.

Germany is by no means alone among major European countries lacking the resolve needed for a victory in Ukraine. However, given its size and economic strength Germany should be the leader of a united European front against Putin's Russia.

Other unimpressive major European countries include France under Emmanuel Macron, who has shown very bad judgment in trying to position himself as a great peacemaker in Ukraine instead of a staunch ally for Kyiv.

Nevertheless, some major European countries—notably Britain under Boris Johnson, Liz Truss and Rishi Sunak, as well as Italy under its fiery

---

15. Mateusz Morawiecki. January 22, 2023. *Polish PM vows to aid Ukraine with or without German consent.* Polish Press Agency (PAP).

new premier Giorgia Meloni—have shown a real understanding of the threat Europe faces from Putin and the need for a forceful response.

However, the countries of Western Europe as a whole have been exposed as woefully unprepared for a major war and therefore limited in what they can offer Ukraine. The war has rightly sent a shock wave through European governments, alerting them to the need for radical changes.

Many European countries are now moving to address their defense inadequacies. This is long overdue. Germany has committed $100 billion to revamping the Bundeswehr over the next few years, and other countries are also increasing defense spending to at least the minimum NATO requirement of two percent of GDP.[16]

Notably, typical of its outsize influence during this war, little Estonia (population 1.33 million) has called for European countries to uniformly double their defense spending. Estonia is not just talking. It has increased its own defense budget to three percent of GDP.[17]

It's time for Europe to get serious about the threats from Russia, China and other aggressors. And it's time for Germany to acknowledge that it has a responsibility to provide moral leadership for Europe commensurate with its size and wealth.

---

16. Holder Hansen. June 3, 2022. *German lawmakers approve 100 billion Euro military revamp.* Reuters.

17. Tom Balmforth. November 28, 2022. *Estonia says European nations should double defense expenditure.* Reuters.

Chapter 11

Why is the West Bound by Russia's Rules?

The Strange Western Fear of Offending Tyrants

The German disease we discussed in the previous chapter is linked to a widely-held phobia of Russia and a related reluctance to do anything that might upset Russia's rulers. This fear is not much different from that which gripped the West during the Cold War and inspired the policies of containment and détente.

At heart, it is a natural outcome of the application of Western democratic values to the wider world of international relations. According to our Judeo-Christian heritage, we believe we should love all others, treat our enemies with the respect due all God's children, and "turn the other cheek" in response to aggression. This is the root of the flawed 'moral equivalency' thinking and the Western reluctance to confront bullies forcefully.

Thus during the Cold War the West believed that if it treated the Soviet Union with respect, the leaders there would be touched by its virtue and respond in kind. That attitude carried over to the post-Soviet era, and is evident in the diplomatic efforts of the West to get Russia to play by its rules. The intention is good, but problems inevitably arise when we refuse to recognize that Russia is not playing by our rules, and insists that we instead play by its rules.

Things get dangerous when we ignore the fact that we are not operating on a level moral playing field and yet insist that we can anyway have a perfectly fine relationship with a nation that does not share our values. Usually it is commercial interests that are primarily interested in normalizing relations with bad actors, as we discussed in the case of Germany in the previous chapter. The signs of these interests appear in the words of our political leaders who say things like: "We can do business with Putin's Russia," or "We can do business with Communist China."

History has shown the West that it pursues normal relations with tyrants at its peril. For example, the hope that the Soviet Union was a nation with similar values and aspirations as our own was not only naïve, it gave the regime in Moscow an opening to exploit Western goodness to advance its cynical, expansionist ambitions.

The Soviet Union was not founded on the same values that built our Western civilization, but rather on atheistic Marxism-Leninism, which lacked moral absolutes and in their place adhered to the principle that 'ends justify the means.'

The Communist governments that first saw the light of day in Russia after the revolution of 1917 were totally aberrant in the eyes of Westerners who had come to take the freedoms of democracy for granted. Their behavior was literally beyond comprehension. The same was true of the Nazi government led by Adolf Hitler.

Both Communism and Nazism embodied evil on a scale that was truly beyond anything the Western world had experienced or could imagine. Thus it is not difficult to understand why the European leaders of the 1930s wanted to avoid war with Hitler at any cost. They believed that a repetition of WWI was unthinkable. They thought there must be a way to appeal to Hitler's humanity and get him to give up his militaristic ambitions.

The same was true of the West's relationship with Stalin after the end of WWII. Stalin committed one violation of international agreements after another, yet the West feared confronting him, hoping that he would become more decent over time. He never did. As we've discussed, this "convergence theory" was the erroneous hope of FDR and other Western leaders. (It has also been the unfulfilled hope of the West which has invested heavily in Communist China in the expectation that this would cause the regime in Beijing to become more like Western democracies.)

In the meantime, Stalin got away with occupying and then installing puppet Communist governments in eastern and central European countries, as well as helping Mao take over China and Kim Il Sung establish a dictatorship in North Korea.

We have already discussed how containment policy failed to limit the spread of Communism. But it is instructive to look at the mentality that lay behind that policy, and later détente. Both were based on an irrational fear of provoking the Communists to anger. Thus instead of treating these regimes as the evil totalitarians they were—and doing everything possible to isolate them from the rest of the world—the West gave Stalin a seat on the UN Security Council at its founding, and, later, gave Communist China the Security Council seat that originally had gone to the Republic of China.

How on earth could the United Nations play a credible role as the peace-loving arbiter of global conflicts with two of the five permanent Security Council members representing regimes dedicated to inciting and exploiting conflicts wherever and whenever it suited their expansionist agendas? Russia and China are pursuing goals that are diametrically opposed to the stated purpose of the UN.

Putin is Following in the Footsteps of Stalin

Soviet Russia was always a posturing bully. The USSR incorporated 15 'republics' within its vast territory by force, but it was never powerful economically. It covered this economic weakness by investing heavily in its military—and especially in developing nuclear weapons and the missiles to deliver them.

Thus the economic weakling that was called the Union of Soviet Socialist Republics strutted the world stage as the owner of a huge military which was armed with nuclear weapons and missiles. But the USSR and its satellites were never a match for the United States and other NATO members, all of whom benefited from growing capitalist economies. It took Ronald Reagan to call the USSR's bluff and to treat it as the declining power it really was.

Now it is Putin who is swaggering on the world stage, bolstered by a huge army (on paper at least) and a large arsenal of nuclear weapons and missiles. His crony capitalist economy is stronger than its Soviet forebears, but still a far cry from those of major nations. Putin and his army of propagandists love to talk as if Russia was a superpower rather than the mid-sized economy it really is.

The West has feared Putin, as it feared his Soviet antecedents. Thus despite his undeniable responsibility for the war in Ukraine, Putin continues to make the speeches of a major world leader in the apparent belief that he can still sell his duplicitous narratives and continue to intimidate the West into giving him what he wants. Putin and Foreign Minister Sergey Lavrov are frauds and they should not remain unexposed any longer.

As Putin's army faces setback after setback in Ukraine, his bluster and threats sound increasingly hollow. We know too much about the barbarism of Russians in Ukraine to give him the benefit of the doubt. We cannot help but recognize that he does not share our values and does not belong in a community of civilized nations.

Weakness in the West's response to Putin is being replaced with resolve as the deep-seated fear of Russia is being replaced with contempt for its brutal and heartless treatment of Ukraine, as well as its own people. This fear was initially based on ignorance of the reality of the evil of the Soviet regime, and subsequently on ignorance of the reality of Putin's version of a fascist state. As the tyrant shrinks before our eyes, we can dispel the fear for good.

The West Should Not Accept Russia's Rules for the War

The Western hand-wringing over every new step in supplying weapons to Ukraine is simply a reflection of the fact that Russia has been allowed to set the rules for this conflict. In other words, Russia can use all the weapons in its arsenal to attack Ukraine, but NATO cannot do the same to protect Ukraine.

Why does the West play by Russia's rules? Why aren't we simply committed to a Ukrainian victory at the earliest possible time? And if we are so committed, why would we limit the weapons we provide Ukraine? In other words, why do we insist that Ukraine respond to Russia's aggression with its hands tied behind its back?

If this sounds like a distorted characterization of the conflict, consider the following:

1. Why is it OK for Russia to invade Ukraine, a sovereign nation which has never aggressed against Russia, but it is not OK for Ukraine to respond in kind?

2. Why is it OK for Russia to use its full arsenal of weapons, including tanks, infantry fighting vehicles, artillery, drones, missiles and jet fighters to attack Ukraine, but it is an escalation for the West to provide Ukraine with artillery, IFVs, tanks and fighter jets?

3. Why is it OK for Russia to bomb anywhere in Ukraine, including civilian residential buildings and other civilian infrastructure, but it is not OK for Ukraine to use NATO weapons that will enable it to hit Russian military targets on Russian territory?

4. Why is it OK for Russia to bomb Ukraine's capital Kyiv, but not OK for Ukraine to bomb Moscow? (Remember, it was one of the Allies' main objectives in WWII to bomb Berlin and Tokyo.)

5. Why is it OK for Russian soldiers to murder Ukrainian civilians and rape defenseless women, men, and even young girls, to torture captives, and to kidnap and relocate Ukrainian civilians to Russia by force—often separating children from parents—while Ukraine must follow the Geneva Conventions?

6. Why is it OK for Russia to use Russian collaborators in Ukraine as agents to gather intelligence for Russia and spread its propaganda in Ukraine, but it's not OK for Ukraine—which is fighting for its life—to use martial law to prosecute and imprison Russian agents?

7. Why is it OK for Russia to use the thoroughly-corrupted, FSB-infiltrated Russian Orthodox churches in Ukraine to gather intelligence for Russia and spread its propaganda in Ukraine, but it's not OK for Ukraine to shut down these fifth column operations that are hiding behind a religious façade?

8. Why is it OK for Russia to send assassination squads into Ukraine targeting Zelensky and his wife, but it is not OK for Ukraine to send assassination squads into Russia targeting Putin?

9. Why is Russia using Belarus to expand the war not an escalation of the conflict, but NATO sending weapons to Ukraine is?

The sad truth is that Putin's threats and demands do influence Western decision-making, just as Soviet threats and demands influenced Western decision-making during the Cold War. Russian intimidation has worked and does work.

It should not be allowed to work any more. Russia is unquestionably the aggressor in this conflict, and Ukraine the innocent victim. It is high time the West decided that it will no longer let itself be bullied by countries like Putin's Russia and Communist China, and that it will no longer give credence to their insane justifications for aggression. They must be made to follow the modern civilizational norms that we hold one another to in the West.

If we don't insist on our own terms in Ukraine, we will forever be subject to intimidation and threats from regimes that have no legitimacy at all. It is time we believed in our own values and accepted the moral imperative to defend those who share those values against aggression.

Chapter 12

How We Can Help Ukraine Win

Ukraine is Right. Russia is Wrong

Yes, it's as simple as that. Russia invaded Ukraine, not the other way around. It is Russia that is committing massive war crimes in Ukraine—raping, torturing and murdering Ukrainian civilians and turning Ukrainian cities into piles of rubble. Ukraine did not provoke Russia into these actions by expressing a desire to join NATO and the EU. Doing so is fully within Ukraine's rights.

As General Douglas MacArthur told a joint session of Congress at the end of his military career: "In war there is no substitute for victory."[1] Shouldn't this principle of war-fighting apply to all wars, including the war in Ukraine? Why would Ukraine's supporters aim for anything less? And why should the Ukrainian people be subjected to so much suffering if the goal is simply to wear down the Russians until they are willing to negotiate to keep only part of their ill-gotten Ukrainian territory?

The language of war is important. Thus the commitment "to keep supporting Ukraine for as long as it takes" is not the same as the commitment "to give Ukraine whatever it needs to win as soon as possible." Ukraine deserves the latter.

A 'draw' in Ukraine would establish an unacceptable outcome that

---

1. Douglas MacArthur. April 19, 1951. *Farewell Address to Congress.*

143

would inevitably lead to further Russian aggression in the future. The evil embodied in Russia's invasion must be unequivocally defeated, once and for all.

Consider this: Can you imagine the Allies in WWII wringing their hands over the potential dangers of escalating their response to Hitler once his true objectives had become clear? Initially some of the Allies (such as Neville Chamberlain) believed they could negotiate with the Nazis to prevent a war, but they eventually all realized that Hitler had to be thoroughly defeated and forced to surrender unconditionally.

The Allies recognized that they were dealing with a man who would use any and all means to defeat and enslave them. Their righteous response was to marshal all their resources to beat him. Putin is just as transparently evil as Hitler was, and he deserves no better treatment. Thus Ukraine's friends and allies should now be doing everything in their power to make sure that Kyiv can defeat the Russians as quickly and decisively as possible.

Yet all the faulty reasons for not supporting Ukraine, discussed in Chapters 7 and 8, are still voiced by many leaders in the West. This is inexcusable. Apparently the containment and détente theories that became so embedded in Western foreign policy thinking during the Cold War continue to influence many of today's leaders.

The starting point for good policies towards Russia is recognizing that Putin and his regime do not belong in a civilized world. They are evil. They are genocidal terrorists. They cannot be allowed to get their way. Once you come to terms with this reality, it becomes clear that everything must be done to isolate and defeat the Russian regime.

Here are some specific suggestions for how the West can best help Ukraine win.

Recognize that Ukraine is on Our Side

In war, you must be clear about who is on your side. Ukraine is on the side of civilization in this war. It is on the side of NATO and the free and democratic nations in Europe and the rest of the world. It has a lot to offer these countries in the long term. Furthermore, at the moment Ukraine alone is paying with blood to stop the only power threatening European security by confronting the Russian army.

At the same time, it must be recognized that Ukraine is strengthening its democratic institutions despite the difficulties imposed by the invasion. And it is working to weed out the endemic corruption it inherited from its Soviet past and post-Soviet transition to democracy.

President Zelensky and the Ukrainian people as a whole have demonstrated courage and resolve in defending their country from Russian predations. They have suffered enormously under the invasion and they deserve our unwavering and unreserved support. Ukraine belongs in NATO and there is really no good reason to delay its accession. After all, wars are the right time to forge alliances.

Ukraine Must Win. Russia Must Lose

This principle should be the foundation for the Western response to Russia's unjustified and unprovoked invasion of Ukraine. It is the key to righting the wrongs of the invasion and securing justice for Ukraine and peace for Europe.

The Allies Must Not Allow Russia to Divide Them

Russia has demonstrated that it is not on our side. Rather, it constantly seeks to play Western nations off against one another, and uses propaganda to sow discord among the Western Allies. Equivocation by the West in the face of Putin's propaganda and aggression only encourages him to increase his aggression. Western nations must not be intimidated by his constant stream of threats.

We Must Stop Making Moral Equivalency Arguments

We don't need a new incarnation of the Cold War's moral equivalency thinking. We have all the proof we need of Russia's evil intensions and actions, and we should never be shy about pointing out Russia's barbarous behavior in Ukraine. Despite problems of corruption in their country, the Ukrainians are the victims and the Russians the aggressors in this war. Keep it simple and remain resolute.

There is No Better Use for NATO's Weapons at This Time

The continued hand-wringing over which arms systems we can supply to Ukraine is not justified. We do not need to see more Russian atrocities before sending Ukraine the best weapons at our disposal.

If Ukraine needs tanks, give it tanks. If Ukraine needs jet fighters, give it jet fighters. If Ukraine needs munitions that can reach Russian military targets in Russia, give it those munitions.

On January 17, 2023, the former head of the British army, Lord Richard Dannatt, told *Times Radio* essentially the same thing:

> If we are going to give some of our critical equipment then almost by definition our capability is reduced. But, here's the question: "Where is the war in Europe at the present moment?" The answer is: "In Ukraine". It's in everyone's interest, including our British [interest], that the Ukrainians win. We've done a lot to help them not lose. We've now absolutely got to help them win. And they're asking for offensive capabilities—tanks, infantry fighting vehicles, artillery. That's what we should be giving them. Yes, of course, our capabilities will be reduced a little bit. But where is the war now?[2]

He makes an excellent point. Countries will necessarily deplete their arsenals if they send weapons to Ukraine. But what are those weapons for in the first place? Isn't the point of having them to deter and defeat aggressors? And isn't Russia the aggressor of this moment, especially in Europe? In other words, the weapons that NATO nations have for their own defense can best be used to make sure Russian aggression is stopped by Ukraine.

It's Time to Reverse the Disastrous Containment Policy

We have pointed out that a pattern of compromising with evil has proved to be a disastrous policy, both as a basis for managing Cold War relations with

2. Lord Richard Dannatt. January 17, 2023. *Interview*. Times Radio.

Communist regimes as well as in the broader context of responding success-fully to all aggression—Communist, fascist or otherwise.

The containment mindset clearly shaped the lame response to Putin's invasion of Georgia in 2008 as well as Crimea and the Donbas in 2014, which undoubtedly encouraged his invasion of Ukraine in February 2022. Washington and its NATO allies knew that Moscow was planning to invade Ukraine, but adopted a 'wait and see' stance instead of imposing anticipatory sanctions and warning Russia in no uncertain terms that if it proceeded with an invasion there would be a massive Western response.

Now that the fight is on, a unified West must demonstrate that it will no longer tolerate Russian aggression. The West must also insist that Russia abandon all of its territorial gains and compensate all who have suffered from its aggression. (See the next chapter for details regarding reparations Russian must make for its invasion.)

Stop Apologizing for Putin and His Regime

There is no excuse for justifying Putin's acts of aggression. These attacks are all wrong and violate the international, rules-based norms that have kept the peace in most of Europe since WWII.

Russian propagandists make a career out of justifying Putin's aggression. They are paid to do so, and when he falls they will likely disappear as well—like the ex-Nazis that were driven from office and positions of influence once Hitler was defeated. They are a cancer on Russian society and it is shameful for people in the West to parrot their lies. There should be no apologists for Putin or his regime.

Remain United and Resolute

Above all else, it is critical for the world to remain united and resolute in demanding Russia exit Ukraine, and in continuing to assist Ukraine until that objective is achieved. No other outcome to this war is acceptable. This is the best thing we can do for Ukraine. All other good things (such as sup-plying the arms Kyiv needs to win) will flow from this.

To remain united and resolute, Ukraine's allies must never forget that

Putin has the instincts of a predator and therefore will always look for divisions and weakness in the West that he can exploit to his own benefit. He has everything to gain from weakening the unity and resolve of the West. He must not be allowed to succeed in this.

To maintain the posture of an implacable and indivisible foe to Putin, the West has to reshape its policy towards Russia (and China for that matter) based on first principles and not transactional considerations. We know that initially Germany and France were shamefully bent on negotiating a settlement that would achieve peace on Russia's terms and at Ukraine's expense. If they have not already abandoned this dishonorable position, they must now.

We cannot allow our focus on victory to be clouded by other considerations and conflicting interests.

In war, there is no substitute for victory.

Chapter 13

Russia Must Pay For Its Crimes

Putin's Genocide Cannot Go Unpunished

When Vladimir Putin used his army to take territory from Georgia in 2008 and Ukraine in 2014, he got the equivalent of a slap on the hand from the international community—in the form of ineffective sanctions. This feeble response encouraged him to undertake the much bolder step of trying to seize the whole of Ukraine in 2022.

This time, the world has seen the reality of Putin's evil in graphic images of his genocidal attacks on the people of Ukraine—their families, homes, livelihoods and culture. Already indicted by the International Criminal Court for the forcible removal of Ukrainian children to Russia, he stands to be prosecuted for genocide.

If found guilty, the 150 countries that are signatories to the *Convention on the Prevention and Punishment of the Crime of Genocide* are bound to see to it that he and other Russians responsible for these crimes are punished, as Article I stipulates:

> The Contracting Parties confirm that genocide, whether committed in time of peace or in time of war, is a crime under international law which they undertake to prevent and to punish.[1]

---

1. For an explanation of Genocide and a copy of the full text of the Convention, see: https://www.un.org/en/genocideprevention/genocide.shtml

Article IV specifies that all individuals that have participated in genocide are liable for prosecution. Holding office, however senior, is no shield:

> Persons committing genocide or any of the other acts enumerated in article III shall be punished, whether they are constitutionally responsible rulers, public officials or private individuals

In no previous war has there been so much evidence of crimes against humanity gathered by credible eyewitnesses, who use their cell phones to record relevant scenes and information contemporaneously with the commitment of crimes, or shortly thereafter. This evidence is enormously useful for investigators whose job it is to pinpoint specific crimes and identify those responsible for them.

The Responsibility of the International Community

Prosecuting crimes against humanity is uniquely the responsibility of the international community, because a civilized world cannot tolerate genocide and other atrocities against its members. Those who perpetrate these crimes must be stopped and punished. They cannot be allowed to participate in the normal relationships among civilized people and nations.

Furthermore, as Article I specifies, signatories to the Convention on Genocide are not only responsible for punishing those guilty, they are also responsible for preventing genocide in the first place.

That Putin's earlier aggressions were genocidal in nature (i.e. aimed at destroying a specific group of people) should have prompted Convention members to respond forcefully to Putin at the time. This time, thank God, there has been a fairly strong, albeit delayed, reaction to Putin's aggression —and the allies supporting Ukraine in this conflict deserve recognition for that.

However, it should also be noted that many of the 150 signatories to the Convention have not done anything to stop Putin's invasion and destruction of Ukraine and its people, or anything to punish Russia for it. This should change. If countries want the protection of the international community when they are faced with aggression and genocide, they should show their commitment to protecting human rights in Ukraine today.

Russia Will Have to Pay for Putin's Crimes

Russia itself is a signatory to the Convention on Genocide. In allowing Putin to abuse his position as President of the Russian Federation by attacking Ukraine, the government of Russia and the people of Russia who have not opposed Putin's war have failed their responsibility to hold their leadership to account, and lost their opportunity to be treated with respect by the international community. The price Russia will pay for Putin's crimes will be very high.

The grim truth is that there is no way that Russia (or anyone else) can repay the Ukrainians for the lives lost in this war, for the injuries suffered by soldiers and civilians alike, for the lives crushed through imprisonment, torture, rape or forced deportation, and for the homes and businesses destroyed.

But Russia must be made to do the next best thing: it must take responsibility for crimes committed under Putin and do whatever possible to compensate the victims. What will all of this cost? There is no way to assess the cost accurately until the war is over, and even then there will be much work to do to monetize the damage in a meaningful way.

In the meantime, there have been several estimates of the cost of the war after one year. A March 23, 2023 report compiled by the Government of Ukraine, the European Commission and the World Bank, estimated that 7.1 million Ukrainians have been reduced to living in poverty by the war, and that to rebuild Ukraine would take an estimated $411 billion over a decade.[2]

This, then, is a starting point for calculating what Russia must pay for Putin's crimes. But only a beginning. Consider the following that must be included in any fair calculation of what Russia must do to be once more included in the family of civilized nations.

---

2. March 23, 2023. *Updated Ukraine Recovery and Reconstruction Assessment.* World Bank, European Commission and the Government of Ukraine.

Keeping in mind that human and material losses are inextricably intertwined and must be compensated for together:

1. Russia must provide a complete accounting of its crimes in Ukraine, to the maximum extent possible. This means it must identify every Ukrainian it has killed, injured, tortured, raped, imprisoned, or taken by force to Russia. It must also list all the Ukrainian property its army has either destroyed or stolen.

2. Russia must release all Ukrainian prisoners and citizens forced into exile in Russia, and return them to Ukraine. It must also return any Ukrainian property of value that was taken to Russia, or pay for its replacement (this includes expensive farm and factory machinery).

3. Russia must compensate monetarily all Ukrainians it has harmed, whether directly or indirectly. This compensation must include damages as assessed by Ukraine for death, injury, and destruction or theft of property.

4. Russia must pay for all the damage it has inflicted on Ukraine's infrastructure, including buildings, roads, bridges, railway lines and stations, ports, airports, etc.

Furthermore, Russia has faced no significant costs for its earlier aggressions (against Georgia and Ukraine's Crimea and the Donbas). The only way to achieve a measure of justice for the victims of those aggressions is to make Moscow pay reparations to them once Ukraine has won this war.

Only the pain of meaningful consequences will make Russia think twice before trying this type of aggression again. Taking strong measures will also have the benefit of making other would-be aggressors consider carefully before acting on their unjust ambitions.

How Russia Can Pay for Putin's Crimes

Russia has sizable sovereign deposits in the West that it cannot access under the sanctions in place. According to a press release issued by the US Treasury Department on February 24, 2023, sovereign cash held in the West under the

Russian sanctions regime is currently $300 billion.[3] This money should be used by Ukraine to compensate its people and rebuild its infrastructure.

Russia is also rich in natural resources, especially oil and gas. The international community has already caused Russia's sale of these resources to be severely limited, capping the price of oil at a little above the cost of extraction and delivery. As part of a settlement ending this war, there should be a 'Ukraine Tariff' imposed on all Russian commodity exports, including oil and gas. This would remain in force until Russia has paid its obligations to Ukraine in full. (Because of the extensive sanctions evasion Russia and some of its enablers are currently engaged in, the implementation of a scheme like this may well require control of all Russian oil and gas exports by a third party until Ukraine is made whole.)

Whatever mechanisms are put in place to manage this repayment process, there must be tight supervision of the disbursement of funds to make sure that the process does not fall prey to corruption.

There Need to be Long-Term Consequences for Russia

The war in Ukraine must be recognized for what it really is: a fundamental breach of the rules-based international order that underpins our civilization. As such, Russia must be ejected from the community of civilized countries until it has been thoroughly reformed. The following are ten measures that should be taken, as soon as possible—although many will have to wait for the war to end and Putin to be replaced by a democratic leader:

1. Russia has no business being one of five permanent members of the United Nations Security Council. It inherited this seat from the Soviet Union, which itself never played by the rules of civilized nations. It should lose this seat immediately. If the UN lacks the mechanisms to do this, then it should establish them. If it is unable to do so, then it is time to reconstitute the organization with only democratic countries permitted as members. A new Security Council would be made

---

3. Press Release. February 24, 2023. *FACT SHEET: Disrupting and Degrading— One Year of U.S. Sanctions on Russia and its Enablers*. US Department of the Treasury.

up only of free, democratic countries, or representatives of regional groupings of democratic countries, such as the European Union. No Communist or other totalitarian country—such as China, Russia, Cuba, North Korea or Iran—would be members. (See Chapter 15 for a proposal to establish a new international organization with the sole purpose of securing world peace.)

2.   Russia must be expelled from other international organizations, including UN agencies, until it proves itself worthy to be a member. Non-UN organizations would include the OSCE, APEC, ARF, EAS and G-20.

3.   Russia must be excluded from participating in all international events, such as the Olympic Games and other sporting competitions and conferences.

4.   Russia must shut down its propaganda apparatus, including RT, and cease all funding for propaganda activities.

5.   Russia must be designated a state sponsor of terror by the United States, European Union and other nations or national groupings. The crimes Moscow has perpetrated in Ukraine fit the definition of state terrorism—the violent targeting of civilians to achieve political ends.

6.   Russia must denuclearize. This war has shown that Moscow is willing to use its nuclear weapons to threaten other nations, destabilizing the world order. It has no need for these weapons in the world today, and it should be made to give them up—in the same way that Ukraine, Belarus and Kazakhstan gave up the Soviet nukes on their territories when they became independent states.

7.   Russia must withdraw its army and all support from South Ossetia and Abkhazia—the two provinces of Georgia that Putin occupied in 2008. It must return sovereignty to Georgia, and allow the return of all Georgian refugees to their homes there.

8.   Moscow must withdraw its army and all financial and political support from Transnistria, which must then be restored to full union with Moldova.

9.   There are also older, Soviet-era wrongs that Russia must right. Moscow was never supposed to occupy permanently Japan's Kuril Islands after WWII. They should be returned to Tokyo. Then there is Western Karelia that should be returned to Finland, and Kaliningrad that should go to Poland and/or Lithuania.

10. Sanctions on Russia must be tightened until Russia has met these demands. This means first cracking down on Russian evasion of sanctions—including by imposing and implementing effectively secondary sanctions on those countries and parties that are violating the sanction rules. More broadly, all investment in Russia and trade with Russia must be limited to non-military and non-dual-use goods and services. Third party violators of these sanctions must likewise be sanctioned. International travel by Russian nationals should be strictly limited to those individuals who have played no part in Russia's wars of aggression.

The Breakup of The Russian Federation

The measures listed above are severe consequences for Russia, but Moscow's crimes have been massive. Furthermore, the war in Ukraine has shown fundamental inequalities in the Russian Federation that should be addressed at this moment of transition.

There is considerable speculation about a possible break-up of Russia in the wake of a defeat by Ukraine. This might be a good step to address the deeply ingrained regional disparities in Russian society, while permanently removing Russia from the list of countries threatening the world.

Several observers have noted that the bulk of men mobilized to fight in Ukraine come from remote regions of Russia such as Buryatia, Dagestan and Chechnya. Far fewer are coming from the wealthy regions of Moscow and St. Petersburg.

There are 21 member-states of the Russian Federation, and several are likely candidates for independence if the opportunity arises in the wake of a Russian defeat.

If this breakup were to happen, it would be a self-inflicted punishment for Putin's renewed empire-building for Russia, but it would likely set Russia on a path of constructive reform and open the way for Moscow to return to the world community as a peaceful and constructive nation.

Looking ahead, there is no reason a reformed Russia could not itself be part of NATO and thereby contribute to the global effort to counter Communism, and especially expansionist Communist China.

Chapter 14

A World of Good Will Come From Ukraine's Victory

A New Ukraine Is Emerging from This War

Ukraine is being transformed by this war. Putin's aggression has inadvertently resulted in the people of Ukraine uniting as never before. Ever since the Soviet Union collapsed and Ukraine became independent, many in the large Russian-speaking populations in Crimea and the south and east of the country have been conflicted over their allegiances. This ambivalence has long been exploited by Putin in his efforts to peel parts of Ukraine off and incorporate them into Russia.

To cement the annexation of Crimea, Putin in 2016 began the construction of a massive road and rail bridge across the Kerch Strait that separates Russia from Crimea. Finished in 2018, the bridge cost $3.7 billion—a huge investment in infrastructure that demonstrated Putin's determination to make his control of Ukraine permanent.

Encouraged by his army of agents in Ukraine, Putin has apparently continued in the belief that Ukrainians whose first language is Russian would indeed prefer to be part of the motherland—while the rest of the population could be intimidated into accepting an inevitable surrender to the much greater power of Russia.

However, Putin's calculations have been faulty. The brutality of his army in its wholesale destruction of Ukraine and oppressive occupation of large swaths of its territory have shown Ukrainians just what they can expect if they do surrender to Putin.

The Ukrainians living in Crimea and the Donbas have not faired well under Moscow's rule over the nine years since the first Russian invasion in February 2014. Those in regions occupied since February 2022 have fared even worse. Men have been conscripted into Russian or pro-Russian military units, and residents have been robbed, raped, tortured and murdered by brutal, puppet regimes. Many Ukrainian adults and children have been forcibly relocated to Russia.

Today, after seeing the true nature of the Russian intervention, the people of Ukraine have become increasingly united in their opposition to making any concessions to Russia. The vast majority do not want to join Russia. They want Ukraine to regain its pre-2014 borders.

According to a poll conducted by the Kyiv International Institute of Sociology (KIIS) before the February 2022 invasion, only 64.4 percent of Ukrainians identified, first and foremost, as Ukrainian citizens, showing how strong pro-Russian sentiment was in parts of Ukraine. However, a similar poll conducted by KIIS six months later showed this number had leaped to 85 percent. Anton Hrushetskiy, the deputy director of the Institute, explained in an interview with *Radio Free Europe* the significance of this change in attitudes:

> The ideas that there is no such thing as the Ukrainian nation and that the Ukrainian state is a failed state, were crucial to Russian propaganda. Nothing could have had such a unifying effect as the war waged by Putin and his cynical justification of it.[1]

The change in support among Ukrainians for a total victory over Russia is truly remarkable. The article reports:

> As many as 96 percent of Ukrainians support their country joining the European Union, and 91 percent now favor joining NATO. Some

---

1. Aleksander Palikot. August 23, 2022. *Hard-Won Unity: Polls show Russian Invasion Is Transforming Ukrainian Self-Identity.* Radio Free Europe.

92 percent profess a "bad" attitude toward Russia, while only 2 percent declare a "good" one.

This huge swing of sentiment against Russia is Putin's doing. After tasting his brand of government they want nothing to do with him.

And if his purpose in invading Ukraine was to prevent it joining NATO, his "special military operation" has had the exact opposite effect from that intended, as the numbers just referenced prove—91 percent of Ukrainians now want to be protected from Putin by joining NATO.

In other words, Putin has forced all but a very small minority of Ukrainians to become clear about who they are and what kind of country they want to belong to. They now fully embrace being part of a new Ukraine that has chosen the path leading to full integration with the West, and complete separation from its former masters in Moscow.

The government in Ukraine has taken additional steps to make this divorce permanent. Even before the invasion, a 2019 state language law included several provisions to end Ukraine's bilingual status. Now only Ukrainian can be used for education and most public purposes, and, as of January 16, 2023, all print media must be in Ukrainian (except for small minority language publications, such as English periodicals.)[2]

For decades Ukraine has been stuck on a fence between Russia and the West. National elections have been bitterly contested over which way it should go, but now there is no doubt regarding its direction. As the polls above indicate, all but a handful of Ukrainians now—unequivocally—want to be part of the European Union and NATO, following the path taken by the Baltic States and ex-Soviet satellites in East and Central Europe.

A New Ukraine is Helping Shape a New Europe and NATO

In less than a year, Putin has managed not only to unite Ukrainians in opposition to him but also to bring European nations and the United States closer together as allies. Given the weak Western reaction to Putin's aggression

---

2. Rachel Denber. January 19, 2022. *New Language Requirement Raises Concerns in Ukraine.* Human Rights Watch.

in Georgia and Crimea, a firm European response to his invasion in 2022 was not to be taken for granted. But Europe has responded with surprising vigor and effectiveness. This bodes well for Europe and NATO but not at all well for an ambitious Russia that we can now see is not the military giant it claimed to be.

Almost all NATO members are now revamping, modernizing and expanding their militaries—as we discussed in Chapter 10. Weapons systems that have been sitting in storage are being brought out and reconditioned, and some countries—notably Poland—have embarked on very ambitious armament programs, all with the renewed Russian threat in mind.

The secretary general of NATO, Jens Stoltenberg, has emerged as a good unifier, rallying support for Ukraine by taking a clear position on the need to make sure Ukraine has the weapons it needs to drive Russia from its territory.

As usual, it is the United States that has offered the most support—both in military hardware and training as well as in budget support—for the Kyiv government during the war. The Biden administration and the US Congress have been extremely generous with support for Ukraine, even authorizing a resurrected version of the WWII-era Lend-Lease Act that was critical in enabling FDR to support Britain before America officially entered the war.[3]

The decision of Finland and Sweden to join NATO is a very good step too, strengthening NATO's very long frontier with Russia. Finland became a member on April 4, 2023, and Sweden should follow once Turkey and Hungary sign off on its accession to the alliance.

Turkey's president Recep Erdogan used the NATO rule that all current members must approve the addition of any new member to hold up the accession of Finland and Sweden. He pressured the two Scandinavian countries to crack down on their Kurdish populations by tightening their terrorism laws, and requested the extradition of some Kurds to Turkey.

---

3. David Vergun. May 9, 2022. *Biden Signs Lend-Lease Act to Supply More Security Assistance to Ukraine.* DOD News.

For his part, Hungary's Prime Minister Viktor Orbán delayed approval for both countries as a way of putting pressure on the European Union which has been holding up some seven billion Euros earmarked for Hungary, claiming Budapest was not in compliance with the EU's rule of law standards.[4] (This dispute is related in part to a lawsuit the EU brought against Hungary for a law limiting the use of educational books with gay content for certain grades.)

Ukraine's Success Reverberates Throughout the World

While Ukraine is fighting for its life successfully against a much larger and more powerful neighbor, there have been stirrings in other places around the world where ordinary people are resisting oppression in order to gain their freedom.

In China this resistance is new, and it was prompted by draconian government control of the population in the name of limiting the spread of the COVID-19 virus. Despite a severe government crackdown, demonstrators called not only for an end to COVID restrictions, but also for newly re-elected President Xi Jinping to be replaced and for Communist rule to be ended.[5]

At the same time, Beijing's constant threats to take Taiwan by force if necessary, are sounding a lot less credible in the light of Ukraine's successes against Russia on the battlefield. No one doubts now that Taiwan would also put up a very fierce fight to preserve its independence—and the rulers in Beijing might well suffer a regime-ending defeat at the hands of their cousins across the Taiwan Strait if they do invade Taiwan.

Other Socialist or Communist dictatorships would do well to take note, too, in particular the Kim dynasty in North Korea, the Castros in Cuba, Maduro in Venezuela and Ortega in Nicaragua. All of these dinosaur regimes lack legitimacy and have no place in a civilized world.

---

4. Samuel Petrequin. November 30, 2022. *EU Commission proposes blocking billions in funds to Hungary.* AP.

5. Dake Kang and Huizhong Wu. November 27, 2022. *Crowd angered by lockdowns calls for China's Xi to step down.* AP

The same is true for Iran, where primarily young rebels—led by unarmed women demonstrators—have been seeking the overthrow of the Islamist regime with its freedom-crushing policies and brutal punishments for dissidents. The Iranians truly deserve freedom, and Ukraine is likely offering them some hope.

If victorious, Ukraine could prove to be a turning point towards freedom for hundreds of millions of people who continue to be trapped in dictatorships. With their intelligence and determination, the Ukrainians are showing the world how to fight evil.

Chapter 15

We Need a Global NATO to Secure World Peace

The World Still Has Dangerous Totalitarian Regimes

Few ever thought that in the 21st century an ever-more prosperous Europe would once more be threatened by a hostile power unleashing a great army against a peaceful neighbor. Not since Hitler mounted a blitzkrieg against Poland in 1939 and the Soviet Union occupied East and Central Europe at the end of WWII had anything like this been seen—and then only by the parents and grandparents of today's Europeans.

There is a message for the peace-loving world in this. As much as we would like to believe that our developed societies are immune to the threat of war, as long as there is evil in the world we should expect violence and aggression from totalitarian regimes created, maintained and expanded through force of arms.

Communist and fascist governments are of this type, and the world continues to have a collection of these unsavory and often dangerous regimes. They include the fascist states of Putin's Russia, Myanmar, and the Islamist regime in Iran. In the Communist column they include the world's most dangerous country, Communist China, as well as North Korea under the Kim dynasty and Cuba under the Castro dynasty. Lesser threats come from Communist regimes in Vietnam, Laos and Nicaragua, and the socialist regime in Venezuela.

All of these regimes maintain themselves in power through force and by preventing free and fair elections. As such, they all pose a threat to a world order based on freedom, democracy and self-determination. Without exception, they prevent their own citizens from exercising their God-given rights without government interference and suppression.

The aim of civilization is to create a world in which individuals can fulfill their original purpose as children of God. The aim of evil is to prevent the realization of that ideal. We must expect, then, that as long as evil holds sway in the hearts and minds of some rulers those nations will continue to pose a threat to the civilized world we are building.

Which is why we need strong alliances of civilized nations to protect one another in the face of evil regimes that would destroy them.

Ukraine is Paying a High Price to Preserve Our Security

By absorbing the full brunt of Russia's aggression by itself, Ukraine is paying a very high price in blood and treasure to protect Europe from a dangerous and predatory foe. But it is doing more than that. By standing up to Russia it is showing a world swaddled in the comforts of modern life how to deal with a clear manifestation of evil by confronting it fearlessly and making whatever sacrifices necessary to defeat it.

By Ukraine taking a clear and courageous stand in defending itself against this Russian aggression it has exposed Putin's government for the corrupt and evil regime it is. At the same time, Ukraine has inadvertently shown the Western nations—and the NATO alliance in particular—the serious deficiencies in policy and military readiness that have eroded the West's ability to respond effectively to aggression. (For one, most NATO members have for decades depended on the United States' military for their protection, and have failed in their obligation to spend two percent of their GDP on defense.)

Nevertheless, other than the courageous stand the Ukrainian people have taken in opposing Putin, NATO's support for Ukraine has emerged as the single most important factor contributing to Ukraine's success in this war.

NATO Has Proved its Effectiveness

NATO was created in 1949 to prevent a repetition of the just-ended WWII which had been started by an empire-building Adolph Hitler. During the Cold War, this defensive alliance proved largely effective in limiting Communist expansion in Europe. Through its support of Ukraine in the current war, NATO has proved its enduring value as protector of peaceful nations in the post-Cold War era.

Because of NATO's effectiveness, there is little doubt that Ukraine would have been spared the suffering and destruction of the Russian invasion if it had been a member of the alliance in 2014. In that case, Kyiv would have automatically enjoyed the protection provided by Article 5 of NATO's governing treaty, which obliges all members to come to the defense of any member facing aggression:

Article 5

The Parties agree that an armed attack against one or more of them in Europe or North America shall be considered an attack against them all and consequently they agree that, if such an armed attack occurs, each of them, in exercise of the right of individual or collective self-defense recognized by Article 51 of the Charter of the United Nations, will assist the Party or Parties so attacked by taking forthwith, individually and in concert with the other Parties, such action as it deems necessary, including the use of armed force, to restore and maintain the security of the North Atlantic area.

Any such armed attack and all measures taken as a result thereof shall immediately be reported to the Security Council. Such measures shall be terminated when the Security Council has taken the measures necessary to restore and maintain international peace and security.[1]

Putin would not have risked going to war with the 30 countries that belong to NATO and which together have unrivaled military power.

Even without Article 5 protection, Ukraine has benefited from being a

---

1. For the full text of The North Atlantic Treaty see Appendix 3.

country aligned with the Euro-Atlantic order as it seeks membership in both the European Union and NATO. Without the support of NATO, Ukraine would not have been able to put up a sustained defense against Russia, and the prospect of it regaining control of its territory after the invasion would have been bleak indeed.

Which raises a very important point: How can countries that do not belong in the Euro-Atlantic space be protected against aggression by other nations?

The United Nations Has Proven Useless

NATO's principled and effective support for Ukraine points up a glaring feature of this war—the total failure of the United Nations to prevent Russia's invasion or to help Ukraine defeat the Russian army once it had invaded.

Somewhat ironically, the NATO Treaty begins with a statement aligning its purpose with the principles of the United Nations:

> The Parties to this Treaty reaffirm their faith in the purposes and principles of the Charter of the United Nations and their desire to live in peace with all peoples and all governments.

In other words, NATO derives its ideals from an organization that has proved totally incapable of defending those ideals in the real world. This irony is underscored by the Treaty's Article 5 instruction for members to report aggression to the Security Council: "Any such armed attack and all measures taken as a result thereof shall immediately be reported to the Security Council."

Why report attacks to the Security Council? What will the Security Council do other than—perhaps—issue some sort of statement of concern or condemnation—words that a predatory country like Putin's Russia will dismiss out of hand?

There is a particular irony in Ukraine's case. It was Stalin himself who insisted at Yalta in 1945 that the Ukraine Soviet Socialist Republic should be treated as an independent nation and admitted to the United Nations as such when the UN was founded (which took place a few months later). Stalin was, of course, lying, since at that time Ukraine was an integral part of the USSR and thus totally under Moscow's control. Now Russia has invaded Ukraine with the justification that it is not really a separate country!

With Washington estimating that Russia had moved 150,000 troops to the border with Ukraine, *Reuters* reported that on February 23, 2022 Kyiv appealed to the United Nations to stop Russia's "aggressive plans."[2] Russia responded to Ukraine's appeal by saying it could not ignore "the blatant genocide" of Russian-speakers in eastern Ukraine—another outrageous, Stalinesque lie since it was Russia that had illegally occupied Ukrainian territory where it was targeting Ukrainians for ethnic cleansing.

Reuters noted that no action was taken by the UN. Instead, Secretary-General Antonio Guterres simply stated that a wider conflict in Ukraine "could see a scale and severity of need unseen for many years." There was no condemnation of Russia. There was no warning to Moscow that it would face severe consequences if it invaded—as if a new level of need in Ukraine would be the result of a conflict for which Russia and Ukraine shared equal responsibility. Guterres lamely called for a ceasefire and return to dialogue!

Russia launched its full-scale invasion the very next day.

Nothing has changed in the course of the war. While Ukraine has suffered much greater harm than Guterres could have envisioned, the UN has remained irrelevant. It has no influence over Russia at all, and even its most die-hard supporters must realize that the deployment of its 'blue helmet' peacekeepers to Ukraine to stop the fighting there is not an option.

The irony is, then, that under Stalin an enslaved Ukraine was used illicitly to give Moscow more leverage in the United Nations, but under Putin, when an independent Ukraine deserves the protection of the international community, it has been virtually abandoned by the UN. Thus when the UN

---

2. Michael Nichols. February 23, 2022. *Ukraine appeals for UN help, Russia says can't ignore 'genocide'*. Reuters.

was founded it mistreated the people of Ukraine by allowing Stalin to use their country for his own ambitions, and now that Ukraine is truly independent the UN is once more unable to protect its people from Moscow's selfish ambitions and illicit predatory behavior.

The UN Has Been Almost Entirely Irrelevant Since the Korean War

The inability of the United Nations to stop aggression and prevent wars is not a new phenomenon. Only in the Korean War was the Security Council able to play a useful role in countering international aggression—by voting to support the South against Kim Il Sung's invasion from the North. With this mandate—achieved only because the Russians were not present when the vote was taken—21 UN members, led by the United States, came to Seoul's defense, and saved the South from being conquered by the Soviet-backed Communist North.

Even so, it was only due to America's commitment to Seoul that the UN-mandated allies came to the South's defense with enough military power to defeat the North. And with the Soviet Union still a member of the Security Council, the United Nations was unable to make sure that the war ended successfully for all Koreans. An armistice was signed without Kim Il Sung being removed from power in Pyongyang and without the Soviet Union and Communist China being forced to end their support for the North so that the people there could determine the system of government they wanted. The North Koreans have been oppressed by the successive regimes of the Kim dynasty ever since.

And since the Korean War, the UN has been helpless to stop Communist aggression because Russia has remained a member of the Security Council. The situation only got worse when the UN General Assembly in October 1971 expelled the Republic of China (Taiwan) from the Security Council and gave that seat to the People's Republic of China.

This remains the situation at the UN to this day, and explains why the UN has done little more than wring its hands over the invasion of Ukraine. The deleterious influence of Russia and China at the top of the organization has been multiplied by a large portion of the membership being heavily influenced by Moscow and/or Beijing—two governments that don't respect the UN's altruistic purposes but use the organization to advance their self-interested agendas.

The UN's Problem Originated With Its Founding

In many respects, from its founding the United Nations has embodied what would soon become known as containment policy. This is reflected in its structure, which gives equal status to both free and totalitarian states. Furthermore, from the outset the Soviet Union held one of five permanent seats on the all-powerful Security Council, a seat inherited by the Russian Federation after the collapse of the USSR. Since all five members can exercise a veto over Council decisions, this structure gave the Soviets de facto control over the UN. Today it gives the same power to Russia.

For some people, the UN's respectful treatment of the Soviet Union may have appeared a just reward for the part the Soviets played in defeating Hitler—as an ally of Britain, France, the United States and other Western countries. After all, Stalin claimed to share the same interests as the Allies in wanting an international organization to be created after WWII that would prevent the rise of another Nazi-like aggressor.

However, the United States and Great Britain were not sufficiently alert to the dangers they faced in trying to establish an international organization to keep the peace that included in its leadership a Communist state that was in the vanguard of a worldwide movement that promoted violent revolutions against the existing order, and that had a long history of oppression, aggression and human rights violations.

The Western Allies could be forgiven for this—in part, at least—because the proposal to create the UN was mooted when they were fully occupied with defeating Nazi Germany and Imperialist Japan, and believed they needed the Soviet Union to defeat these two fascist enemies. They did not want to antagonize Stalin before these objectives had been attained.

With the war in Europe winding down to what seemed an inevitable

Allied victory, the main goal of Churchill and Roosevelt at Yalta was to get Stalin to commit to helping them defeat Japan once Hitler had surrendered. So eager were they to secure Stalin's support in the East that they made a number of unwise (and as it would prove unnecessary) concessions to Stalin to achieve this goal.

History would show that the concessions made to Stalin at Yalta and Potsdam would prove disastrous for the European and Asian countries that Stalin occupied at the end of the war. Even more harmful was the way that Stalin was able to co-opt the altruistic purposes of the United Nations to make it into a durable tool of Communist influence and expansionism.

All of these damaging outcomes were to be expected from Stalin. For him the Soviet alliance with Western powers offered a great opportunity to extend Moscow's reach both westward and eastward, and through the UN he would be able to spread Communism into the colonial world that the European powers had created—the so-called Third World. Stalin was not interested in building a peaceful post-WWII world order, but in Communizing the world.

Hundreds of millions of people have suffered under brutal Communist regimes because Stalin was able to advance his dark plans so successfully after WWII, thanks in large part to the failure of the Western allies to recognize what he was up to, and to stop him while they still could.

Stalin Perfected the Communist Playbook for Securing Power

Beginning with the Russian Revolution in 1917, the Soviets became expert at subverting democratic organizations and governments. Always numerically a minority in society and national populations, the Communists knew that they could not gain power through winning fair elections. The alternative path was to control countries by engineering the takeover of ruling bodies and coalitions, and then keeping power by blocking a return to democracy.

The tactics they employed to achieve this end were cultivated through the practice of subverting and then controlling key societal organizations, including workers unions, social clubs, advocacy groups and political parties.

How did this work? The path for a minority to dominate a majority is for minority members to work harder than the other members until they win the leadership positions in the organization. On the way up, a useful ploy for consolidating power in the organization is to prolong decision-making meetings until most or all non-Communist members have tired and left, leaving the Communists with the majority they need to win a vote.

Once in power, the Communists can shape policies and fund activities that advance their cause—likely at the expense of the majority. To keep power indefinitely, where possible they can then adopt Lenin's invention—Democratic Centralism. This is a system in which only candidates chosen or approved by the Communist Party can run for office.

If the Communists are unable to solve their minority status problems by using these maneuvers, the next best option is for them to gain veto power over the decision-making process, which gives them de facto control of the organization.

In taking over governments, there is another tool the Communists have often used. They join ruling coalitions but then seek to secure the key security portfolios, giving them control over everyone in the government with a gun—the police, secret service and/or army. They then infiltrate these forces with their own cadres until they are ready to mount a coup and take power.

Stalin used all these techniques when he consolidated Communist rule in the countries the Soviets occupied after WWII. In these cases, the subversion of existing governments would be carried out by Moscow-supported and trained agents, followed by local Communist party leaders gaining power—with Russian troops providing the muscle to secure them in office long enough to establish a full Communist regime.

In the parts of the world shaking off colonial rule after WWII, similar stratagems were employed by Communists who incited Moscow-backed wars of national liberation and violent coups d'état.

The United Front Stratagem

The Communists adopted many of their tactics as a result of what they had learned from a disaster they had brought on themselves in Germany's national elections in 1932. The German Communist Party (KPD) had attacked the ruling SPD, thereby splitting the vote on the Left and inadvertently handed power to the Nazis, who then set about destroying the Communists.

In hindsight, it was clear that the KPD should have formed an alliance with the SPD to beat the Nazis and then they could have found a way to wrest control of the German government from the Socialists. At this time, the KPD was the largest communist party outside Russia.

As a result of this huge setback, the Comintern (the Communist International which was responsible for coordinating the work of Communist parties around the world) changed its strategy. It instructed its international network to work with organizations that they could influence to support Moscow's policies. This meant that instead of fighting all non-Communist groups, Communist cadres should infiltrate local, national and international organizations that could be bent to Moscow's purposes.

Thus otherwise innocuous or altruistic-sounding groups such as the World Council of Churches were infiltrated by Communists who hid their true identity in order to influence the group's policies.

This 'United Front' strategy has been in use by Communists everywhere since the mid-1930s. The granddaddy of all United Front operations engineered by Moscow was its participation in the creation of the United Nations as a tool of the Soviet agenda to spread Communism worldwide.

The Sinister Soviet Plot Behind the Founding of the UN

Stalin used his status as an ally fighting Hitler to manipulate the way the United Nations was structured at its founding, so that the new organization would serve his purposes.

The chief architect of the United Nations structure was Alger Hiss, who headed the State Department's Office of Special Political Affairs, which was responsible for all matters related to the formation of the United Nations organization.[3] Hiss came from a privileged American family and was a grad-

---

3. John Earl Haynes and Harvey Klehr. 2000. *Venona: Decoding Soviet Espionage*

uate of Harvard Law School. But his loyalties were not to America. He was a dues-paying member of the Communist Party USA—whose first loyalties were to Communism and the Soviet Union—and in the mid-1930s he was recruited from the Party to work as a spy for the Kremlin.[4]

Hiss was extremely valuable to Stalin not only because of his years of espionage for Moscow and the influence he had in drafting the founding documents of the United Nations, but also because he was an important member of the American delegation to Yalta—where the allies agreed on the UN's structure and membership. Better still, Hiss would become the Secretary-General of the founding conference of the United Nations that was held in San Francisco in the Spring of 1945. In this position he was able to make sure that Moscow's interests were fully protected in the UN's structure.

The Yalta summit was convened by the leaders of the three main Allies in WWII: Churchill, FDR and Stalin. It was held from February 4 to 11, 1945 in the Crimean city of that name. Hiss was a key assistant to a relatively new US Secretary of State, Edward Stettinius, as well as an influential voice in the ear of FDR and his top advisor, Harry Hopkins, who also attended.

By the time these leaders gathered in Yalta, President Roosevelt was very ill. Although he had only just started his fourth term, his energy was rapidly draining from him and he would die on April 12, just two months after the conference ended. He was hardly up to negotiating vigorously for US and Allied interests—especially since he had to deal with the wily and duplicitous Stalin. The Soviet leader had a clear set of objectives for the meeting and was expert at wearing down Churchill and—especially—FDR over issues dear to his heart, such as the future of Poland and the structure and membership of the United Nations.[5]

---

in America. Yale Nota Bene, p 168.

4. For the full story of Alger Hiss, his espionage for the Soviet Union and his eventual trial and conviction, see the 1952 book *Witness* by his one-time handler and friend, Whittaker Chambers.

5. For minutes of the meetings at Yalta, see the State Department records: https://history.state.gov/historicaldocuments/frus1945Malta/ch8

Stalin had every reason to be pleased with himself at Yalta. By this juncture in the war Britain's power had been reduced by years of fighting Hitler—weakening Churchill's leverage with his Allies. In contrast, America's influence had only grown as it provided most of the soldiers and weapons for the war, making the United States the emergent global superpower.

Thus Stalin faced two men who were not at the peak of their powers—one a strong leader of a fading empire; the other a weak leader of an emerging superpower. But he also had a secret ace up his sleeve—Alger Hiss, who sat in on many important meetings. Hiss was therefore able to influence the decision-making of FDR and Churchill in Stalin's favor.

There is perhaps no better evidence of Stalin's outsize influence on the founding of the United Nations than the fact that at Yalta he was able to persuade Britain and the US to accept his preposterous claim that Ukraine and Belorussia (now Belarus) were independent countries that should therefore enjoy full member status in the United Nations. And, more important still, his success in getting his partners to agree that each member of the Security Council should have veto power over its decisions.

As is so often the case with the evil machinations of corrupt people, the secret role of Stalin and Hiss in the founding of the UN only came to light long after the damage had been done. The extent of Hiss's treachery was not confirmed until the mid-1990s, when the work of a secret US signals operation called Venona was published. Starting in 1943, Venona decoded cable traffic between Moscow and its agents in the United States. Among the Venona revelations was proof that Hiss was a spy for Moscow and that on this way back to Washington from Yalta he stopped in Moscow, where he received an award for his service to the Soviet Union.[6]

Is it Possible to Fix the UN?

Because of the flawed way in which the UN was established, it has always been ineffective in dealing with the world's many bad actors. In 2023, UN

---

6. John Earl Haynes and Harvey Klehr. 2000. *Venona: Decoding Soviet Espionage in America*. Yale Nota Bene, p172.

peacekeeping operations could be found in 10 hot spots around the world—including some decades-long conflicts in places like Cyprus, Lebanon and Congo—at an annual cost of $6.45 billion.[7]

An obvious concern regarding these operations is that while they appear to have some beneficial peace-preserving functions, they do not offer a way to end conflicts. Furthermore, all of them exist because the international community was unable to prevent the outbreak of fighting in the first place and has been unable to forge lasting solutions since. How long will this continue?

The message to UN members is clear: If you are the target of aggression don't expect the UN to save you. For one, the perpetrators of the aggression are almost certainly also members of the UN and, worse yet, they may well be under the influence of Russia or China.

Thus the war in Ukraine is only the most recent demonstration of the inability of the UN to be taken seriously by anyone seeking protection from aggressors and human rights violators. As we have noted, this will not change so long as fascist Russia and Communist China occupy two of the five permanent seats on the Security Council, and countries of their ilk hold positions of power in the UN's many organizations.

A case in point is the UN's Human Rights Council. Several countries that are responsible for massive human rights violations—like Iran, Russia and Libya—have held seats in the 47-member HRC, despite complaints from more civilized UN members, including the US and other countries that cover the bulk of the UN's huge annual budget. The complaints are ignored and serious human rights violators continue to be elected to Council membership by the General Assembly. In 2023, HRC members included China and Cuba![8]

To fix the UN, countries like Russia, China, North Korea, Cuba, Ven-

---

7. July 20, 2022. *The 2022 UN Peacekeeping Budget: Signs of Progress or a Fleeting Moment of Consensus?* Reliefweb.

8. January 1 to December 31, 2023. Members of the United Nations Human Rights Council.

ezuela, Nicaragua and Iran should be expelled, since they are causing the most conflicts and suffering in the world while doing nothing to ameliorate disputes or improve the lives of those in need.

According to the United Nations Charter, the founding member states were those invited to join by the three main allies at Yalta: Britain, the US and Soviet Union. In general, they were countries that supported the allied effort to defeat Hitler. However, Article 4 provides for other countries to join if they are "peace-loving states":

> Article 4
>
> Membership in the United Nations is open to all other peace-loving states which accept the obligations contained in the present Charter and, in the judgment of the Organization, are able and willing to carry out these obligations.
>
> The admission of any such state to membership in the United Nations will be effected by a decision of the General Assembly upon the recommendation of the Security Council.[9]

This article should have served to exclude from membership fascist and Communist countries that are governed by dictators and violence-advocating Marxist ideologies, and which are chronic violators of human rights. And it should have prevented Communist China from replacing Taiwan on the Security Council.

There is a mechanism for expelling members who are in violation of UN principles, but that process requires the recommendation of the Security Council:

> Article 6
>
> A Member of the United Nations which has persistently violated the Principles contained in the present Charter may be expelled from the Organization by the General Assembly upon the recommendation of the Security Council.

---

9. June 26, 1945. United Nations Charter, Articles 4 and 6. https://www.un.org/en/about-us/un-charter.

Thus the Charter that enshrined the Soviet Union as a founding member gave evil a permanent leadership position in the organization. And since Putin's Russia and Communist China now enjoy the privileges of Security Council membership, the chances of fundamental reform of the UN are zero.

In conclusion, the United Nations is not only unable to perform the core tasks of maintaining peace in the world and defending the weak and innocent against predators, but it is also unable to reform itself. The UN should be shut down. If any of its services are deemed effective, they can be spun off to parties interested in their continuation, albeit free from affiliation to a central global bureaucracy such as the UN is today.

A New Defense Alliance is Needed to Secure World Peace

Since the war in Ukraine has demonstrated the continued relevance of NATO and irrelevance of the United Nations, it can also serve to catalyze the creation of an international defense alliance that will actually fulfill its security objectives.

A good starting point would be to use NATO as a model for this new alliance, since it already has a 74-year record of success. NATO works well in part because of the way it is structured to provide maximum freedom to its members while having clear mechanisms that oblige them to come to one another's aid in times of crisis. NATO does not have a standing army, but the armies of all its members are bound to contribute to joint military actions.

Throughout its history, NATO has preserved its defensive purpose, which is a vitally important principle that prevents it from violating its own reason for existence by engaging in aggression towards others. The new alliance should also state in its founding documents that its primary purpose is to defend its members against violations of their national borders. It should not waver from this purpose, or allow itself to be drawn into other important but distracting missions.

A central objective behind establishing a new worldwide alliance is to avoid the mistakes inherent in the founding of the United Nations, in particular the inclusion of member states that do not share the same values as those of free nations. This means that the new organization must be made up of members who are committed to upholding the principles of individual freedom, democratic government and free markets. No Communist, fascist or similar totalitarian regime can be allowed to join—and any member that becomes totalitarian must be expelled.

Furthermore, membership should be aspirational: To qualify, a candidate nation must have a democratically-elected government, universal suffrage, elections with secure and secret ballots, and the rule of law administered by an independent judiciary. It must recognize its citizens' individual rights—such as those in the US Bill of Rights.

As with NATO, the vetting process for potential new members must be rigorous, and those members who do not keep up the agreed level of defense spending for more than three years should be suspended, pending compliance. And while there should be unanimous (or perhaps close to unanimous) agreement of existing members to the accession of new countries to membership, there should also be provisions for the expulsion of members for extended delinquency in defense spending or non-conformity with the organizations core principles. Expulsion could require a two-thirds vote.

The social and economic activities of the UN should not transfer to the new organization, nor should they be added to its mandate. It should be understood that the best way to help countries reduce poverty, hunger and disease is to enable its citizens to become prosperous, and the best way to foster prosperity is to provide a secure environment for social development and private enterprise.

It's Time for America to Exit the UN

The one country with the political, economic and military power needed to establish an effective, worldwide defense alliance is the United States. It is also the one country whose support for the United Nations is critical for that organization to function as it does. US support for the UN generally accounts for about a fifth of the organization's total budget. In 2021 this support amounted to $12 billion.[10]

Why is the United States supporting Ukraine with tens of billions of dollars in aid while at the same time pouring tens of billions of dollars into an organization that is supposed to be providing Ukraine with the security it needs against Russian aggression, but failing to do so?

Furthermore, what is the point of committing so much money to an organization that all too often votes against American interests—for example by condemning Washington's ally Israel while staffing its Human Rights Council with representatives of countries that are sworn enemies of the United States?

It's time for Washington to come to terms with the fact that the UN has failed in its core mission to provide its members with security, and that it is a very inefficient and costly agency to trust with delivering assistance to the world.

There is no need for the United States to use the UN as an intermediary for its humanitarian aid. Through USAID and other programs, America—the most generous nation on earth—is already supporting needy people in countries everywhere. It hardly needs to pass this assistance through an often corrupt and hostile UN bureaucracy.

Finally, the UN should be made to move its headquarters out of America. The iconic New York skyscraper has long been the home of foreign officials and secret agents who are bent on destroying America, enemies the US as host to the UN headquarters is obliged to allow into the country. This should end.

The war in Ukraine has shown how urgently a defensive alliance for all responsible nations is needed, and just how useless for this purpose the United Nations is. Let this lesson from the war in Ukraine be used to make the long-overdue changes that we are advocating for in these pages.

---

10. Editors. March 13, 2023. *Funding the United Nations: How Much Does the U.S. Pay?* The Council on Foreign Relations.

By making a decisive move to exit the United Nations and remove its headquarters from New York, America will provide the leadership necessary for a radical shift away from the compromising entanglements of a leadership and membership that includes the enemies of freedom and democracy. This will pave the way for the formation of a new global organization designed to meet the security needs of the peace-loving people and nations of the world.

Chapter 16

This Could Be a Providential Inflection Point

The War to End All Wars

In 1914, H.G. Wells published a book on his thoughts about the war unfolding in Europe. The title, *The War That Will End War*, reflected his belief that a war of such unprecedented dimensions should be a lesson to humanity that war itself is wrong and must end.

To prevent the repetition of such 'unnecessary' wars, he believed the aim of the war should be to thoroughly defeat German imperialism so that it could not raise its ugly head once more. He pointed out that such a decisive victory could not be achieved through diplomacy, but had to be realized through force of arms. After all, Britain had not sought out the war but was obliged to fight it for its own preservation:

> And war is mortal conflict. We have now either to destroy or be destroyed. We have not sought this reckoning, we have done our utmost to avoid it; but now that it has been forced upon us it is imperative that it should be a thorough reckoning. This is a war that touches every man and every home in each of the combatant countries...

> And it is a war that must be fought to such a finish that every man in each of the nations engaged understands what has happened. There can be no diplomatic settlement that will leave German Imperialism free to explain away its failure to its people and start new prepara-

tions. We have to go on until we are absolutely done for, or until the Germans as a people know that they are beaten, and are convinced that they have had enough of war.[1]

He also made the important point that while Britain was fighting to destroy the evil of German imperialism it was not seeking to harm the German people or their country:

> We are fighting Germany. But we are fighting without any hatred of the German people. We do not intend to destroy either their freedom or their unity. But we have to destroy an evil system of government and the mental and material corruption that has got hold of the German imagination and taken possession of German life. We have to smash the Prussian Imperialism as thoroughly as Germany in 1871 smashed the rotten Imperialism of Napoleon III. And also we have to learn from the failure of that victory to avoid a vindictive triumph.

Wells was an influential writer, and his book captured the imagination of many in Britain. The title was adapted into a slogan that was widely used to encapsulate the purpose of the war: "The war to end all wars." Wells was serious when he wrote his book, but WWI did not end with an unconditional surrender of Germany and war itself would rage on in the 20th century, turning the slogan into a popular term used to mock the aspirations it represented.[2]

WWI had not even ended before Russia's losses in the war became the pretext for the violent 1917 Russian Revolution, which in turn ignited a series of conflicts as the Bolsheviks conquered several countries to establish the Soviet Union and then spread Marxist-Leninist revolutions around the world, creating one new war after the other.

Meanwhile, Germany's loss in WWI gave birth to the German Communist Party and Nazism, both of which appealed to the worst in German nature. By the time Hitler took power in 1933 and began to militarize Ger-

---

1. H.G. Wells. 2014. *The War That Will End War*. H.G. Wells Library, p8.
2. November 10, 1998. *The war to end all wars*. BBC News.

many in preparation for what would become another world war, the hopes that WWI would prevent further wars was a distant fantasy. If there were any doubts remaining as to Hitler's real intensions, they were killed when Germany invaded Poland on September 1, 1939, starting WWII.

As we have discussed, it was the lack of a decisive Allied victory in WWI that led to a resurgence of a predatory and militarized Germany and the start of another major war—a war that would prove much more lethal than WWI. Fortunately, the Allies did learn their lesson from WWI—in part at least—and ended WWII by demanding the unconditional surrender of Germany, Italy and Japan, and then by making sure these aggressors disarmed and became peaceful members of the world community.

However, to defeat Hitler, the Western nations made the Soviet Union an ally in the war against Germany, supplying Moscow with massive quantities of armaments and other assistance. These supplies enabled Russia to beat back the Nazi invasion and then occupy and Communize much of eastern and central Europe as the German army collapsed.

Meanwhile, in China a US administration riddled with Soviet agents worked with Mao's Chinese Communist Party during and after WWII to help the Red Army defeat Chiang Kai-shek's Nationalists.[3] The outcome was the creation in 1949 of the largest Communist country by population in the world—the People's Republic of China.

Thus through being far too accommodating to Stalin and Mao at the end of WWII, the Allies set in motion the spread of a lethal Communist cancer that would prove even more devastating than Hitler's Nazis had been.

The Cold War is Not Over

We call the post-WWII conflict between the Communist countries and the Free World the Cold War, although it has been responsible for countless hot

---

3. For authoritative books on this history, see Diana West's 2014 *American Betrayal: The Secret Assault on Our Nation's Character*, and M. Stanton Evans' 2009 *Blacklisted by History: The Untold Story of Senator Joe McCarthy and His Fight Against America's Enemies.*

wars and a death toll in the tens of millions, topping the toll of WWII.[4] As we have discussed, the Western policies of containment and détente have contributed mightily to the prolongation and proliferation of Cold War conflicts, greatly increasing human suffering around the world.

The collapse of the Soviet Union at the beginning of the 1990s marked an important milestone in rolling back global Communism, but Marxism-Leninism survived in China, North Korea, Cuba and elsewhere. And now the world is threatened by an aggressive Communist China, which is more powerful than its Soviet parent. The Cold War is far from over.

Which brings us to Russia's invasion of Ukraine in February 2022. The shocking barbarity of the Russian army confirms that the evils of the Soviet system have not yet been expunged from today's Russian state. Russians themselves have increasingly faced fascistic limits to their freedoms of speech, press and religion, while Putin's invasion has inflicted on Ukraine a catastrophe that matches any of the horrors of WWI and WWII.

A Deeper Meaning to the War in Ukraine

We contend that the war now raging in Ukraine has a deeper meaning than just another bilateral conflict. It is a war of aggression by a post-Communist nation that has morphed into a fascist regime that continues to harbor imperial ambitions and—echoing Soviet practices—is willing to use any and all means to achieve those ambitions. Its target is a country that has turned away from its Communist past and is determined to join the countries that have embraced democracy and adhere to the rules-based international system.

The resolve of President Volodymyr Zelensky and the Ukrainian people in the face of the Russian onslaught has turned Ukraine into a nation that stands in the vanguard against the forces of evil in the modern world. The

---

4. Estimates of the death toll of Communism vary greatly. *The Black Book of Communism* puts the total death toll of Communism since the Russian Revolution in 1917 at 94 million. *The Epoch Times* has calculated that the murderous activities of Mao and the Chinese Communist Party in the Great Leap Forward, the Cultural Revolution and other oppressive activities have cost the lives of some 80 million people in China alone.

suffering incurred by the Ukrainian people in taking this stand is evident in their bombed-out cities and in the death and maiming of their finest young people, who are sacrificing their lives to preserve liberty and the continued independence of their country. The injustice of their suffering should be evident to all righteous-minded people.

Insights From a Mythological War Between Good and Evil

In an all too realistic demonstration of reality imitating art, the Ukrainians call the Russian invaders "Orcs"[5]—after the ugly mythological creatures that carry out the evil purposes of Sauron, the Dark Lord of Mordor, in J.R.R. Tolkien's *The Lord of the Rings* trilogy.[6] Russia is Mordor and Putin Sauron. The transformation of Ukrainian cities into post-apocalyptic wastelands indeed mirrors the destruction of life and human goodness that follows the Orcs wherever they go.

The forces that gather to defeat Sauron are diverse but united in goodness. From humble hobbits to magnificent Elven warriors, Rohan horsemen and great kings of earlier times, these allies take on what seem like impossible odds because fighting Mordor's evil to protect good is the right thing to do to save Middle Earth from destruction. In the end the good side is victorious.

Once the magical ring that controls great powers—that were originally to be used for good but which Sauron wanted to use for evil purposes—is destroyed by the Hobbits, the evil forces behind Mordor crumble and suddenly Sauron's evil empire collapses.

The humble hobbits emerge as heroes.

Meanwhile, those who had once been allies on the side of good but who had secretly harkened to Sauron's whispered promises of power—like the white wizard, Saruman—were exposed as traitors through the separation of good and evil forces in the lead-up to the final confrontation with Mordor.

---

5. Christopher MacLachlan. April 10, 2022. *Why are Ukrainians calling Russian invaders 'orcs'?* The Spectator.

6. J.R.R. Tolkien. 1968. *The Lord of the Rings*. Allen & Unwin.

The Propaganda Myth of Russian Virtue

At the heart of all successful propaganda there is a kernel of truth that is wrapped in a great lie. In Soviet times the kernel of truth was that the West was far from perfect. The big lie was that Communism was the solution to Western ills. The truth was quite the opposite: the West had the culture and institutions to improve itself while the Communist world could do nothing more than create an ever-worsening hell on earth.

In Russian propaganda today, the kernel of truth is that Ukraine is far from perfect, and the big lie is that Russia is a better country than Ukraine and justified in invading its neighbor. However, Ukraine is demonstrating its intention and ability to improve itself—through its anti-corruption campaign and its willingness to undergo the rigors of joining the European Union and NATO—while Russia is becoming increasingly fascistic, totalitarian and corrupt.

Yet Putin and his army of propaganda acolytes have shown themselves to be masters at exploiting confusion about the war to spread their false narratives around the world as part of a massive disinformation campaign. Most glaring for its falsehood, Moscow claims to own the moral high ground in this war. Putin would have the world believe that Russia today is guided by Judeo-Christian values of faith and family, while Ukraine is infected with Western depravity and ruled by Nazis.

This is an obscene claim when you consider that the Ukrainian side is showing decency in its conduct of the war—including in its treatment of prisoners—while Russia has broken every civilizational norm with its indiscriminate bombing of civilians, its rape, torture and murder of prisoners, and its abduction of Ukrainians to Russia.

Russia's Propaganda Lies Must be Exposed

The bogus arguments against supporting Ukraine in this war that we have highlighted in this book all originated in Russian propaganda that has been spread far and wide, and foolishly accepted by many in the West—as if these lies provide a credible Russian narrative. Russian propagandists have tailored their messages for each target audience—whether Conservative or Liberal, globalist or nationalist—feeding each group the lies and half-truths required for them to form an anti-Ukraine opinion.

It must be said plainly: Russian deceptions and disinformation about Ukraine are just that—lies and distortions of the truth. Western media should be called out when they quote Russian sources as if they were just as credible as those from Ukraine or other bona fide sources. Russia counts on the appearance of fairness enjoyed by most Western media to get its lies treated with the same respect as the truth.

Given the barbaric behavior of Russia in Ukraine, which itself exposes the propaganda lies, the Ukrainian narrative should be given the benefit of the doubt, since it comes from the side that is undeniably the victim in the conflict.

Furthermore, the West should recognize that Russian propaganda against Ukraine didn't start with the invasion in February 2022. It has been used by Moscow for years to prepare the way for the invasion by conditioning the West to accept Russia's justifications for expansion.[7] And the West should recognize that in the face of pushback against its narratives, Russia does not admit wrongdoing but simply adjusts its messaging as it looks for alternative disinformation that will stick.

NATO members and other supporters of Ukraine have to be aware of the danger posed by these deceptions and remain firmly committed to a Ukrainian victory. Many good people have been duped by Russian propaganda, and winning this war must include exposing and debunking Moscow's lies that have been used to justify it. Any peace settlement must include an admission by Russia that it has lied about Ukraine for decades.

After all, this war really is a conflict between good and evil and it is of vital global importance that only the truly good prevails.

---

7. Christopher Paul and Miriam Matthews. 2016. *The Russian "Firehose of Falsehood" Propaganda Model: Why it Might Work and Options to Counter It*. RAND Corporation. https://www.rand.org/pubs/perspectives/PE198.html

The Age-Old Conflict Between Good and Evil

In this book we have frequently referred to good and evil in the belief that they are the real and irreconcilable forces at play in this war, which is just the latest in the millennia-long history of these contests. It is this perspective that makes the war in Ukraine so important for the world.

What do we mean by good and evil? And is there any hope that good can ultimately vanquish evil?

If you are religious, you likely recognize good and evil as irreconcilable forces that represent God and Satan, respectively. If you don't have a religious belief, you likely nevertheless recognize both good and evil through the opposite results they produce—good improves the world while evil harms it; and doing good brings satisfaction and joy while doing evil produces misery.

The reality of good and evil becomes clear through the extremes of their opposite behaviors: the selfless service of others by saintly individuals, in the case of good, compared with the brutal destruction of others by totalitarians like Hitler, Stalin and Mao, in the case of evil.

Aleksandr Solzhenitsyn described the internal struggle between good and evil, and the problem of overcoming evil, in this way:

> If only it were all so simple! If only there were evil people somewhere insidiously committing evil deeds, and it were necessary only to separate them from the rest of us and destroy them. But the line dividing good and evil cuts through the heart of every human being. And who is willing to destroy a piece of his own heart?

He continued:

> The line separating good and evil passes not through states, nor between classes, nor between political parties either—but right through every human heart... even within hearts overwhelmed by evil, one small bridgehead of good is retained. And even in the best of all hearts, there remains... an uprooted small corner of evil.[8]

---

8. Aleksandr Solzhenitsyn. 1974. *The Gulag Archipelago*. Collins, p168.

188

This may be a dark reality, but it also contains the seeds of hope. For two reasons. First, since all people have both good and evil tendencies they can all become better versions of themselves through a process of education and improvement. Second, the relative difference in individuals' standards of goodness and evil means that those who are more advanced in goodness can provide leadership and guidance to help others become better.

Experience teaches us that the goodness within us can be strengthened through our practice of goodness towards others, and vice versa. In the Christian tradition, Christ represents an absolute standard of good and therefore by following him we too can aspire to an absolute standard of good. As Jesus said: "Be perfect, therefore, as your heavenly Father is perfect." (Matthew 5:48)

This perspective underscores the importance of being able to discern the difference between the relatively better and the relatively worse sides in conflicts, so that you can align yourself with the better side. For the war in Ukraine, this means recognizing Ukraine is on the side of good compared with Russia.

As we have noted, both Russia and Ukraine emerged from the Soviet Union and therefore inherited many of the evils of Communism. However, while Russia under Putin is continuing many dark Soviet practices, Ukraine under Zelensky is doing what it can to leave its Soviet past behind in order to become a peace-loving, democratic country.

The current war is all the evidence we need of the opposite directions these two countries are taking: Russia has invaded Ukraine to deprive it of its separate identity and independence, while Ukraine is seeking to join the democracies of the West in the European Union and to protect itself from aggression by joining NATO. The difference between the two is clearly evident, yet there is still confusion in many parts of the world as to which side to support.

The Invisible Hand of the Divine Providence

Given the invisible nature of good and evil, is there a sure way to distinguish one from the other except by examining their fruits, as we have discussed here? The Bible provides just such a paradigm in the story of Cain and Abel, which is explained in some detail in Appendix 5. However, beyond the Biblical account of the origin of evil, there is an almost universal consciousness of the operation of these conflicting invisible forces that have shaped our history and continue to influence our world today.

In this book we recognize the forces of good as those aligned with the invisible operation of the Divine Providence, which is God's original purpose for the creation being worked out over time. You can think of the providence as the invisible hand of God guiding humanity to its ultimate destiny in a heavenly world—a Garden of Eden as it was before the Fall.

Contesting with this Divine Providence for the hearts and minds of all people are the invisible forces of a Satanic Anti-Providence that is bent on destroying the world of God's original ideal. Thus evil is anything that aligns with the destructive forces of the Satanic Anti-Providence.

The founders of the United States believed their work to be guided by the Divine Providence, as they declared in the Declaration of Independence:

> For the support of this Declaration, with a firm reliance on the Protection of Divine Providence, we mutually pledge to each other our Lives, our Fortunes and our sacred Honor.

The founders were faithful men for whom receiving God's blessing for their work was vitally important. Because of this, the fruits of their labors not only benefited all in America but also people around the world. Sooner or later, countless millions living beyond America's shores would have their lives improved in countries that also embraced liberty, self-determination and government based on Judeo-Christian or similar religious values.

The Divine Providence that guided the American founders embodied the goodness of the Creator's original purpose. And since God is only good, that purpose is likewise only good. Thus the Divine Providence is unchangingly aimed at the realization of the original good purpose for the creation.

In our own lives we may well see the results of the invisible hand of God working to guide us to our Godly destiny, so that our lives have meaning within the providence. In the same way, the invisible hand of God guides groups and nations to fulfill their own providential purposes.

As creatures endowed with free will, in order for us to receive blessings from our Creator within the compass of the providence (including the rights described in the Declaration of Independence) we must choose to fulfill our portion of responsibility.

Ukraine's responsibility has been to stand up to Russia's aggression and to make sure that this aggression is not rewarded with success. By doing exactly this, the people of Ukraine have earned a place in the vanguard of the worldwide conflict between good and evil. They are on the side of the Divine Providence and therefore deserve the wholehearted support of the rest of the world.

To return to the words of H.G. Wells: If one substitutes Putin's Russia for the Kaiser's Germany, there is a clear parallel between the operation of evil in WWI and in the war in Ukraine, as well as a similar need to sacrifice in order to defeat evil. Wells believed that Germany had been overtaken by the evil of war-making:

> But the evil was started; the German imagination was captured and enslaved. On every other European country that valued its integrity there was thrust the overwhelming necessity to arm and drill—and still to arm and drill. Money was withdrawn from education, from social progress, from business enterprise, and art and scientific research, and from every kind of happiness; life was drilled and darkened.

> So that the harvest of this darkness comes now almost as a relief, and it is a grim satisfaction in our discomforts that we can at last look across the roar and torment of battlefields to the possibility of an organized peace.

> For this is now a war for peace.[9]

_____

9. H.G. Wells. 2014. *The War That Will End War*. H.G. Wells Library, p9.

Indeed, the war in Ukraine is a war for peace, a war to end the seemingly endless aggression of Russia. Victory will mean that Ukraine regains sovereignty over its own territory, but also that Russia will be deterred from its evil behavior into the future.

This Could be an Inflection Point in the Providence

As we noted in the Preface, today the front line in the global conflict between good and evil is in Ukraine. Thus we believe that if Ukraine achieves a clear victory this could be an inflection point in the providence, a turning point in humanity's march towards the fulfillment of our original purpose—a peaceful world.

The Ukrainian people are shedding their blood to stop an unjust invasion and the expansion of power by a regime that has demonstrated its evil intentions and practices. If Russia is allowed to succeed, the world will witness more evil and more suffering as an emboldened Putin expands his dark influence. Meanwhile, other totalitarians—like the Chinese Communist Party, the North Korean Communist regime, the Communists in Cuba and the dictatorial Islamist state in Iran—are likely to take heart from a Russian victory and imitate Moscow's aggressions with their own.

On the other hand, if Ukraine is victorious, Russia will be forced to give up its predatory behavior and accept a diminished role in the world. Putin's government is likely to fall, creating an opportunity for the installation of a more ethical and responsible leadership with a mandate to guide Russia to become a peaceful member of the community of nations.

The repercussions from a decisive win by Ukraine could reverberate far beyond Russia. China would likely lose a major ally to its north and west, and will have to think twice before trying to conquer Taiwan by force of arms. The survival of the Chinese Communist Party itself could be in danger as the long-suffering Chinese people will be encouraged to take on their oppressive rulers.

With a weakened Russia and China, North Korea will lose support from its major backers—in particular Beijing. Without them, Pyongyang cannot survive. Other dictatorial client states of Russia and China—in particular Cuba, Venezuela, Nicaragua and Iran—will also face new pressures from citizens seeking freedom.

In Iran, resistance to the fascistic Islamist regime is already growing stronger, especially now that the country's women are becoming active in opposing the government. A reformed Russia will cut or downgrade its ties with the aggressive, terrorist-supporting regime in Tehran, and join the world community in helping the Iranian people win their freedom.

Wherever there is tyranny, oppressed people hunger for freedom and aspire to live free in a peaceful and prosperous world. A decisive victory for Ukraine will give these people new hope, a hope that will brighten the future of all humanity.

Ukraine can win. Ukraine must win. Ukraine will win!

Slava Ukraini!

APPENDICES

Address by the President of the Russian Federation

February 21, 2022

The Kremlin, Moscow

President of Russia Vladimir Putin: Citizens of Russia, friends,

My address concerns the events in Ukraine and why this is so important for us, for Russia. Of course, my message is also addressed to our compatriots in Ukraine.

The matter is very serious and needs to be discussed in depth.

The situation in Donbass has reached a critical, acute stage. I am speaking to you directly today not only to explain what is happening but also to inform you of the decisions being made as well as potential further steps.

I would like to emphasize again that Ukraine is not just a neighboring country for us. It is an inalienable part of our own history, culture and spiritual space. These are our comrades, those dearest to us—not only colleagues, friends and people who once served together, but also relatives, people bound by blood, by family ties.

Since time immemorial, the people living in the southwest of what has historically been Russian land have called themselves Russians and Orthodox Christians. This was the case before the 17th century, when a portion of this territory rejoined the Russian state, and after.

It seems to us that, generally speaking, we all know these facts, that this is common knowledge. Still, it is necessary to say at least a few words about the history of this issue in order to understand what is happening today, to explain the motives behind Russia's actions and what we aim to achieve.

So, I will start with the fact that modern Ukraine was entirely created by Russia or, to be more precise, by Bolshevik, Communist Russia. This process started practically right after the 1917 revolution, and Lenin and his associates did it in a way that was extremely harsh on Russia—by separating, severing what is historically Russian land. Nobody asked the millions of people living there what they thought.

Then, both before and after the Great Patriotic War, Stalin incorporated in the USSR and transferred to Ukraine some lands that previously belonged to Poland, Romania and Hungary. In the process, he gave Poland part of what was traditionally German land as compensation, and in 1954, Khrushchev took Crimea away from Russia for some reason and also gave it to Ukraine. In effect, this is how the territory of modern Ukraine was formed.

But now I would like to focus attention on the initial period of the USSR's formation. I believe this is extremely important for us. I will have to approach it from a distance, so to speak.

I will remind you that after the 1917 October Revolution and the subsequent Civil War, the Bolsheviks set about creating a new statehood. They had rather serious disagreements among themselves on this point. In 1922, Stalin occupied the positions of both the General Secretary of the Russian Communist Party (Bolsheviks) and the People's Commissar for Ethnic Affairs. He suggested building the country on the principles of autonomization that is, giving the republics—the future administrative and territorial entities—broad powers upon joining a unified state.

Lenin criticized this plan and suggested making concessions to the nationalists, whom he called "independents" at that time. Lenin's ideas of what amounted in essence to a confederative state arrangement and a slogan about the right of nations to self-determination, up to secession, were laid in the foundation of Soviet statehood. Initially they were confirmed in the Declaration on the Formation of the USSR in 1922, and later on, after Lenin's death, were enshrined in the 1924 Soviet Constitution.

This immediately raises many questions. The first is really the main one: why was it necessary to appease the nationalists, to satisfy the ceaselessly growing nationalist ambitions on the outskirts of the former empire? What was the point of transferring to the newly, often arbitrarily formed administrative units—the union republics—vast territories that had nothing to do with them? Let me repeat that these territories were transferred along with the population of what was historically Russia.

Moreover, these administrative units were de facto given the status and form of national state entities. That raises another question: why was it necessary to make such generous gifts, beyond the wildest dreams of the most zealous nationalists and, on top of all that, give the republics the right to secede from the unified state without any conditions?

At first glance, this looks absolutely incomprehensible, even crazy. But only at first glance. There is an explanation. After the revolution, the Bolsheviks' main goal was to stay in power at all costs, absolutely at all costs. They did everything for this purpose: accepted the humiliating Treaty of Brest-Litovsk, although the military and economic situation in Kaiser Germany and its allies was dramatic and the outcome of the First World War was a foregone conclusion, and satisfied any demands and wishes of the nationalists within the country.

When it comes to the historical destiny of Russia and its peoples, Lenin's principles of state development were not just a mistake; they were worse than a mistake, as the saying goes. This became patently clear after the dissolution of the Soviet Union in 1991.

Of course, we cannot change past events, but we must at least admit them openly and honestly, without any reservations or politicking. Personally, I can add that no political factors, however impressive or profitable they may seem at any given moment, can or may be used as the fundamental principles of statehood.

I am not trying to put the blame on anyone. The situation in the country at that time, both before and after the Civil War, was extremely complicated; it was critical. The only thing I would like to say today is that this is exactly how it was. It is a historical fact. Actually, as I have already said, Soviet Ukraine is the result of the Bolsheviks' policy and can be rightfully called "Vladimir Lenin's Ukraine." He was its creator and architect. This is fully and comprehensively corroborated by archival documents, including Lenin's harsh instructions regarding Donbass, which was actually shoved into Ukraine. And today the "grateful progeny" has overturned monuments to Lenin in Ukraine. They call it decommunization.

You want decommunization? Very well, this suits us just fine. But why stop halfway? We are ready to show what real decommunizations would mean for Ukraine.

Going back to history, I would like to repeat that the Soviet Union was established in the place of the former Russian Empire in 1922. But practice showed immediately that it was impossible to preserve or govern such a vast and complex territory on the amorphous principles that amounted to con-federation. They were far removed from reality and the historical tradition.

It is logical that the Red Terror and a rapid slide into Stalin's dictator-ship, the domination of the communist ideology and the Communist Par-ty's monopoly on power, nationalization and the planned economy—all this transformed the formally declared but ineffective principles of government into a mere declaration. In reality, the union republics did not have any sov-ereign rights, none at all. The practical result was the creation of a tightly centralized and absolutely unitary state.

In fact, what Stalin fully implemented was not Lenin's but his own prin-ciples of government. But he did not make the relevant amendments to the cornerstone documents, to the Constitution, and he did not formally revise Lenin's principles underlying the Soviet Union. From the look of it, there seemed to be no need for that, because everything seemed to be working well in conditions of the totalitarian regime, and outwardly it looked won-derful, attractive and even super-democratic.

And yet, it is a great pity that the fundamental and formally legal foun-dations of our state were not promptly cleansed of the odious and utopian fantasies inspired by the revolution, which are absolutely destructive for any normal state. As it often happened in our country before, nobody gave any thought to the future.

It seems that the Communist Party leaders were convinced that they had created a solid system of government and that their policies had settled the ethnic issue for good. But falsification, misconception, and tampering with public opinion have a high cost. The virus of nationalist ambitions is still with us, and the mine laid at the initial stage to destroy state immunity to the disease of nationalism was ticking. As I have already said, the mine was the right of secession from the Soviet Union.

In the mid-1980s, the increasing socioeconomic problems and the apparent crisis of the planned economy aggravated the ethnic issue, which essentially was not based on any expectations or unfulfilled dreams of the Soviet peoples but primarily the growing appetites of the local elites.

However, instead of analyzing the situation, taking appropriate measures, first of all in the economy, and gradually transforming the political system and government in a well-considered and balanced manner, the Communist Party leadership only engaged in open doubletalk about the revival of the Leninist principle of national self-determination.

Moreover, in the course of power struggle within the Communist Party itself, each of the opposing sides, in a bid to expand its support base, started to thoughtlessly incite and encourage nationalist sentiments, manipulating them and promising their potential supporters whatever they wished. Against the backdrop of the superficial and populist rhetoric about democracy and a bright future based either on a market or a planned economy, but amid a true impoverishment of people and widespread shortages, no one among the powers that be was thinking about the inevitable tragic consequences for the country.

Next, they entirely embarked on the track beaten at the inception of the USSR and pandering to the ambitions of the nationalist elites nurtured within their own party ranks. But in so doing, they forgot that the CPSU no longer had—thank God—the tools for retaining power and the country itself, tools such as state terror and a Stalinist-type dictatorship, and that the notorious guiding role of the party was disappearing without a trace, like a morning mist, right before their eyes.

And then, the September 1989 plenary session of the CPSU Central Committee approved a truly fatal document, the so-called ethnic policy of the party in modern conditions, the CPSU platform. It included the following provisions, I quote: "The republics of the USSR shall possess all the rights appropriate to their status as sovereign socialist states."

The next point: "The supreme representative bodies of power of the USSR republics can challenge and suspend the operation of the USSR Government's resolutions and directives in their territory."

And finally: "Each republic of the USSR shall have citizenship of its own, which shall apply to all of its residents."

Wasn't it clear what these formulas and decisions would lead to?

Now is not the time or place to go into matters pertaining to state or constitutional law, or define the concept of citizenship. But one may wonder: why was it necessary to rock the country even more in that already complicated situation? The facts remain.

Even two years before the collapse of the USSR, its fate was actually predetermined. It is now that radicals and nationalists, including and primarily those in Ukraine, are taking credit for having gained independence. As we can see, this is absolutely wrong. The disintegration of our united country was brought about by the historic, strategic mistakes on the part of the Bolshevik leaders and the CPSU leadership, mistakes committed at different times in state-building and in economic and ethnic policies. The collapse of the historical Russia known as the USSR is on their conscience.

Despite all these injustices, lies and outright pillage of Russia, it was our people who accepted the new geopolitical reality that took shape after the dissolution of the USSR, and recognized the new independent states. Not only did Russia recognize these countries, but helped its CIS partners, even though it faced a very dire situation itself. This included our Ukrainian colleagues, who turned to us for financial support many times from the very moment they declared independence. Our country provided this assistance while respecting Ukraine's dignity and sovereignty.

According to expert assessments, confirmed by a simple calculation of our energy prices, the subsidized loans Russia provided to Ukraine along with economic and trade preferences, the overall benefit for the Ukrainian budget in the period from 1991 to 2013 amounted to $250 billion.

However, there was more to it than that. By the end of 1991, the USSR owed some $100 billion to other countries and international funds. Initially, there was this idea that all former Soviet republics will pay back these loans together, in the spirit of solidarity and proportionally to their economic potential. However, Russia undertook to pay back all Soviet debts and delivered on this promise by completing this process in 2017.

In exchange for that, the newly independent states had to hand over to Russia part of the Soviet foreign assets. An agreement to this effect was reached with Ukraine in December 1994. However, Kiev failed to ratify these agreements and later simply refused to honor them by making demands for a share of the Diamond Treasury, gold reserves, as well as former USSR property and other assets abroad.

Nevertheless, despite all these challenges, Russia always worked with Ukraine in an open and honest manner and, as I have already said, with respect for its interests. We developed our ties in multiple fields. Thus, in 2011, bilateral trade exceeded $50 billion. Let me note that in 2019, that is before the pandemic, Ukraine's trade with all EU countries combined was below this indicator.

At the same time, it was striking how the Ukrainian authorities always preferred dealing with Russia in a way that ensured that they enjoy all the rights and privileges while remaining free from any obligations.

The officials in Kiev replaced partnership with a parasitic attitude acting at times in an extremely brash manner. Suffice it to recall the continuous blackmail on energy transits and the fact that they literally stole gas.

I can add that Kiev tried to use dialogue with Russia as a bargaining chip in its relations with the West, using the threat of closer ties with Russia for blackmailing the West to secure preferences by claiming that otherwise Russia would have a bigger influence in Ukraine.

At the same time, the Ukrainian authorities—I would like to emphasize this—began by building their statehood on the negation of everything that united us, trying to distort the mentality and historical memory of millions of people, of entire generations living in Ukraine. It is not surprising that Ukrainian society was faced with the rise of far-right nationalism, which rapidly developed into aggressive Russophobia and neo-Nazism. This resulted in the participation of Ukrainian nationalists and neo-Nazis in the terrorist groups in the North Caucasus and the increasingly loud territorial claims to Russia.

A role in this was played by external forces, which used a ramified network of NGOs and special services to nurture their clients in Ukraine and to bring their representatives to the seats of authority.

It should be noted that Ukraine actually never had stable traditions of real statehood. And, therefore, in 1991 it opted for mindlessly emulating foreign models, which have no relation to history or Ukrainian realities. Political government institutions were readjusted many times to the rapidly growing clans and their self-serving interests, which had nothing to do with the interests of the Ukrainian people.

Essentially, the so-called pro-Western civilizational choice made by the oligarchic Ukrainian authorities was not and is not aimed at creating better conditions in the interests of people's well-being but at keeping the billions of dollars that the oligarchs have stolen from the Ukrainians and are holding in their accounts in Western banks, while reverently accommodating the geopolitical rivals of Russia.

Some industrial and financial groups and the parties and politicians on their payroll relied on the nationalists and radicals from the very beginning. Others claimed to be in favor of good relations with Russia and cultural and language diversity, coming to power with the help of their citizens who sincerely supported their declared aspirations, including the millions of people in the southeastern regions. But after getting the positions they coveted, these people immediately betrayed their voters, going back on their election promises and instead steering a policy prompted by the radicals and sometimes even persecuting their former allies—the public organizations that supported bilingualism and cooperation with Russia. These people took advantage of the fact that their voters were mostly law-abiding citizens with moderate views who trusted the authorities, and that, unlike the radicals, they would not act aggressively or make use of illegal instruments.

Meanwhile, the radicals became increasingly brazen in their actions and made more demands every year. They found it easy to force their will on the weak authorities, which were infected with the virus of nationalism and corruption as well and which artfully replaced the real cultural, economic and social interests of the people and Ukraine's true sovereignty with various ethnic speculations and formal ethnic attributes.

A stable statehood has never developed in Ukraine; its electoral and other political procedures just serve as a cover, a screen for the redistribution of power and property between various oligarchic clans.

Corruption, which is certainly a challenge and a problem for many countries, including Russia, has gone beyond the usual scope in Ukraine. It has literally permeated and corroded Ukrainian statehood, the entire system, and all branches of power.

Radical nationalists took advantage of the justified public discontent and saddled the Maidan protest, escalating it to a coup d'état in 2014. They also had direct assistance from foreign states. According to reports, the US Embassy provided $1 million a day to support the so-called protest camp on Independence Square in Kiev. In addition, large amounts were impudently transferred directly to the opposition leaders' bank accounts, tens of millions of dollars. But the people who actually suffered, the families of those who died in the clashes provoked in the streets and squares of Kiev and other cities, how much did they get in the end? Better not ask.

The nationalists who have seized power have unleashed a persecution, a real terror campaign against those who opposed their anti-constitutional actions. Politicians, journalists, and public activists were harassed and

203

publicly humiliated. A wave of violence swept Ukrainian cities, including a series of high-profile and unpunished murders. One shudders at the memories of the terrible tragedy in Odessa, where peaceful protesters were brutally murdered, burned alive in the House of Trade Unions. The criminals who committed that atrocity have never been punished, and no one is even looking for them. But we know their names and we will do everything to punish them, find them and bring them to justice.

Maidan did not bring Ukraine any closer to democracy and progress. Having accomplished a coup d'état, the nationalists and those political forces that supported them eventually led Ukraine into an impasse, pushed the country into the abyss of civil war. Eight years later, the country is split. Ukraine is struggling with an acute socioeconomic crisis.

According to international organizations, in 2019, almost 6 million Ukrainians—I emphasize—about 15 percent, not of the workforce, but of the entire population of that country, had to go abroad to find work. Most of them do odd jobs. The following fact is also revealing: since 2020, over 60,000 doctors and other health workers have left the country amid the pandemic.

Since 2014, water bills increased by almost a third, and energy bills grew several times, while the price of gas for households surged several dozen times. Many people simply do not have the money to pay for utilities. They literally struggle to survive.

What happened? Why is this all happening? The answer is obvious. They spent and embezzled the legacy inherited not only from the Soviet era, but also from the Russian Empire. They lost tens, hundreds of thousands of jobs which enabled people to earn a reliable income and generate tax revenue, among other things thanks to close cooperation with Russia. Sectors including machine building, instrument engineering, electronics, ship and aircraft building have been undermined or destroyed altogether. There was a time, however, when not only Ukraine, but the entire Soviet Union took pride in these companies.

In 2021, the Black Sea Shipyard in Nikolayev went out of business. Its first docks date back to Catherine the Great. Antonov, the famous manufacturer, has not made a single commercial aircraft since 2016, while Yuzhmash, a factory specializing in missile and space equipment, is nearly bankrupt. The Kremenchug Steel Plant is in a similar situation. This sad list goes on and on.

As for the gas transportation system, it was built in its entirety by the Soviet Union, and it has now deteriorated to an extent that using it creates major risks and comes at a high cost for the environment.

This situation begs the question: poverty, lack of opportunity, and lost industrial and technological potential—is this the pro-Western civilizational choice they have been using for many years to fool millions of people with promises of heavenly pastures?

It all came down to a Ukrainian economy in tatters and an outright pillage of the country's citizens, while Ukraine itself was placed under external control, directed not only from the Western capitals, but also on the ground, as the saying goes, through an entire network of foreign advisors, NGOs and other institutions present in Ukraine. They have a direct bearing on all the key appointments and dismissals and on all branches of power at all levels, from the central government down to municipalities, as well as on state-owned companies and corporations, including Naftogaz, Ukrenergo, Ukrainian Railways, Ukroboronprom, Ukrposhta, and the Ukrainian Sea Ports Authority.

There is no independent judiciary in Ukraine. The Kiev authorities, at the West's demand, delegated the priority right to select members of the supreme judicial bodies, the Council of Justice and the High Qualifications Commission of Judges, to international organizations.

In addition, the United States directly controls the National Agency on Corruption Prevention, the National Anti-Corruption Bureau, the Specialized Anti-Corruption Prosecutor's Office and the High Anti-Corruption Court. All this is done under the noble pretext of invigorating efforts against corruption. All right, but where are the results? Corruption is flourishing like never before.

Are the Ukrainian people aware that this is how their country is managed? Do they realize that their country has turned not even into a political or economic protectorate but has been reduced to a colony with a puppet regime? The state was privatized. As a result, the government, which designates itself as the "power of patriots" no longer acts in a national capacity and consistently pushes Ukraine towards losing its sovereignty.

The policy to root out the Russian language and culture and promote assimilation carries on. The Verkhovna Rada has generated a steady flow of discriminatory bills, and the law on the so-called indigenous people has already come into force. People who identify as Russians and want to preserve their identity, language and culture are getting the signal that they are not wanted in Ukraine.

Under the laws on education and the Ukrainian language as a state language, the Russian language has no place in schools or public spaces, even in ordinary shops. The law on the so-called vetting of officials and purging their ranks created a pathway for dealing with unwanted civil servants.

There are more and more acts enabling the Ukrainian military and law enforcement agencies to crack down on the freedom of speech, dissent, and going after the opposition. The world knows the deplorable practice of imposing unilateral illegitimate sanctions against other countries, foreign individuals and legal entities. Ukraine has outperformed its Western masters by inventing sanctions against its own citizens, companies, television channels, other media outlets and even members of parliament.

Kiev continues to prepare the destruction of the Ukrainian Orthodox Church of the Moscow Patriarchate. This is not an emotional judgement; proof of this can be found in concrete decisions and documents. The Ukrainian authorities have cynically turned the tragedy of the schism into an instrument of state policy. The current authorities do not react to the Ukrainian people's appeals to abolish the laws that are infringing on believers' rights. Moreover, new draft laws directed against the clergy and millions of parishioners of the Ukrainian Orthodox Church of the Moscow Patriarchate have been registered in the Verkhovna Rada.

A few words about Crimea. The people of the peninsula freely made their choice to be with Russia. The Kiev authorities cannot challenge the clearly stated choice of the people, which is why they have opted for aggressive action, for activating extremist cells, including radical Islamist organizations, for sending subversives to stage terrorist attacks at critical infrastructure facilities, and for kidnapping Russian citizens. We have factual proof that such aggressive actions are being taken with support from Western security services.

In March 2021, a new Military Strategy was adopted in Ukraine. This document is almost entirely dedicated to confrontation with Russia and sets the goal of involving foreign states in a conflict with our country. The strategy stipulates the organization of what can be described as a terrorist underground movement in Russia's Crimea and in Donbass. It also sets out the contours of a potential war, which should end, according to the Kiev strategists, "with the assistance of the international community on favorable terms for Ukraine," as well as—listen carefully, please—"with foreign military support in the geopolitical confrontation with the Russian Federation." In fact, this is nothing other than preparation for hostilities against our country, Russia.

As we know, it has already been stated today that Ukraine intends to create its own nuclear weapons, and this is not just bragging. Ukraine has the nuclear technologies created back in the Soviet times and delivery vehicles for such weapons, including aircraft, as well as the Soviet-designed Tochka-U precision tactical missiles with a range of over 100 kilometers. But they can do more; it is only a matter of time. They have had the groundwork for this since the Soviet era.

In other words, acquiring tactical nuclear weapons will be much easier for Ukraine than for some other states I am not going to mention here, which are conducting such research, especially if Kiev receives foreign technological support. We cannot rule this out either.

If Ukraine acquires weapons of mass destruction, the situation in the world and in Europe will drastically change, especially for us, for Russia.

We cannot but react to this real danger, all the more so since, let me repeat, Ukraine's Western patrons may help it acquire these weapons to create yet another threat to our country. We are seeing how persistently the Kiev regime is being pumped with arms. Since 2014, the United States alone has spent billions of dollars for this purpose, including supplies of arms and equipment and training of specialists. In the last few months, there has been a constant flow of Western weapons to Ukraine, ostentatiously, with the entire world watching. Foreign advisors supervise the activities of Ukraine's armed forces and special services and we are well aware of this.

Over the past few years, military contingents of NATO countries have been almost constantly present on Ukrainian territory under the pretext of exercises. The Ukrainian troop control system has already been integrated into NATO. This means that NATO headquarters can issue direct commands to the Ukrainian armed forces, even to their separate units and squads.

The United States and NATO have started an impudent development of Ukrainian territory as a theatre of potential military operations. Their regular joint exercises are obviously anti-Russian. Last year alone, over 23,000 troops and more than a thousand units of hardware were involved.

A law has already been adopted that allows foreign troops to come to Ukraine in 2022 to take part in multinational drills. Understandably, these are primarily NATO troops. This year, at least ten of these joint drills are planned.

Obviously, such undertakings are designed to be a cover-up for a rapid buildup of the NATO military group on Ukrainian territory. This is all the more so since the network of airfields upgraded with US help in Borispol, Ivano-Frankovsk, Chuguyev and Odessa, to name a few, is capable of transferring army units in a very short time. Ukraine's airspace is open to flights by US strategic and reconnaissance aircraft and drones that conduct surveillance over Russian territory.

I will add that the US-built Maritime Operations Center in Ochakov makes it possible to support activity by NATO warships, including the use of precision weapons, against the Russian Black Sea Fleet and our infrastructure on the entire Black Sea Coast.

At one time, the United States intended to build similar facilities in Crimea as well but the Crimeans and residents of Sevastopol wrecked these plans. We will always remember this.

I would like to repeat that today such a center has already been deployed in Ochakov. In the 18th century, soldiers of Alexander Suvorov fought for this city. Owing to their courage, it became part of Russia. Also in the 18th century, the lands of the Black Sea littoral, incorporated in Russia as a result of wars with the Ottoman Empire, were given the name of Novorossiya (New Russia). Now attempts are being made to condemn these landmarks of history to oblivion, along with the names of state and military figures of the Russian Empire without whose efforts modern Ukraine would not have many big cities or even access to the Black Sea.

A monument to Alexander Suvorov was recently demolished in Poltava. What is there to say? Are you renouncing your own past? The so-called colonial heritage of the Russian Empire? Well, in this case, be consistent.

Next, notably, Article 17 of the Constitution of Ukraine stipulates that deploying foreign military bases on its territory is illegal. However, as it turns out, this is just a conventionality that can be easily circumvented.

Ukraine is home to NATO training missions which are, in fact, foreign military bases. They just called a base a mission and were done with it.

Kiev has long proclaimed a strategic course on joining NATO. Indeed, each country is entitled to pick its own security system and enter into military alliances. There would be no problem with that, if it were not for one "but." International documents expressly stipulate the principle of equal and indivisible security, which includes obligations not to strengthen one's own security at the expense of the security of other states. This is stated in the 1999 OSCE Charter for European Security adopted in Istanbul and the 2010 OSCE Astana Declaration.

In other words, the choice of pathways towards ensuring security should not pose a threat to other states, whereas Ukraine joining NATO is a direct threat to Russia's security.

Let me remind you that at the Bucharest NATO summit held in April 2008, the United States pushed through a decision to the effect that Ukraine and, by the way, Georgia would become NATO members. Many European allies of the United States were well aware of the risks associated with this prospect already then, but were forced to put up with the will of their senior partner. The Americans simply used them to carry out a clearly anti-Russian policy.

A number of NATO member states are still very skeptical about Ukraine joining NATO. We are getting signals from some European capitals telling us not to worry since it will not happen literally overnight. In fact, our US partners are saying the same thing as well. "All right, then" we respond, "if it does not happen tomorrow, then it will happen the day after tomorrow. What does it change from the historical perspective? Nothing at all."

Furthermore, we are aware of the US leadership's position and words that active hostilities in eastern Ukraine do not rule out the possibility of that country joining NATO if it meets NATO criteria and overcomes corruption.

All the while, they are trying to convince us over and over again that NATO is a peace-loving and purely defensive alliance that poses no threat to Russia. Again, they want us to take their word for it. But we are well aware of the real value of these words. In 1990, when German unification was discussed, the United States promised the Soviet leadership that NATO jurisdiction or military presence will not expand one inch to the east and that the unification of Germany will not lead to the spread of NATO's military organization to the east. This is a quote.

They issued lots of verbal assurances, all of which turned out to be empty phrases. Later, they began to assure us that the accession to NATO by Central and Eastern European countries would only improve relations with Moscow, relieve these countries of the fears steeped in their bitter historical legacy, and even create a belt of countries that are friendly towards Russia.

However, the exact opposite happened. The governments of certain

Eastern European countries, speculating on Russophobia, brought their complexes and stereotypes about the Russian threat to the Alliance and insisted on building up the collective defense potentials and deploying them primarily against Russia. Worse still, that happened in the 1990s and the early 2000s when, thanks to our openness and goodwill, relations between Russia and the West had reached a high level.

Russia has fulfilled all of its obligations, including the pullout from Germany, from Central and Eastern Europe, making an immense contribution to overcoming the legacy of the Cold War. We have consistently proposed various cooperation options, including in the NATO-Russia Council and the OSCE formats.

Moreover, I will say something I have never said publicly, I will say it now for the first time. When then outgoing US President Bill Clinton visited Moscow in 2000, I asked him how America would feel about admitting Russia to NATO.

I will not reveal all the details of that conversation, but the reaction to my question was, let us say, quite restrained, and the Americans' true attitude to that possibility can actually be seen from their subsequent steps with regard to our country. I am referring to the overt support for terrorists in the North Caucasus, the disregard for our security demands and concerns, NATO's continued expansion, withdrawal from the ABM Treaty, and so on. It raises the question: why? What is all this about, what is the purpose? All right, you do not want to see us as friends or allies, but why make us an enemy?

There can be only one answer—this is not about our political regime or anything like that. They just do not need a big and independent country like Russia around. This is the answer to all questions. This is the source of America's traditional policy towards Russia. Hence the attitude to all our security proposals.

Today, one glance at the map is enough to see to what extent Western countries have kept their promise to refrain from NATO's eastward expansion. They just cheated. We have seen five waves of NATO expansion, one after another—Poland, the Czech Republic and Hungary were admitted in

1999; Bulgaria, Estonia, Latvia, Lithuania, Romania, Slovakia and Slovenia in 2004; Albania and Croatia in 2009; Montenegro in 2017; and North Macedonia in 2020.

As a result, the Alliance, its military infrastructure has reached Russia's borders. This is one of the key causes of the European security crisis; it has had the most negative impact on the entire system of international relations and led to the loss of mutual trust.

The situation continues to deteriorate, including in the strategic area. Thus, positioning areas for interceptor missiles are being established in Romania and Poland as part of the US project to create a global missile defense system. It is common knowledge that the launchers deployed there can be used for Tomahawk cruise missiles—offensive strike systems.

In addition, the United States is developing its all-purpose Standard Missile-6, which can provide air and missile defense, as well as strike ground and surface targets. In other words, the allegedly defensive US missile defense system is developing and expanding its new offensive capabilities.

The information we have gives us good reason to believe that Ukraine's accession to NATO and the subsequent deployment of NATO facilities has already been decided and is only a matter of time. We clearly understand that given this scenario, the level of military threats to Russia will increase dramatically, several times over. And I would like to emphasize at this point that the risk of a sudden strike at our country will multiply.

I will explain that American strategic planning documents confirm the possibility of a so-called preemptive strike at enemy missile systems. We also know the main adversary of the United States and NATO. It is Russia. NATO documents officially declare our country to be the main threat to Euro-Atlantic security. Ukraine will serve as an advanced bridgehead for such a strike. If our ancestors heard about this, they would probably simply not believe this. We do not want to believe this today either, but it is what it is. I would like people in Russia and Ukraine to understand this.

Many Ukrainian airfields are located not far from our borders. NATO's tactical aviation deployed there, including precision weapon carriers, will be capable of striking at our territory to the depth of the Volgograd-Kazan-Samara-Astrakhan line. The deployment of reconnaissance radars on Ukrainian territory will allow NATO to tightly control Russia's airspace up to the Urals.

Finally, after the US destroyed the INF Treaty, the Pentagon has been openly developing many land-based attack weapons, including ballistic missiles that are capable of hitting targets at a distance of up to 5,500 km. If deployed in Ukraine, such systems will be able to hit targets in Russia's entire European part. The flying time of Tomahawk cruise missiles to Moscow will be less than 35 minutes; ballistic missiles from Kharkov will take seven to eight minutes; and hypersonic assault weapons, four to five minutes. It is like a knife to the throat. I have no doubt that they hope to carry out these plans, as they did many times in the past, expanding NATO eastward, moving their military infrastructure to Russian borders and fully ignoring our concerns, protests and warnings. Excuse me, but they simply did not care at all about such things and did whatever they deemed necessary.

Of course, they are going to behave in the same way in the future, following a well-known proverb: "The dogs bark but the caravan goes on." Let me say right away—we do not accept this behavior and will never accept it. That said, Russia has always advocated the resolution of the most complicated problems by political and diplomatic means, at the negotiating table.

We are well aware of our enormous responsibility when it comes to regional and global stability. Back in 2008, Russia put forth an initiative to conclude a European Security Treaty under which not a single Euro-Atlantic state or international organization could strengthen their security at the expense of the security of others. However, our proposal was rejected right off the bat on the pretext that Russia should not be allowed to put limits on NATO activities.

Furthermore, it was made explicitly clear to us that only NATO members can have legally binding security guarantees.

Last December, we handed over to our Western partners a draft treaty between the Russian Federation and the United States of America on security guarantees, as well as a draft agreement on measures to ensure the security of the Russian Federation and NATO member states.

The United States and NATO responded with general statements. There were kernels of rationality in them as well, but they concerned matters of secondary importance and it all looked like an attempt to drag the issue out and to lead the discussion astray.

We responded to this accordingly and pointed out that we were ready to follow the path of negotiations, provided, however, that all issues are considered as a package that includes Russia's core proposals which contain three key points. First, to prevent further NATO expansion. Second, to have the Alliance refrain from deploying assault weapon systems on Russian borders. And finally, rolling back the bloc's military capability and infrastructure in Europe to where they were in 1997, when the NATO-Russia Founding Act was signed.

These principled proposals of ours have been ignored. To reiterate, our Western partners have once again vocalized the all-too-familiar formulas that each state is entitled to freely choose ways to ensure its security or to join any military union or alliance. That is, nothing has changed in their stance, and we keep hearing the same old references to NATO's notorious "open door" policy. Moreover, they are again trying to blackmail us and are threatening us with sanctions, which, by the way, they will introduce no matter what as Russia continues to strengthen its sovereignty and its Armed Forces. To be sure, they will never think twice before coming up with or just fabricating a pretext for yet another sanction attack regardless of the developments in Ukraine. Their one and only goal is to hold back the development of Russia. And they will keep doing so, just as they did before, even without any formal pretext just because we exist and will never compromise our sovereignty, national interests or values.

I would like to be clear and straightforward: in the current circumstances, when our proposals for an equal dialogue on fundamental issues have actually remained unanswered by the United States and NATO, when the level of threats to our country has increased significantly, Russia has every right to respond in order to ensure its security. That is exactly what we will do.

With regard to the state of affairs in Donbass, we see that the ruling Kiev elites never stop publicly making clear their unwillingness to comply with the Minsk Package of Measures to settle the conflict and are not interested in a peaceful settlement. On the contrary, they are trying to orchestrate a blitz-krieg in Donbass as was the case in 2014 and 2015. We all know how these reckless schemes ended.

Not a single day goes by without Donbass communities coming under shelling attacks. The recently formed large military force makes use of attack drones, heavy equipment, missiles, artillery and multiple rocket launchers. The killing of civilians, the blockade, the abuse of people, including chil-dren, women and the elderly, continues unabated. As we say, there is no end in sight to this.

Meanwhile, the so-called civilized world, which our Western colleagues proclaimed themselves the only representatives of, prefers not to see this, as if this horror and genocide, which almost 4 million people are facing, do not exist. But they do exist and only because these people did not agree with the West-supported coup in Ukraine in 2014 and opposed the transition towards the Neanderthal and aggressive nationalism and neo-Nazism which have been elevated in Ukraine to the rank of national policy. They are fighting for their elementary right to live on their own land, to speak their own language, and to preserve their culture and traditions.

How long can this tragedy continue? How much longer can one put up with this? Russia has done everything to preserve Ukraine's territorial integ-rity. All these years, it has persistently and patiently pushed for the imple-mentation of UN Security Council Resolution 2202 of February 17, 2015, which consolidated the Minsk Package of Measures of February 12, 2015, to settle the situation in Donbass.

Everything was in vain. Presidents and Rada deputies come and go, but deep down the aggressive and nationalistic regime that seized power in Kiev remains unchanged. It is entirely a product of the 2014 coup, and those who then embarked on the path of violence, bloodshed and lawlessness did not recognize then and do not recognize now any solution to the Donbass issue other than a military one.

In this regard, I consider it necessary to take a long overdue decision and to immediately recognize the independence and sovereignty of the Donetsk People's Republic and the Luhansk People's Republic.

I would like to ask the Federal Assembly of the Russian Federation to support this decision and then ratify the Treaty of Friendship and Mutual Assistance with both republics. These two documents will be prepared and signed shortly.

We want those who seized and continue to hold power in Kiev to immediately stop hostilities. Otherwise, the responsibility for the possible continuation of the bloodshed will lie entirely on the conscience of Ukraine's ruling regime.

As I announce the decisions taken today, I remain confident in the support of Russia's citizens and the country's patriotic forces.

Thank you.

Appendix 2

The Budapest Memorandum of 1994

The following is the text of the Memorandum on Security Assurances, known as the Budapest Memorandum, in connection with Ukraine's accession to the Treaty on the Non-Proliferation of Nuclear Weapons, signed December 5, 1994.

The United States of America, the Russian Federation, and the United Kingdom of Great Britain and Northern Ireland,

Welcoming the accession of Ukraine to the Treaty on the Non-Proliferation of Nuclear Weapons as a non-nuclear-weapon State, Taking into account the commitment of Ukraine to eliminate all nuclear weapons from its territory within a specified period of time,

Noting the changes in the world-wide security situation, including the end of the Cold War, which have brought about conditions for deep reductions in nuclear forces.

Confirm the following:
1. The United States of America, the Russian Federation, and the United Kingdom of Great Britain and Northern Ireland, reaffirm their commitment

to Ukraine, in accordance with the principles of the CSCE [Commission on Security and Cooperation in Europe] Final Act, to respect the Independence and Sovereignty and the existing borders of Ukraine.

2. The United States of America, the Russian Federation, and the United Kingdom of Great Britain and Northern Ireland, reaffirm their obligation to refrain from the threat or use of force against the territorial integrity or political independence of Ukraine, and that none of their weapons will ever be used against Ukraine except in self-defense or otherwise in accordance with the Charter of the United Nations.

3. The United States of America, the Russian Federation, and the United Kingdom of Great Britain and Northern Ireland, reaffirm their commitment to Ukraine, in accordance with the principles of the CSCE Final Act, to refrain from economic coercion designed to subordinate to their own interest the exercise by Ukraine of the rights inherent in its sovereignty and thus to secure advantages of any kind.

4. The United States of America, the Russian Federation, and the United Kingdom of Great Britain and Northern Ireland, reaffirm their commitment to seek immediate United Nations Security Council action to provide assistance to Ukraine, as a non-nuclear-weapon State Party to the Treaty on the Non-Proliferation of Nuclear Weapons, if Ukraine should become a victim of an act of aggression or an object of a threat of aggression in which nuclear weapons are used.

5. The United States of America, the Russian Federation, and the United Kingdom of Great Britain and Northern Ireland, reaffirm, in the case of the Ukraine, their commitment not to use nuclear weapons against any non-nuclear-weapon State Party to the Treaty on the Non-Proliferation of Nuclear Weapons, except in the case of an attack on themselves, their territories or dependent territories, their armed forces, or their allies, by such a state in association or alliance with a nuclear weapon state.

6. The United States of America, the Russian Federation, and the United Kingdom of Great Britain and Northern Ireland will consult in the event a situation arises which raises a question concerning these commitments.

This Memorandum will become applicable upon signature.

Signed in four copies having equal validity in the

English, Russian and Ukrainian languages

Source: Harvard Kennedy School. Harvard University.
https://policymemos.hks.harvard.edu/links/ukraine-budapest-memorandum-1994

Appendix 3

The North Atlantic Treaty

Washington D.C. - 4 April 1949

The Parties to this Treaty reaffirm their faith in the purposes and principles of the Charter of the United Nations and their desire to live in peace with all peoples and all governments.

They are determined to safeguard the freedom, common heritage and civilization of their peoples, founded on the principles of democracy, individual liberty and the rule of law. They seek to promote stability and well-being in the North Atlantic area.

They are resolved to unite their efforts for collective defense and for the preservation of peace and security. They therefore agree to this North Atlantic Treaty:

Article 1
The Parties undertake, as set forth in the Charter of the United Nations, to settle any international dispute in which they may be involved by peaceful means in such a manner that international peace and security and justice are not endangered, and to refrain in their international relations from the threat or use of force in any manner inconsistent with the purposes of the United Nations.

Article 2

The Parties will contribute toward the further development of peaceful and friendly international relations by strengthening their free institutions, by bringing about a better understanding of the principles upon which these institutions are founded, and by promoting conditions of stability and well-being. They will seek to eliminate conflict in their international economic policies and will encourage economic collaboration between any or all of them.

Article 3

In order more effectively to achieve the objectives of this Treaty, the Parties, separately and jointly, by means of continuous and effective self-help and mutual aid, will maintain and develop their individual and collective capacity to resist armed attack.

Article 4

The Parties will consult together whenever, in the opinion of any of them, the territorial integrity, political independence or security of any of the Parties is threatened.

Article 5

The Parties agree that an armed attack against one or more of them in Europe or North America shall be considered an attack against them all and consequently they agree that, if such an armed attack occurs, each of them, in exercise of the right of individual or collective self-defense recognized by Article 51 of the Charter of the United Nations, will assist the Party or Parties so attacked by taking forthwith, individually and in concert with the other Parties, such action as it deems necessary, including the use of armed force, to restore and maintain the security of the North Atlantic area.

Any such armed attack and all measures taken as a result thereof shall immediately be reported to the Security Council. Such measures shall be terminated when the Security Council has taken the measures necessary to restore and maintain international peace and security .

Article 6[1]

For the purpose of Article 5, an armed attack on one or more of the Parties is deemed to include an armed attack:

on the territory of any of the Parties in Europe or North America, on the Algerian Departments of France[2], on the territory of Turkey or on the Islands under the jurisdiction of any of the Parties in the North Atlantic area north of the Tropic of Cancer;

on the forces, vessels, or aircraft of any of the Parties, when in or over these territories or any other area in Europe in which occupation forces of any of the Parties were stationed on the date when the Treaty entered into force or the Mediterranean Sea or the North Atlantic area north of the Tropic of Cancer.

Article 7

This Treaty does not affect, and shall not be interpreted as affecting in any way the rights and obligations under the Charter of the Parties which are members of the United Nations, or the primary responsibility of the Security Council for the maintenance of international peace and security.

Article 8

Each Party declares that none of the international engagements now in force between it and any other of the Parties or any third State is in conflict with the provisions of this Treaty, and undertakes not to enter into any international engagement in conflict with this Treaty.

---

1. The definition of the territories to which Article 5 applies was revised by Article 2 of the Protocol to the North Atlantic Treaty on the accession of Greece and Turkey signed on 22 October 1951.

2. On January 16, 1963, the North Atlantic Council noted that insofar as the former Algerian Departments of France were concerned, the relevant clauses of this Treaty had become inapplicable as from July 3, 1962.

Article 9

The Parties hereby establish a Council, on which each of them shall be represented, to consider matters concerning the implementation of this Treaty. The Council shall be so organised as to be able to meet promptly at any time. The Council shall set up such subsidiary bodies as may be necessary; in particular it shall establish immediately a defense committee which shall recommend measures for the implementation of Articles 3 and 5.

Article 10

The Parties may, by unanimous agreement, invite any other European State in a position to further the principles of this Treaty and to contribute to the security of the North Atlantic area to accede to this Treaty. Any State so invited may become a Party to the Treaty by depositing its instrument of accession with the Government of the United States of America. The Government of the United States of America will inform each of the Parties of the deposit of each such instrument of accession.

Article 11

This Treaty shall be ratified and its provisions carried out by the Parties in accordance with their respective constitutional processes. The instruments of ratification shall be deposited as soon as possible with the Government of the United States of America, which will notify all the other signatories of each deposit. The Treaty shall enter into force between the States which have ratified it as soon as the ratifications of the majority of the signatories, including the ratifications of Belgium, Canada, France, Luxembourg, the Netherlands, the United Kingdom and the United States, have been deposited and shall come into effect with respect to other States on the date of the deposit of their ratifications.[3]

Article 12

After the Treaty has been in force for ten years, or at any time thereafter, the

----

3. The Treaty came into force on 24 August 1949, after the deposition of the ratifications of all signatory states.

Parties shall, if any of them so requests, consult together for the purpose of reviewing the Treaty, having regard for the factors then affecting peace and security in the North Atlantic area, including the development of universal as well as regional arrangements under the Charter of the United Nations for the maintenance of international peace and security.

Article 13

After the Treaty has been in force for twenty years, any Party may cease to be a Party one year after its notice of denunciation has been given to the Government of the United States of America, which will inform the Governments of the other Parties of the deposit of each notice of denunciation.

Article 14

This Treaty, of which the English and French texts are equally authentic, shall be deposited in the archives of the Government of the United States of America. Duly certified copies will be transmitted by that Government to the Governments of other signatories.

Source: The North Atlantic Treaty Organization:
https://www.nato.int/cps/en/natohq/official_texts_17120.htm

Appendix 4

Letter to Biden from Concerned Republicans in Congress

April 20, 2023

The Honorable Joseph R. Biden
President of the United States
The White House
1600 Pennsylvania Avenue NW
Washington, DC 20500

Dear President Biden,

We write to express concern regarding the U.S. response to Ukraine. Over a year ago, Russia launched an invasion that has upended decades of peace in Europe. We are deeply concerned that the trajectory of U.S. aid to the Ukrainian war effort threatens further escalation and lacks much-needed strategic clarity.

Over the past year, the U.S. has been the principal financier of the Ukrainian defense effort. As the war enters its second year, there is no end in sight and no clear strategy to bring this war to a close. A proxy war with Russia in Ukraine is not in the strategic interest of the United States and risks an escalation that could spiral out of control.

The recently announced shipments of M1 Abrams tanks will require months of training and transport.[1] Ground Launched Small Diameter Bombs will similarly take months to arrive.[2] These announcements signal that your administration is settling in for a long-term conflict. The current strategy of sanctions and drawn-out aid will only prolong the conflict, leading to escalation and more violence. Our national and economic security demand an alternative. Unrestrained U.S. aid for Ukraine must come to an end, and we will adamantly oppose all future aid packages unless they are linked to a clear diplomatic strategy designed to bring this war to a rapid conclusion.

To date, the U.S. has committed over $113 billion in military, economic, and humanitarian assistance to Ukraine,[3] becoming its single largest bene-factor. The contributions of our NATO allies pale in comparison. Beyond dollar value, there is also a stark difference in substance and motivation. As the U.S. is further indebting itself to provide tanks, air defense systems, missiles, and long-range rockets to a battlefield an ocean away, those with conflict at their borders have been content to send uniforms and personal protective equipment. Our allies condition their contributions of major military equipment on a corresponding U.S. commitment - all while calling for the U.S. to do more.[4]

With every new aid package and every new weapon provided to Ukraine,

---

1. Matthew Lee & Lolita Baldor, "In reversal, US poised to approve Abrams tanks for Ukraine." Associated Press, January 24, 2023.

2. David Axe, "Ukraine's new rocket-boosted glide-bombs can turn around and hit targets on the backs of hills, 90 miles away." Forbes, February 3, 2023.

3. Committee for a Responsible Federal Budget, "Congress approved $113 billion of aid to Ukraine in 2022." January 5, 2023.

4. Elena Cherney & Bojan Pancevski, "Berlin won't allow exports of German tanks to Ukraine unless U.S. sends its own." The Wall Street Journal, January 18, 2023.

the risk of direct conflict with Russia climbs. The decision to issue High Mobility Artillery Rocket Systems (HIMARS) to Ukraine last June was seen as a serious provocation, given the enhanced capabilities these weapons afforded.[5] At the time, the HIMARS sent by the U.S. doubled Ukraine's strike range. Now, casting risk aside, we seem prepared to double Ukraine's range yet again with even longer-range weapons systems. Similarly, the U.S. reversed course on sending tanks, an action that was once considered to be too inflammatory.

Our military assistance goes beyond tangible assets to include military training[6] and intelligence support.[7] The extent of our aid makes it increasingly difficult to deny Russian accusations of U.S. complicity in a proxy war. Vladimir Putin's advisors are already framing the conflict as "a military confrontation between Russia and NATO, and above all the United States and Britain.[8]" Russian tolerance for fighting a proxy war with NATO could run out at any point. The decision to invade Ukraine should be evidence enough of Putin's willingness to use military force and should give us pause in continuing to push the limits at the risk of catastrophe.

While the pace of our aid would suggest otherwise, the U.S. is in no position to expend $113 billion reinforcing a foreign military as our own military atrophies. Time and again, the executive branch has used debt as a tool to finance foreign wars to the detriment of the American taxpayer. Of the total aid allocated for Ukraine, $27 billion is designated for economic support including funding the Ukrainian government, repairing infrastructure, and

---

5. Valerie Insinna, "US to provide 4 HIMARS systems to Ukraine in latest $700M arms package." Breaking Defense, June 1, 2022.

6. C. Todd Lopez, "Ukrainian troops headed to U.S. for Patriot missile training." U.S. Department of Defense, January 10, 2023.

7. Warren Strobel, "U.S. has eased intelligence-sharing rules to help Ukraine target Russians." The Wall Street Journal, December 21, 2022.

8. Guy Faulconbridge, "Russia is now fighting NATO in Ukraine, top Putin ally says." Reuters, January 10, 2023.

food security.[9] Meanwhile, the U.S. reached the $31.4 trillion debt ceiling weeks ago and is risking the first-ever default. To prop up a foreign government that is historically mired in corruption while the American people suffer from record inflation and a crippling national debt is wildly irresponsible on its own - but to do so while our military contends with aging weapons systems and depleted stockpiles is disgraceful.

For nearly a year, your administration has poured aid into Ukraine at the expense of U.S. military readiness. Supplies that will take years to replenish are being exhausted by Ukraine in a matter of weeks. Ukraine is currently burning through more 155mm artillery rounds in one month than the U.S. can produce in six. We have given more Javelins to Ukraine than can be made in four years.[10] As we demand that industry ramp up production of HIMARS, Javelins, and Stingers to support Ukraine, our allies are left with delivery backlogs for these same weapons. Should our actions entangle us in a confrontation with Russia now or should conflict erupt in the Indo-Pacific in the coming years, we fear that our military will be woefully unprepared to meet these challenges as a direct result of what has been shipped to Ukraine. The top responsibility of the President and the only mission of the Department of Defense is to ensure U.S. national security. To push the limits of our readiness is to disregard this mission.

As the U.S. capacity to respond to threats is being degraded, your strategy in Ukraine is pushing our two greatest adversaries closer together. Russia and China's burgeoning alliance has only become stronger in the past year. In early February 2022, Putin and Xi reminded the world of their "no limits"

---

9. Committee for a Responsible Federal Budget, "Congress approved $113 billion of aid to Ukraine in 2022." January 5, 2023.

10. Per the State Department fact sheet "U.S. Security Cooperation with Ukraine," last updated March 20, 2023, the U.S. has provided over 1,500,000 155mm artillery rounds to Ukraine and over 8,500 Javelin anti-armor systems. Current production of 155mm artillery is 14,000 per month - Ukraine's monthly consumption is approximately 100,000. Current production of Javelins is 2,100 per year.

partnership in their first face-to-face meeting in two years.[11] Russia would invade Ukraine by the end of that month, with no condemnation from China. In the months since, trade and energy cooperation soared to new highs, with plans for a Power of Siberia 2 gas pipeline gaining momentum. Multiple air and naval drills in the past year also signal deepening military cooperation between the two countries. These drills have been days long and have involved thousands of troops, dozens of warships, and nuclear-capable bombers. Both China and Russia see the U.S. as inextricably opposed to their interests and security. The depth of U.S. involvement in Ukraine only gives credence to this narrative.

Open-ended U.S. aid to Ukraine is fundamentally incompatible with our strategic interests. A simple reading of the 2022 National Security Strategy admits as much. The strategy acknowledges China as "the only competitor with both the intent to reshape the international order and, increasingly, the economic, diplomatic, military, and technological power to do it.[12]" Yet, U.S. action in the past year would suggest otherwise.

There are appropriate ways in which the U.S. can support the Ukrainian people, but unlimited arms supplies in support of an endless war is not one of them. Our national interests, and those of the Ukrainian people, are best served by incentivizing the negotiations that are urgently needed to bring this conflict to a resolution. We strongly urge you to advocate for a negotiated peace between the two sides, bringing this awful conflict to a close.

Sincerely,

(Signed)

---

11. Guy Faulconbridge & Simon Lewis, "U.S. concerned by China-Russia ties as Putin signals Xi visit." Reuters, February 22, 2023.

12. White House "National Security Strategy," October 2022.

United States Senators:

Michael S. Lee
Rand Paul, M.D.
JD Vance

Members of Congress:

Laurne Boebert
Tim Burchett
Matt Gaetz
Anna Paulina Luna
Mary E. Miller
Eli Crane
Andy Biggs
Dan Bishop
Josh Brecheen
Matt Rosendale
Marjorie Taylor Greene
Barry Moore
Ralph Norman
Andy Ogles
Mike Collins
Paul A. Gosar, D.D.S.

The Biblical Roots for the Divine Providence

Why War is Sometimes Necessary

We would all like to live in a world that is without war. We imagine that world to be a place where weapons would not be needed as all the people would be committed to solving their differences peacefully. This aspiration is beautifully expressed in Isaiah 2:4:

> He shall judge between the nations,
>   and shall decide for many peoples;
> and they shall beat their swords into plowshares,
>   and their spears into pruning hooks;
> nation shall not lift up sword against nation,
>   neither shall they learn war any more.

The "He" in this passage is God, and the great prophet Isaiah is describing a world under the dominion of God. This is the world of God's original intension, which was lost through the Fall of Adam and Eve. As discussed in Chapter 16, the purpose of the Divine Providence is to recreate that original world, but the path the providence must take to get to its destination cannot avoid war because evil stands in the way of the providence. The nature of evil is violent and destructive, and if it cannot be countered and defeated by peaceful means, it must be stopped by force.

There are some favorite cliches about war and peace that miss this point. One comes from British Labour Party politician Tony Benn: "All war represents a failure of diplomacy."[1] If this statement was true, history would judge Chamberlain right and Churchill wrong. Britain went to war against Hitler's Germany not because Chamberlain failed in his diplomacy but because he did not recognize that Hitler was using diplomacy not to seek peace but to prepare for war. Churchill did recognize this truth and concluded that no diplomacy could stop Hitler's aggression. Only a stronger army could stop Hitler—making war with Germany inevitable.

Thus war itself is not necessarily evil. It can be a necessary tool to end evil. By the same token, diplomacy and negotiations are not necessarily preferable to war—if they lead to more evil they can be worse than war. Thus wars of aggression, such as the Russian invasion of Ukraine, are unjustified and therefore evil. But wars fought to protect human freedom and defeat evil, are justified and therefore good.

The moral position to take vis a vis the war in Ukraine is that the Russian aggressors are on the side of evil and the Ukrainians on the side of good. Thus to advance good it is not sufficient to simply *end* the war, but rather to support Ukraine so that it can *win* the war.

Aggressors Exploit the Universal Desire for Peace

The predatory mind of the aggressor knows that most people prefer peace to war and will therefore seek to exploit this desire by employing the language of peace to shroud his war-making in the hope that this will lull his enemies into a pacifist posture. This was Hitler's stratagem with Chamberlain.

There is another perfect example of this stratagem. On December 4, 1959, the Soviet Union gifted the United Nations a large bronze statue of

1. Tony Benn. February 28, 1991. *Speech to the House of Commons.*

a man beating a sword into plowshares. The artwork took its title from the passage in Isaiah quoted above: "Let Us Beat Swords Into Plowshares."[2]

At the time, the USSR was the leading Communist nation in the world. It had been created through a violent revolution and then wars of conquest. It had consistently expanded its global influence through aggression, including the military occupation of its neighbors and the sponsorship of numerous violent revolutions around the world. Furthermore, the ruling ideology of the Soviet Union, Marxism-Leninism, was an atheistic theory of revolution and dictatorial rule based on the necessity of using violence to acquire and retain power.

In other words, Moscow had no interest whatsoever in promoting world peace but it did see the benefit of making a show of giving a statue to the UN in the name of working for peace, since this would likely deceive many into believing Communist propaganda and thereby making the rapid expansion of the USSR that much easier.

The same type of deception is at the heart of Russian propaganda today. Putin would have us believe that his invasion of Ukraine was in the interest of protecting the Russian minorities there, freeing the Ukrainian people from Nazi tyranny, and preventing the dangerous expansion of NATO—which he said could lead to a new world war.

All too many people in the West have taken Putin at his word and blame the US and NATO for causing this war by helping Ukraine defend itself against the Russian invasion. The truth is that Ukraine—like Britain in 1939—has been given no alternative but to respond to Russia's invasion with all the military power it can muster. If it did not resist militarily, Ukraine would have been overrun by the Russian army in a matter of days.

With everything we know about the Soviet legacy of Russia under Putin, there should be no confusion as to which side is responsible for this war or

---

2. United Nations. December 5, 1959. *Let us beat swords into plowshares.* United Nations Gifts. https://www.un.org/ungifts/let-us-beat-swords-ploughshares

the legitimacy and importance of the West supporting Ukraine so that it can defeat Russia.

The ultimate significance of the war in Ukraine can best be understood in terms of the contest between good and evil. This framework exposes Russia's barbaric behavior as typical of the forces of destruction that have plagued the world since the first humans walked the earth. It also provides a deeper meaning to the current suffering of Ukraine and the reasons it is so necessary for the world to support Ukraine if we are to see the better world we all aspire to live in.

The Origin of Good and Evil in Scriptures

The origin of good and evil can be found in the scriptures of the Abrahamic faiths: Judaism, Christianity and Islam. These scriptures contain accounts of the original creation of the world in the image of a good God, the subsequent deception and seduction of the first woman, Eve, by the jealous archangel Lucifer, the consequent seduction of Adam by Eve, and finally the resultant alienation from God of the original family.

This, then, is the story of the advent of evil on earth through the Fall of the first man and woman into sin and ignorance. Through the Fall, the once-good Lucifer became Satan and the once sinless Adam and Eve became the ancestors of a world under Satan's dominion.

Furthermore, the Fall set up what became a contest between the forces of good and evil that manifests in history and the world around us as a contest between the Divine Providence and a Satanic Anti-Providence. The Divine Providence is God's work to realize the original ideal of creation—a sinless world of peace-loving individuals and families—which we call heaven, while the Satanic Anti-Providence aims to destroy this ideal and put in its place a Godless Utopia, which we call hell.

Some will likely complain that the scriptural story cannot be trusted as truth because it comes to us from pre-history, which of course it does. But we would argue that its value lies not in its historical accuracy but in what it reveals about the origin and nature of good and evil, which themselves are primordial.

And we would point out that myth can be a powerful way to communicate truth, as we showed in our discussion of J.R.R. Tolkien's *The Lord of the Rings*, in Chapter 16. Tolkien explained why myth is particularly important for understanding good and evil:

> Just as speech is invention about objects and ideas, so myth is invention about truth. We have come from God, and inevitably the myths woven by us, though they contain error, will also reflect a splintered fragment of the true light, the eternal truth that is with God. Indeed, only by mythmaking, only by becoming a 'sub-creator' and inventing stories, can Man ascribe to the state of perfection that he knew before the Fall.[3]

The Cain and Abel Archetypes of Good and Evil

It's worth examining the Genesis story of the Fall in some detail, especially as it describes the inception of the Divine Providence and the Satanic Anti-Providence through Cain and Abel, the sons of Adam and Eve.

Here is the Genesis account of Lucifer's deception of Eve that led to the Fall:

> And the woman said to the serpent, "We may eat of the fruit of the trees of the garden; but God said, 'You shall not eat of the fruit of the tree which is in the midst of the garden, neither shall you touch it, lest you die.'" But the serpent said to the woman, "You will not die. For God knows that when you eat of it your eyes will be opened, and you will be like God, knowing good and evil.'" (RSV: Genesis 3:2-5)

Genesis goes on to explain that first Eve and then Adam succumbed to the temptation to "eat of the fruit." Once they had ignored the risk of (spiritual) death and engaged in illicit relationships (Eve with Lucifer and then with an immature Adam), they immediately recognized that they had been

---

3. J.R.R. Tolkien in Humphrey Carpenter. 1977. *J.R.R. Tolkien: A Biography*. George Allen & Unwin, pp197-198.

deceived into making a catastrophic mistake. They hid their nakedness from God in shame, but were expelled from the Garden of Eden because they no longer had the purity to remain there.

Thus evil took hold in the first human family, from which point it was embedded in human nature and lineage as a tendency to misuse God's blessings for selfish and Satanic purposes. This corruption of the original image of God in human beings became a tool for Satan to attack people and induce them to sin.

And because sinfulness became part of every person, men and women lacked the pure nature that would have allowed them to recognize the difference between good and evil, and thereby rid themselves of evil. Thus it became necessary for relative good to be separated from that which was more evil, so that the better could lead the worse towards participation in the Divine Providence.

This process of separation and purification was first attempted in the providence when Cain and Abel revealed different attitudes to God and each other. Cain was the oldest son who inherited the brunt of fallen nature from his parents and therefore represented relative evil. Abel was the second son who was relatively closer to God than Cain and therefore represented relative good.

The difference between Cain and Abel became evident when they were called by God to offer sacrifices—Cain's was rejected by God while Abel's was accepted. As the New Testament letter to Hebrews explained:

> By faith Abel offered to God a more acceptable sacrifice than Cain, through which he received approval as righteous, God bearing witness by accepting his gifts. (Hebrews 11:4)

However, a jealous and resentful Cain could not accept his seemingly lesser status and was unwilling to humble himself to his younger brother, Abel, whom he murdered in a fit of jealous rage. His bitter jealousy mirrored that of Lucifer towards Adam and Eve, whom the angel saw growing in beauty and goodness as they prepared to receive great blessings from God.

Jordan Peterson explained the historical significance of Cain's murder of Abel:

> Cain and Abel are "prototypical human beings… Humanity enters history at the end of the story of Adam and Eve, and then the archetypal patterns of human behavior are instantaneously presented… The first two human beings engage in a fratricidal struggle that ends in the death of the best one of them. That's the story of human beings in history."[4]

Indeed it is. History is replete with examples of Cain and Abel relationships that are typically conflictual. Out of this history the Cain-type character emerges as irresponsible: selfish, jealous, accusatory and willing to kill Abel to get his way. In contrast, the Abel-type character is responsible: selfless, forgiving and loving of others. And Abel's virtue is best demonstrated by the fact that he is willing to sacrifice himself in order to save Cain from evil.

Because Cain murdered his brother, no purification of fallen humanity occurred in the first family and evil multiplied instead.

The Cain-Abel Paradigm

Because we all inherit both good and evil tendencies in our nature, getting rid of evil is not just a matter of identifying and then eliminating evil people, institutions and governments. That would be relatively simple. Rather, for good to prevail evil must be defeated and ultimately removed from the nature of fallen humanity altogether. This is the only way for God's original good purpose to be realized.

The Cain-Abel paradigm is the process by which this can be accomplished, and therefore the process through which the Divine Providence unfolds.

How does it work? The good and evil in fallen humanity are externalized and represented by two individuals. One is closer to God and therefore

---

4. Jordan B. Peterson. 2017. Biblical Series V: *Cain and Abel: The Hostile Brothers*. Video: https://www.youtube.com/watch?v=44f3mxcsI50; Transcript: https://www.jordanbpeterson.com/transcripts/biblical-series-v/

able to guide the other away from the path of the Satanic Anti-Providence and to the path of the Divine Providence.

Using the first family as the template for this process, Abel was closer to God than Cain and therefore responsible to overcome his own fallen nature in order to love his older brother and save him from evil. For his part, Cain had to overcome his own fallen nature and accept the love and guidance of Abel by humbling himself to his younger brother.

Thus for the providence to advance, both Cain and Abel have to overcome their tendencies to do evil in order to undergo internal purification and to be reconciled on God's terms. When they accomplish this reconciliation, they are both elevated spiritually and contribute to the fulfillment of God's will.

The notion that human beings can live at peace in a world under God's dominion (as Isaiah prophesized) may well seem fantastical for us who live in a world that often seems to be dominated by evil. This is especially so since even the men and women who are normally held up as examples of virtue—such as the saints—themselves experience internal struggles between their desire to do good and the reality of their fallen nature which wants them to do evil.

Saint Paul described this universal struggle in his letter to Romans:

> For I do not do the good I want, but the evil I do not want is what I do. Now if I do what I do not want, it is no longer I that do it, but sin which dwells within me. So I find it to be a law that when I want to do right, evil lies close at hand. For I delight in the law of God, in my inmost self, but I see in my members another law at war with the law of my mind and making me captive to the law of sin which dwells in my members. Wretched man that I am! Who will deliver me from this body of death? (RSV: Romans 7:19-24)

What answer does Paul offer to this rhetorical question? He says that Jesus is the solution to his problem of sin, although he continued to experience an internal conflict:

> Thanks be to God through Jesus Christ our Lord! So then, I of myself
> serve the law of God with my mind, but with my flesh I serve the law
> of sin. (Romans 7:25)

This testimony of Paul to the saving grace of Jesus is consistent with the hope of humankind that a sinless man, a second Adam, will appear and provide an absolute standard of good that enables us to recognize the dark side of our fallen nature, and work to overcome it.

In this context, Benjamin Franklin offered some hope and practical advice regarding how we can grow in maturity as individuals and thereby contribute to a more peaceful world. The key is for individuals to overcome their fallen, Cain-type nature.

He said "Be at war with your vices, at peace with your neighbors, and let every new year find you a better man."[5] This is the process that prepares us to recognize and follow the absolute Abel.

The Cain-Abel paradigm is the key to understanding our inner struggles with evil, but it also explains the relationship between the Divine Providence and Satanic Anti-Providence. In the same way that a person becomes better when he or she overcomes their vices, so too the world becomes a better place when Abel-type people, institutions, nations and ideas win out over Cain-type counterparts. This is how the Divine Providence advances.

For a Biblical example: When Jacob (in the Abel position) prevailed against Esau (in the Cain position) the two brothers were eventually reconciled on God's terms, enabling both to be blessed and the providence to advance from the level of Jacob's family to the establishment of the chosen nation of Israel.

The ultimate goal of this Cain-Abel process in the Old Testament era was to prepare a nation for a sinless Adam to come as an Absolute Abel who could fulfill the purpose of the providence. Thus the mission of the 12 tribes of Israel (Jacob was called Israel after he won a contest with an angel) was to prepare that nation to accept the Messiah, their savior.

---

5. Benjamin Franklin. 1755. *Poor Richard's Almanac.*

Cain and Abel in the Divine Providence

The Cain-Abel paradigm reveals how the invisible hand of the Divine Providence has worked in the past and is working today. The ultimate destiny of the providence is unchanging and so God is constantly seeking out Abel-type figures to guide those willing to follow along the providential path to the realization of heaven on earth.

History shows that when Abel is successful in winning over Cain, the providence advances and both Abel and Cain receive God's blessings. However, when Cain refuses to follow Abel, the providence is delayed, and neither is blessed. In other words, when Abel wins, both Cain and Abel win and are blessed, but when Cain wins, both Cain and Abel lose.

We gave the Biblical example of both Jacob and Esau being blessed once they had reconciled on God's terms. There is also the example of Cain and Abel themselves. When Cain killed Abel he was cursed. Abel was prevented from serving the providence, which then shifted to the lineage of their younger brother, Seth. But it was many generations before God could raise up another major Abel figure, Noah.

To choose a more recent example that we have already touched on, we can look to the major conflicts of the 20th century for examples of the Cain-Abel paradigm at work. Because WWI did not end with a complete German surrender to the Allies, Cain-type German militarism was able to survive this initial defeat, regroup, rearm and then initiate an even bigger war. Both Germany and its Central Powers allies, as well as the more Abel-type allies opposing them, lost millions of lives and much treasure in the First World War, but they lost even more in the Second World War.

Only after Germany was thoroughly defeated and surrendered unconditionally to the Allies to end WWII in Europe was its Cain-type militarism finally stamped out, and both Germany and its former enemies could then both prosper and work together to create a more peaceful world.

The examples of Jacob and Esau, the Allies and Germany, do offer hope that humanity can progress towards a more Godly world. And, as the words from Saint Paul and Benjamin Franklin indicate, the key to realizing the ideal of a heavenly world is for every person to be purified and made better through overcoming their fallen, Cain-type nature. This is precisely what Jesus instructed his disciples to do in his Sermon on the Mount:

> "You, therefore, must be perfect, as your heavenly Father is perfect."
> (Matthew 5:48)

But how does the Cain-Abel paradigm apply to the war in Ukraine?

Cain and Abel in the Ukraine War

If you overlay the war in Ukraine with the Cain-Abel template it is clear that Russia is the aggressor who has manifested Cain-type behavior throughout this war. Thus not only was the invasion of Ukraine a Cain-type aggression in itself, Russia's brutal occupation of Ukraine represents another manifestation of Russia's Cain-type nature as well.

In contrast to this pure evil, the Abel-type Ukrainian military is fighting a just war of self-defense and taking pains to follow the Geneva Convention by avoiding civilian targets and treating the Russian prisoners in its care with decency.

All too many critics of Ukraine seem reluctant to recognize the evil that Russia's military has demonstrated in Ukraine. You have to harden your heart to the suffering of the Ukrainian people to be able to justify Putin's invasion in any way.

For those cheering Russia on, be aware that you are encouraging a Cain-type regime that is unrepentantly perpetrating against Ukraine the Cain-type crimes of blaming, torturing and murdering Abel.

The Importance of Recognizing and Supporting Abel

Which brings us full circle to the purpose of this appendix. The value of the Cain-Abel paradigm in the context of the war in Ukraine is that it explains perfectly which side is in the position of Cain and which in the position of Abel. Both Ukraine and Russia are far from perfect, but while Putin's Russia is increasingly returning to the evil of Russia's Soviet past, Ukraine is moving in the opposite direction—demonstrating Abel-type behavior as it seeks integration into the European Union and NATO.

Russia's behavior is linked to its Soviet history as the dominant Marxist state in the world in the last century. Marxism is a theory that embodies the resentment, anger and murderous impulses of Cain. This nature was fully on display during the 20th century when Marxist movements (Socialist and Communist) conquered much of the world and imposed ruthless dictatorships over hundreds of millions of people. (Nazism was also a variant of socialism, albeit under the label of fascism).

The predations of all the Cain-type dictatorial regimes of the last century inflicted death in the tens of millions, and untold additional suffering for those imprisoned, raped, tortured, displaced and generally mistreated under totalitarian oppression.

Cain is not all bad, nor Abel all good. But it is their relative goodness or evil in comparison to each other that is all important, since it is this difference that enables God to advance the providence. As we have explained, for both Russia and Ukraine to emerge from this war improved, the Abel side must win. That is, Ukraine must win and Russia lose.

It is our responsibility to do whatever we can to end the evil invasion of Russia as soon as possible, and to help Ukraine recover from this aggression as fully and quickly as possible. Not only will Ukraine benefit from this success, but so too will Russia, which will be forced to undergo major changes for the better.

(For an in-depth discussion of the Cain-Abel paradigm and its operation in history, see my book: *The Triumph of Good: Divine Providence, The Cain-Abel Paradigm, And the End of Marxism.*)

Index